MURDER, INC.

MURDER, INC.

**HOW UNREGULATED INDUSTRY KILLS OR INJURES
THOUSANDS OF AMERICANS EVERY YEAR ...
AND WHAT YOU CAN DO ABOUT IT**

DR. GERALD M. GOLDHABER

"THE WARNINGS DOCTOR"

PUBLISH
YOUR
PURPOSE®
PRESS

Photo and Artwork Credits:
Dr. Gerald M. Goldhaber: Figures 2.1, 2.2, 4.1, 4.2, 5.1, 7.4; Natalie Williams: Figure 5.2.

For permission requests, write to the publisher, addressed "Attention: Permissions Coordinator," at the address below.

Publish Your Purpose Press
141 Weston Street, #155
Hartford, CT, 06141

The opinions expressed by the Author are not necessarily those held by Publish Your Purpose Press.

Ordering Information: Quantity sales and special discounts are available on quantity purchases by corporations, associations, and others. For details, contact the publisher at orders@publishyourpurposepress.com.

Edited by: Karen Ang
Cover design by: Jon Silver
Typeset by: Medlar Publishing Solutions Pvt Ltd., India

Printed in the United States of America.
ISBN: 978-1-946384-84-3 (hardcover)
ISBN: 978-1-946384-79-9 (paperback)
ISBN: 978-1-946384-85-0 (ebook)

Library of Congress Control Number: 2019910594

First edition, March 2020.

The information contained within this book is strictly for informational purposes. The material may include information, products, or services by third parties. As such, the Author and Publisher do not assume responsibility or liability for any third-party material or opinions. The publisher is not responsible for websites (or their content) that are not owned by the publisher. Readers are advised to do their own due diligence when it comes to making decisions.

Publish Your Purpose Press works with authors, and aspiring authors, who have a story to tell and a brand to build. Do you have a book idea you would like us to consider publishing? Please visit PublishYourPurposePress.com for more information.

CONTENTS

PART I: BEHAVIORS

PART II: THE SAFETY TRIAD

A NOTE FROM GERRY

Do you ever wonder if big companies do things that fit inside regulations but aren't necessarily what's best for you, the consumer? Well, the answer to that question is yes! That's why I'm here (Gerry Goldhaber, AKA "The Warnings Doctor") … to let you know about these kinds of things so you can make better decisions for you and your family.

With that in mind, I have a special gift for you that will tell you a lot more about this. Go to www.TopFiveSafetyTips.com and get your copy of "The Top 5 Things Big Companies Don't Want You To Know That Will Keep You, & Your Loved Ones, Safe & Healthy."

You might be surprised to know what's happening out there that you aren't being made aware of. That's why "The Warnings Doctor" (Gerry Goldhaber, the author of this book) is here to help … and continues to fight to make the big companies do the right thing.

Go to www.TopFiveSafetyTips.com for your FREE copy of "The Top 5 Things Big Companies Don't Want You To Know That Will Keep You, & Your Loved Ones, Safe & Healthy."

A NOTE FROM ERIN BROCKOVICH

We have become comfortable and complacent, and I oftentimes think we believe that Superman, the EPA, or some agency that is in place will come and automatically fix the issues we are having. But we're just now waking up and realizing that isn't true. We have started to ask ourselves, "What can we do?" And that's the thing—we can do something about it.

This book is a good first step, filled with explanations and stories, a great deal of information that we didn't know, and a how-to road map for what it is we CAN do.

It has subtle humor and is told in a way that we can understand, giving us the tools we need to push forward and become aware that WE have to ask the questions and WE have to know how and where to go look, and not take for granted that someone has our backs.

In the new industry we live in—with all the technology we have—we are able to find out things faster than ever, to sort through information, to become more self-aware, and to protect ourselves better than ever. That is a good thing, but most won't know how to use that technology for research. This book is a wonderful tool that can help people navigate their way through a plethora of information. We must learn that with technology and using our own motivation, we might just change companies and their way of doing business. By being the watchdog, being informed, and fighting back, we the consumers get more and more savvy to what is really going on.

I want to thank Gerry for writing this important book. Great job!

Erin Brockovich
Public Advocate

FOREWORD

The 20th century—and, so far, the 21st—have been, by most measures, a triumph of new and improved products, industrial progress, and marketplace innovation. We have some better and faster motor vehicles, mostly purer foods and drugs, and millions of new, efficient homes to live in. But are they really better, newer, and faster? What is the downside—to our health, safety, and lives—of this forward march of our civilization? How can we have the benefits and not pay for them with our lives and health?

This is the issue squarely put by Dr. Gerald Goldhaber in this book. The author is highly qualified to make that judgment. He is a teacher, lecturer, and expert advisor to government and industry in the analysis and disclosure to the consumer of the use and safety of home, workplace, and consumer products.

His answer to the question of our real progress is a qualified *yes*, but with major warnings about hidden dangers and a new threat to the worker, consumer, and the environment due to the aggressive deregulation efforts of the current administration.

Why do some companies produce products that are poorly designed and often flat-out dangerous? Why does the government have to be a revolving door for the industries it is supposed to be watching on our behalf? Why are the Food and Drug Administration (FDA), the National Highway Traffic Safety Administration (NHTSA), the Environmental

Protection Agency (EPA), and other safety agencies generally underfunded and unable to adequately protect workers and consumers? Is it partially our own fault as consumers and voters?

The author suggests answers to these questions in this book. We are partly to blame. But he offers a methodology for the three groups (manufacturers, government, and consumers) involved in product safety production, use, and warnings to reduce the dangers in the future.

Murder, Inc. educates purchasers, workers, and users to take steps to protect themselves and, hopefully, induce companies to use proactive production methods and recognize that the public wants safer products and will pay for them.

Dr. Goldhaber closes with an appeal to all parties to work together in a "triad" of cooperation to reduce death and injury on the roads, in the home, in the workplace, and in the environment. He notes that principled disclosure by manufacturers would be a major step. It is an approach that the author suggests is essential since it appears the government is exposing all of us to greater risk and injury.

This review of the safety of the products we use daily is a book for our times. We need to read and understand it. While we benefit from this era of progress, we are all at great risk, especially when our government is determined to let us down.

Michael R. Lemov, former counsel to the House Commerce Committee for motor vehicle and product safety, is the author of Car Safety Wars: One Hundred Years of Technology, Politics, and Death *(Fairleigh Dickinson Press, 2015) and* People's Warrior: John Moss and the Fight for Freedom of Information and Consumer Rights *(Fairleigh Dickinson Press, 2011). Mr. Lemov is currently a Member of the Board of Directors of the Center for Auto Safety and was the primary author of the Consumer Product Safety Act.*

INTRODUCTION

On a cool, balmy evening in May 1972, Lily Gray proudly pulled her brand-new Ford Pinto onto the entrance ramp of a Minneapolis highway and began to accelerate. Riding with her was 13-year-old Richard Grimshaw. However, as they entered the highway merge lanes, the 1972-model Pinto began to stall, and Lily's new car was rear-ended by another vehicle at an estimated impact speed of 30 mph. Almost immediately, the Pinto's gas tank ruptured, splattering gasoline into the back seats and mixing highly flammable vapors with the air throughout the passenger compartment. A spark ignited the mixture, and the car exploded in an enormous ball of flames. After several hours of unimaginable agony, Lily Gray died in a nearby hospital emergency room. Richard Grimshaw would survive the accident, but "suffered severe and permanently disfiguring burns on his face and entire body."[1]

Thus began the notorious saga of Ford Motor Company's tooth-and-nail fight—on numerous industrial and political fronts from Dearborn, Michigan, to Washington, D.C.—to keep its highly profitable Pinto (its first foray into the burgeoning and lucrative subcompact market of the day) on the road. And Ford did so openly, despite the company's clear knowledge of a critical design flaw that would result in many more gas tank explosions and, consequently, many more deaths and serious injuries.

---

[1] Grimshaw v. Ford Motor Company.

The facts of the Pinto debacle are legendary in the annals of corporate arrogance—and some would say depravity—in the relentless pursuit of profits over safety. Here are just a few highlights:

- Locked in fierce, cutthroat competition with Volkswagen for the subcompact market, and at the insistence of a man by the name of Lee Iacocca, Ford had rushed the Pinto into production in nearly half the usual schedule. In doing so, they knowingly sacrificed both the time allocated for safety testing and the time allowed for assembly line retooling to eliminate hazards revealed by such testing *before* the cars were released to the public. Determined to increase Ford's market share and profits at any cost or extreme, Iacocca would later become infamous for coldly and callously uttering, "Safety doesn't sell."
- Preproduction crash tests revealed to Ford engineers that rear-end collisions would cause a rupture of the fuel system extremely easily, most often by driving the tank into the differential housing of the rear axle. Internal company documents would later reveal that of 40 crash tests conducted by Ford at an ultrasecret location, every single test conducted at speeds over 25 mph resulted in a ruptured gas tank!
- As a direct consequence, by the time the Ford engineers had discovered this colossal design defect, and because the assembly-line machinery had already been tooled for immediate production, Ford officials made the fateful decision to manufacture the Pinto anyway—exploding gas tank and all. What makes their actions even more incredible is that Ford owned the patent on a much safer fuel tank system.

For the next eight years, Ford Motor Company successfully waged an extraordinarily ferocious and unparalleled lobbying campaign against a key government safety provision that would have forced the company to redesign the Pinto's explosion-prone gas tank and faulty fuel system once and for all. The company's intense and unrelenting lobbying battle occurred even amid an atmosphere of increased public interest in more and better automotive safety standards in the face of staggering increases in highway deaths across the country.

Public awareness had already been heightened by what might be regarded as the birth of the public safety advocacy movement in the 1960s. Numerous advocates argued with particular fervor for the imposition of tougher auto safety standards on the major U.S. auto manufacturers. No individual is more intimately identified with this movement than Ralph Nader, whose seminal, groundbreaking, and highly influential best-selling book, *Unsafe at Any Speed* had outraged the general public and galvanized consumers so powerfully that normally complacent legislators were forced to take action. The book's release catapulted Nader to the very forefront of the gathering public automotive safety advocacy movement. He would famously go on to become America's leading advocate of consumer protection in many other areas, from household products to environmental issues and from health care to nuclear energy.

Nader ceaselessly pursued and badgered the automotive industry, accusing them of blatantly ignoring safety research findings, of knowingly implementing hazardous designs that would unequivocally cause serious injuries and unnecessary deaths, and doing so all in the sole interests of maximizing profits over the protection and safety of the consumer-motorist. When the industry attempted to adopt the sinister ideology and official rallying cry that, "Cars don't cause accidents, people (and highway conditions) do," Nader countered by portraying motorists as uninformed and helpless victims of despicable corporate neglect and greed. His brilliant and shocking 1966 testimony before a Senate subcommittee considering landmark and unprecedented federal legislation to impose safety standards on new cars manufactured in America served to spearhead the passage of the 1966 National Traffic and Motor Vehicle Safety Act. Among other important safety improvements, the Motor Vehicle Safety Act would require, for the first time, the installation of safety belts for all passengers. Later, in 1973, Ralph Nader would also provide revealing and powerfully influential testimony while appearing before yet another congressional subcommittee investigating the Ford Pinto exploding gas tank disaster.

Yet, in the end, the powerful Ford lobbyists were able to successfully put one more outrageous insult over on the American motoring public, and a despicable one at that, because it would mean more people would inevitably die horrifically in their Pintos. Just as regulatory power was finally beginning to coalesce within the National Highway Safety Bureau (established by the 1966 Motor Vehicle Safety Act and now the National Highway Traffic Safety Administration, or NHTSA), Ford's manipulative "experts" managed to elicit a now notorious agreement with the crucial administrators who would soon be making pivotal auto safety decisions for the industry. Bluntly stated, they got the government regulators to agree that "cost-benefit" would be an acceptable mode of analysis by both the Detroit automakers and the regulators themselves. What that meant in real terms was that a monetary value would need to be placed on human life. In an article titled "Pinto Madness" that originally appeared in *Mother Jones* in 1977, investigative reporter Mark Dowie wrote:

> [I]n order to be able to argue that various safety costs were greater than their benefits, Ford needed to have a dollar value figure for the "benefit." Rather than be so uncouth as to come up with such a price tag itself, the auto industry pressured the National Highway Traffic Safety Administration to do so. And in a 1972 report the agency decided a human life was worth $200,725 ...[2]

Subsequent to the NHTSA's mystifying determination of that list-price figure for a human being, in 1973 Ford presented the agency with its cost-benefit analysis, titled *Fatalities Associated with Crash Induced Fuel Leakage and Fires*. The document infamously came to be known as the

---

[2] Dowie, "Pinto Madness."

"Pinto Memo," and argued that the company should not be required to make a relatively simple gas tank design improvement that would prevent 180 fiery deaths a year.[3]

Their reasoning was all in the math: Ford estimated the cost of the fuel system modifications required to reduce the risk of gas tank explosions and fire events to be $11 per car across 12.5 million cars (mostly Pintos but also in some other car models and light trucks), for a total of $137 million. Yet, Ford estimated that the design changes would save *only* about 180 lives and an equal number of 180 serious injuries (injuries valued by NHTSA at a piddling $67,000 each) per year, for a cost to society of a mere $49.5 million. Never mind the fact that, at the time of Mark Dowie's article in August 1977, estimates of deaths resulting from exploding Pinto gas tanks ranged from 500 to 900 in total. And there were many more to come. As reprehensible as it clearly is, cost-benefit analysis quickly became the basis for Ford's—and other automakers'—ongoing and future vigorous arguments *against* safer car design.

The last Ford Pinto models rolled off the assembly line in 1980. Yet today, nearly four decades after the deeply disturbing events that I have only briefly touched on, the question that is begged by this saga of one vehicle's exploding gas tank is simply this:

Have we really learned anything about consumer product safety over the past 40 years?

In a myriad of important ways, I have spent a lifetime examining and looking for answers to that very question. Over the past 42 years as an expert in vital, optimally effective, and potentially lifesaving communications, I have advised over 100 of the top Fortune 500 corporations and over 50 of the nation's most prestigious law firms representing literally over a thousand clients (both plaintiffs and defendants). My expertise includes matters of

---

[3] Leggett, "The Ford Pinto Case."

safety warnings designed to alert consumers to potentially injurious or deadly product, operational, and environmental hazards in the workplace, the home, in schools and on playgrounds, in our food and pharmaceuticals, and out on the road. I have been a consultant to a virtual alphabet soup of government regulatory agencies, from the Consumer Products Safety Commission (CPSC) to the U.S. Department of Agriculture (USDA) to NHTSA to the U.S. Food and Drug Administration (FDA) to the U.S. Department of Defense (DOD), just to name a few. I have authored ten books on these subjects, including two of the all-time bestsellers in the field of communication. At the ground-game level, I have also designed salient and instantly communicative warning label graphics and terminology for innumerable potentially hazardous consumer products and environments.

Additionally, I am the publisher of the *Goldhaber Warnings Report*, an online newsletter now in its eleventh year that advises thousands of attorneys and legal experts nationally. Finally, I have testified and/or consulted for lawyers representing corporations or injured parties in over 1,000 lawsuits since 1978, and am currently CNN's and CNN.com's expert analyst for issues dealing with hazard warnings and/or safety communications issues.

It is fair to say that I have come to be recognized as one of the world's leading experts in the objective science—if I may call it that—of creating proactive and abundantly understandable hazard warnings designed both to alert and protect consumers from harm. In all candor, my expertise also protects corporations and businesses from liability for failure to adequately warn consumers and employees about the hidden hazards that, whether we like it or not, inevitably find their way into the objects and conveniences we use in our conduct of our everyday lives.

Most recently, I have been appointed as a member of the Institute of Electrical and Electronics Engineers' (IEEE) Global Initiative, a worldwide effort of leading scholars, scientists, and government and industrial leaders calling for an ethical and complete identification and disclosure by industry of all product hazards capable of inflicting serious or fatal injuries upon workers and/or consumers. Further, I have also been appointed as an advisor to the Scientific and Technical Advisory Committee of the Conte

Foundation, a nonprofit organization devoted to spotlighting corporations that place safety over profits as well as those that put profits over safety.

With that as qualification, I must state bluntly that my answer to the question posed earlier—whether we have really learned anything about consumer product safety over the past 40 years—is a dishearteningly dubious one at best. I might be inclined to say that, in fact, we have learned little or nothing at all. One need only look at today's headlines to confirm that, in many ways and for many corporations, nothing has changed. Arguably, recent cases have actually raised the diabolical bar of corporate intransigence and their lack of transparency to an even higher level of deliberate nondisclosure, overt and calculated deception, and even premeditated consumer and regulatory criminal fraud.

For example, we have the Takata Corporation shipping out millions of potentially explosive, shrapnel-firing airbag modules that have killed 11 people worldwide, to date, and resulted in the largest and broadest automobile recall in history. It has affected at least ten major auto manufacturers and has impacted millions of lives. We have Volkswagen executives intentionally conspired to rig emissions testing of their vehicles to deceive and defraud the EPA regulators into believing that the cars met current U.S. pollution standards.

In the extreme cases of Takata and Volkswagen, although almost without precedent, criminal indictments of numerous company executives have been handed up. But the stark and unadulterated truth of the matter is that industry and government—through deliberate or inadvertent actions caused by underfunding or sheer incompetence—have, in essence, collaborated in a "devil's agreement" to sacrifice principle for profit and safety for economic growth at all costs. With poor or no safety information, Americans have been denied the ability to make informed choices that would help us lead safer lives in an increasingly dangerous world. At its base, this failure to get vital safety information to workers and consumers effectively denies them the opportunity to make informed decisions about whether and how to use these products safely, resulting in unnecessary injuries and fatalities. Much worse, however, in many situations the denial of disclosure of vital safety information may cross the line into criminally negligent behavior, both by senior corporate management and complicit government regulators who fear the impact of disclosure would drastically slow sales and profits from industrial growth. This notion is *categorically false*, as we will see in this book.

In an article written by Juliet Eilperin and published in the *Washington Post* in February 2017, the new administration under President Donald Trump has begun the most ambitious dismantling of government regulation in a generation, extending across numerous departments and agencies. The *Post* cites figures indicating that in just the first ten days since the new president took office, "Republican lawmakers have taken action to roll back dozens of federal regulations with 37 separate resolutions," noting further that the 37 resolutions signed by Trump are "more than any previous Congress [has] attempted in an entire two-year term."[4]

The full ramifications of this massive and, in my opinion, ill-advised scorched-earth rush to deregulation remain to be seen. Some of these initial resolutions threaten everything from the controlled handling of hazardous substances to consumer product and workplace safety, as well as in the mining industry, in the military, and more. The deregulation may even affect politically volatile issues, such as the trafficking and use of blood diamonds. Moreover, such unreasoned and widespread loosening of deliberative regulatory constraints flies in the face of positive efforts like the IEEE Global Initiative and the work of the Conte Foundation. This book is a direct and forthright objective response to what ominously has already begun to happen in the halls of Washington. *Murder, Inc.* itself may be taken as a serious hazard warning for the future of our country and its people.

The Ford Pinto debacle, along with the hundreds of similar cases that have followed it (as well as many that undoubtedly preceded it), represents what

---

[4] Eilperin, "Regulatory rollback."

I refer to as the "reactive" economic model with respect to a given company's or entity's efforts (or lack thereof) to provide adequate safety warnings to consumers about the hidden hazards in their products. I call this model "reactive" because the manufacturer typically warns about hazards only after either a regulatory body mandates it or litigation verdicts and mounting settlement amounts exceed the perceived cost to sales for providing safety information or endeavoring to eliminate or "design out" the offending hazard altogether.

In contrast, I propose an alternative Proactive Economic Model involving six crucial but entirely practical steps. Fundamentally, I see the Proactive Economic Model as an easily implemented and standardized methodology. It envisions taking every conceivable product-analytic testing precaution toward identifying *in advance* the hidden hazards that may exist in new or redesigned consumer products *before* they are sold or distributed to the open marketplace. The model provides ample opportunity and procedures for creating effective warnings and safety instructions for users—what I refer to as "principled disclosure"—where existing hazards cannot feasibly be eliminated from given products, and before otherwise hidden hazards may cause injury or deaths. Furthermore, the model also would allow manufacturers to go back to the drawing board potentially to retool their products to minimize, or even to design out such hazards entirely, thus eliminating the threat to public safety. It will be shown that through determined and fully dedicated adherence to a Proactive Economic Model, both public safety measures *and* corporate profits may be maximized to the benefit of all.

Throughout this book, we will explore some very blatant and outrageous examples of corporate failure to enact principled disclosure with respect to the unobvious or hidden hazards lurking in their products and the horrendous consequences of their actions (or inaction, as the case may be). However, we will also look at some remarkable instances in which the Proactive Economic Model has served admirably well in saving lives or preventing injuries while, at the same time, *increasing* profits. Perhaps most importantly, the proactive model has also been proven to engender enormous consumer respect and to build substantial customer product loyalty, thus ensuring corporate profitability for the long term.

It is perhaps one of the great paradoxes of human analytic intelligence and technological ingenuity: On the one hand, we have been astonishingly successful in reshaping our world into a much more hospitable place filled with all sorts of modern conveniences to make our everyday lives easier and more enjoyable. Yet on the other hand, all of that intelligence and innovation seems unavoidably destined to create new, ever-expanding, and wholly unintended constellations of potentially detrimental hazards we must face or navigate through—in virtually every moment of our lives. Because, as we will see, these hazards are everywhere. They are as much a part of our environment as the air we breathe. In the next chapter we explore this curious paradox and try to provide an understanding of why this is so.

PART I

BEHAVIORS

Throughout our lives, we confront hundreds of life-threatening situations caused by our exposure to hazardous products without adequate—or even any—product safety information. Nothing can prevent our exposure to hazardous products. However, transparency about these dangers can help us **make informed choices** regarding the risks we choose to take.

CHAPTER 1

ALL THE WORLD'S A HAZARD

The world is a very dangerous place. At any given moment in time, in any given place on any major continent or island, whether remote and uninhabited or a metropolis teeming with humanity, a major catastrophe may strike with little or no warning. Whether it's an earthquake or volcanic eruption, hurricane or blizzard, wildfire or flood, disastrous consequences or the loss of human life abounds. Even with respect to small-scale dangers, the National Oceanic and Atmospheric Administration (NOAA) reports that 51 people are killed annually by lightning strikes in the U.S. alone. According to the Mother Nature Network website, each year an average of 53 people in the U.S. are killed by bee stings. And those are just the natural hazards.

Since the discovery of fire and the invention of the wheel, humankind has sought to make the world a more hospitable place, to make our lives easier and more enjoyable—and safer too. At no time in human history has that been truer than in our modern, technologically advanced, globalized digital age in which seemingly every convenience is being placed at our fingertips. Want to get something done quickly and efficiently and with as little mental or physical exertion as possible? There's an app for that.

Yet an almost perversely ironic consequence of technology is that so often, brilliant, technologically sophisticated innovations exquisitely designed to solve one perceived problem or another almost invariably (and infernally) create altogether new ones with unintended and unanticipated consequences. Those consequences themselves can range from minor inconveniences to the catastrophic. Even more ominously, these potentially catastrophic consequences can be quite unobvious, at least initially.

For example, asbestos when first mined from the ground is relatively harmless. But when it is pulverized in the manufacture of fire-resistant building products, airborne asbestos particles cause deadly pulmonary diseases like mesothelioma and lung cancer. Similarly, coal, whether in the ground or in lump form tossed into furnaces to create heat or electric power, is essentially harmless. However, coal dust is responsible for the deaths of hundreds of thousands of miners due to lung cancer and pneumoconiosis, also called Black Lung. Burning coal under even the cleanest of conditions releases toxic gases, such as sulfur dioxide and nitrogen oxides, that pose critical respiratory, cardiovascular, and even nervous system health risks, not to mention serious damage to the environment in the form of acid rain and other contamination.

Lastly, as an example of unintended consequences, the trace presence of argon gas in residential housing was never a serious problem until the soaring energy cost of fossil fuels like natural gas and home heating oil induced homebuilders to make these structures more airtight. Modern homebuilders' innovations with insulation and other building materials now enable modern houses and office buildings to stay toasty warm in the winter and pleasantly cool in the summer, but in some regions of the country, they may also promote the unwanted and initially unforeseen buildup of dangerous levels of argon gas. This is most true in the northeastern United States, where so many millions of homes that must be kept warm during the long winters actually sit on top of mountainous terrain marked by heavy shale deposits where large quantities of argon exist in the earth, slowly leaching to the surface naturally. Oftentimes, in this way, technology that solves one major problem inadvertently creates a whole new major problem that may—or may not—be so easy to predict.

Anybody who watches network television knows that today there are dozens upon dozens of fantastic prescription pharmaceuticals that are (allegedly) effective in treating everything from depression and anxiety to high blood pressure and bad cholesterol to hepatitis C and type-2 diabetes to eczema and psoriasis. But as all of the infernal and incessant ads on television warn us, an individual taking any single one of those "miracle" drugs faces the not-insignificant risk of a legion of unwanted, potentially hazardous side effects, some of which may be quite serious and life-changing—including death! (By the way, those television ad warnings are grossly ineffective and inadequate, as we will see in Chapter 7.) With some individuals, the benefits of the drugs may very well outweigh the risks. With others, however, the equation may be the reverse.

Throughout our lives, in modern society we confront hundreds of life-threatening circumstances caused by our direct exposure to potentially hazardous products, or by willingly placing ourselves into situations or environments that may be susceptible to accidents. Nothing in the conduct of our daily lives can prevent our being exposed to hazardous products or environments, at least not entirely. Nor can you get away from all these dangers by crawling up in a ball inside your home—because your home is *full* of hazardous products and dangerous environments! Every year, 33 million Americans—that's 10 percent of the total U.S. population—are seriously injured in their own homes. The truth is, most of the time, we are completely oblivious to such exposure.

But here is the truly sinister side to these unobvious hazards: As much as 99 percent of the time, the people and companies responsible for creating these products or designing these environments have all along known about the myriad hazardous risks they pose to health and safety. The companies simply haven't told you about them. And that is why I call them "hidden" hazards. It is not that these hazards are "hidden from view," metaphorically speaking; rather, it is the fact that they are being deliberately hidden *from you.*

HIDDEN HAZARDS: A UBIQUITOUS
CORPORATE CULTURE

In attempting to describe the seemingly endless landscape of hidden hazards that exist in virtually every facet of our lives, it is difficult to decide exactly where to start. In recent years, we have witnessed some terribly disturbing and shockingly blatant examples of corporations attempting to hide—or simply engaging in outright denial of—any knowledge of seriously defective components in their products. It is often only due to scores of horrific incidents resulting in unconscionable numbers of fatalities and injuries that these deceptions come to light in the glare of subsequent media scrutiny. Of these, the Takata exploding, shrapnel-firing airbag scandal probably tops the list.

Regardless, it was difficult, if not impossible, for the automobile industry as a whole to dodge the fact that 2015 was perhaps the all-time banner record year for automotive recalls. In that year alone, the NHTSA, often reluctantly and certainly later than they should have, initiated 123 recall incidents resulting in almost 20 million cars being recalled for safety issues. A whopping 680 additional recalls were initiated *voluntarily* by the auto industry itself, resulting in another 40 million cars being recalled. The grand winner of the century was 2015, with more than 64 million cars recalled.

General Motors' contribution to the recall list stemmed mostly from a defective ignition switch that could cause the engine to shut off, thereby disabling the airbag. It also disabled the power steering and power brakes. Initially, GM sought to address the problem with a warning issued or mailed to every consumer who had bought one of the affected car models across its several divisions. But this proved to be utterly inadequate. The company only issued a fully comprehensive recall—of at least 30 million vehicles worldwide—after as many as 124 deaths had been linked to the ignition key failure.[5] Facing its own hearing before Congress, GM admitted

---

[5] Isadore, "Death toll."

that the fix for the problem was a 57-cent part, yet still lamented that, had the recall been issued in 2007, it would have cost the company over $100 million to fix 30 million cars (through the first half of 2014 alone, as reported by Forbes, GM recalled "about 29 million vehicles for ignition switch defects and other issues, at a cost of $2.5 *billion*" (emphasis mine)).[6]

In perhaps the most infuriatingly blatant disregard for the public trust, 2015 was also the year that the CEO of Volkswagen's America Group finally admitted that VW had deliberately conspired to rig emissions testing of their vehicles to deceive EPA regulators into believing that the cars met current U.S. standards. The German automaker had intentionally programmed the turbocharged direct injection (TDI) diesel engines of 11 million cars worldwide—500,000 in the U.S. alone—so that the emissions controls were activated only during laboratory testing. The programming caused the vehicles' nitric oxide and nitrogen dioxide output (collectively known as NOx level) to meet U.S. standards during regulatory testing, but allowed the engines to emit up to 40 times more NOx in real-world driving.

It needs to be acknowledged here that the actions of Takata and VW may represent a higher plane of evil in that many people might argue that they potentially represent some level of criminality. Takata management allegedly chose to ignore a lethal defect and the deliberate conspiracy perpetrated by VW executives may be tantamount to fraud on a colossal scale. Additionally, we have no way of knowing how many serious injuries or deaths may have been caused to persons suffering with asthma, COPD, and other lung diseases as a result of toxic emissions from 11 million VW engines. Furthermore, while GM might be credited with at least attempting to issue a safety warning to its customers, it was a case of too little too late. And in the end, of course, the warning proved to be a wholly inadequate solution to the problem. In this case, some might contend that GM was civilly negligent, if not criminally so. Whatever the case, all of that is something for the courts to decide.

---

[6] Muller, "GM Profit Plunges on Recall Costs."

On January 11th, 2017, federal prosecutors announced the indictment of six of Volkswagen's top executives, physically arresting one who happened to be on American soil. A U.S. Department of Justice (DOJ) press release stated that, "VW is charged with and has agreed to plead guilty to participating in a conspiracy to defraud the United States ... and to violate the Clean Air Act," as well as obstruction of justice and wire fraud. The *New York Times* reported that the automaker "is set to pay $4.3 billion in criminal and civil penalties in connection with the federal investigation, bringing the total cost of the deception to VW in the United States, including settlements of suits by car owners, to $20 billion—one of the costliest corporate scandals in history."[7] One might ask VW, "Was it worth it?"

Just two days after the indictment of the six VW executives, federal prosecutors also announced the indictment of three Takata executives for their role in the defective airbag inflator scandal. At last report, the DOJ continues to want to bring Shinichi Tanaka, Hideo Nakajima, and Tsuneo Chikaraishi—all of Japan—to the U.S. to face trial.[8]

At least two things are clear from these examples: (1) Takata was never going to get away with plastering a warning on the steering columns of the cars containing its airbag units that read, "**WARNING: airbag may explode with excessive, violent force, sending hot metal shards into your face and neck!**" On January 11, 2017, Toyota issued a recall for another 772,000 vehicles suspected to be equipped with the hazardously faulty Takata airbag inflators. And (2), as we will see time and time again in this book, all of these monumentally foolish decisions were motivated by one simple, monolithic, and pathetically shortsighted principle: "Profits Over Safety."

While Takata, GM, and VW have—to varying degrees—damaged their reputations among direct consumers or the general public, Takata may have committed the biggest sin of all. Because, let's face it, most consumers are incredibly forgiving—perhaps to a fault. Loyal GM and VW

---

[7] Ewing and Tabuchi, "Volkswagen."
[8] Spector, "Takata Executives."

customers will more than likely continue to buy and drive GM and VW cars and trucks. After all, a mildly cynical general public might ask, with all of their technological sophistication, "Aren't periodic motor vehicle recalls pretty much a part of the landscape these days?" Takata, however, manufactured and distributed millions upon millions of potentially defective airbag units to its principal clients, thereby implicating nearly a dozen of the world's largest automobile manufacturers and dragging them down with it. In terms of volume alone, that's a huge market; however, it's a severely narrow one in terms of total customer base. What are there, perhaps two dozen major car companies in the world—the ones that sell standard production-line cars to the general public? Takata's colossal arrogance is thus magnified in that it was willing to piss off its *entire* principal market base, not just a segment of that market base.

In this way, Takata's disastrous decision makes no sense even as a practical matter of good business principles designed to foster partnership-like relationships with trusted, and trusting, long-term customers. It remains to be seen whether his company will be able to survive the scandal he precipitated. It is not clear if a select brotherhood of a dozen or so major automakers, which have lost billions of dollars as a result of Takata's malfeasance, will be quite as willing to forgive the parts manufacturer and let bygones be bygones. This question may now be moot. In June 2017, Takata filed for bankruptcy protection in the U.S. and Japan, and agreed to be largely acquired by Chinese-owned and U.S.-based Key Safety Systems.[9]

It might be said that these three sensational examples represent the worst of the worst, but the fact of the matter is that they are all ripped from headlines that represent the scandals du jour of 2017. The incontrovertible fact remains that incomprehensible, mind-blowing decisions of this kind are made all of the time throughout every sector of business and industry—not just in the automotive industry. Even if, thankfully, such misguided decisions only very rarely result in catastrophic situations, the plain truth is that companies routinely fail to adequately provide for the

---

[9] Tajitsu, "Takata."

safety and well-being of consumers and workers who use and rely on the products the companies manufacture and sell. And government regulatory agencies continue to do a shamefully inadequate job of holding industries accountable for protecting the general public from hazards caused directly or indirectly by their products. To the contrary, government regulators routinely and shockingly collude with industries in helping them to obfuscate or entirely evade the posting or dissemination of critical safety warnings and other vital information—from the actual amount of added sugar in a children's breakfast cereal to the specific toxic chemicals contained in a can of paint or pesticide—that every consumer deserves the right to know before deciding to use that particular product.

Historically speaking, if an accurate and precise cause of death were attached to the millions of consumers' and workers' death certificates, "information underload" or "information obfuscation" would be identified as the proximate cause of their untimely demise. At its base, the failure to get vital safety information to workers and consumers effectively denied them the opportunity to make informed decisions about whether and how to use these products safely.

In short, our leaders have long thought that transparent hazard disclosure and a subsequent outpouring of media stories describing these product hazards to a nervous population would result in our economy taking a disastrous hit on corporate earnings and profits. They are wrong! Yet, even as history, science, and economics have taught us that such fears about the potential for profit loss are unfounded, this same narrow-minded perception persists today. Tragically, across our nation's history and especially over the past 200 years since the flourishing of the industrial revolution in America, the price for the false choice between corporate profits and public safety has been tens of millions of needlessly injured or killed Americans. These were, and continue to be, injuries and deaths that, for the most part, could have been avoided through a sound policy of educational awareness coupled with plainly understandable safety warnings about hidden dangers.

While our country may be 240 years old, the lion's share of the history of effective safety warning policies has unfolded only over the course of the past 45 years since the administration of President Richard Nixon. Prior to that, America's industrial revolution produced 150 years of unconscionable safety and warnings **silence** that resulted in over ten million fatalities and serious injuries. In 1880 alone, five million American workers perished in the national frenzy of industrialization—from building factories and skyscrapers to roads, rails, bridges, and steamships—all to drive the country's monumentally explosive growth.

As we will see, in spite of the lessons that should have been learned over the course of those most dangerous days, as well as in spite of the explosion since the 1980s and 1990s in the field of warnings and safety communications, our current, woefully inadequate safety and warnings policies still have an enormous amount of growing up to do. A virtual alphabet soup of regulatory agencies—from OSHA to CPSC to NHTSA and a host of others—has failed to make citizens safer in their homes, in their places of work, or riding public or private transportation. In many respects, these agencies have collectively added to the informational obfuscation and the burgeoning chaos of codes and regulations that only continues to grow more and more complicated as the number, variety, and sophistication of new and innovative consumer products expands.

Think about this: We are entering a new age of digital "smart" devices or smart technology that will be designed to do more things for people that we used to have to do manually for ourselves—from actual physical or mental or intellectual tasks to home and office systems monitoring. It's plain to see that in the brave new world of smart technology, people will be called upon more and more to put their faith unquestioningly on digital applications and "intelligent" products to perform increasingly vital and, in some cases, life-sustaining, tasks. This fact will put enormous responsibility on the companies that produce these innovations to make sure they must be fail-safe or face potentially hefty lawsuits and liabilities if and when they do fail and cause fatalities and injuries.

I can think of no better example than the autonomous car in which passengers will ultimately be obliged to willingly put themselves and their very lives completely at the mercy of an ostensibly omniscient vehicle (can a noncognitive contraption even have "mercy"?) and trust it to take them to their destination safely and without incident. Some autonomous prototypes featured at recent automobile shows are not even equipped with steering wheels, suggesting that there will be no override mechanisms available to the passengers should the car's computer go haywire, allowing the vehicle to run amok all over the highway! While I do not mean to be cynical, it seems only a matter of time before the filing of the first lawsuit on behalf of someone riding in a conventional automobile who is injured or killed in a collision with an autonomous car, only to have the owner of the driverless car deny any responsibility for the accident and subsequently turn around and sue the vehicle manufacturer! Where will that leave the injured party?

Taking this a bit further, today more and more home and business environments are being converted to wireless control by smart devices that automatically adjust things like heating and cooling. In the very near future, home appliances like refrigerators, ovens, and trash compactors will also be controlled by the same smart technology without any need of oversight by owners or tenants. Might a renegade programming glitch cause a kitchen oven to overheat, eventually igniting a house fire? And who might we suppose will be liable for damages if such an incident should occur?

In the past, if the general public thought government regulators and officials would protect them from harm's way, they were sorely disillusioned. All too often, the regulators were either incompetent or too poorly funded to do their jobs or, worse, they quickly become an integral part of a "revolving-door" system that lets the fox directly into the henhouse. We have a long, storied, and quite unfortunately ongoing history of appointing regulators from the same industries they must regulate and of regulators either joining or rejoining the industries they formerly regulated. The ostensibly well-intended theory underlying this deplorably incestuous practice might be stated as, "Who knows the industry better (and theoretically can better regulate it) than experienced experts from the industry itself?" But the more practically realistic questions might be, "Who knows better how a particular industry might *most easily avoid regulation* than the very experienced experts who formerly ran it? Who knows all the loopholes?"

As for Congress, their incipit role in all of this has historically been relegated to self-righteous grandstanding for the television cameras at highly orchestrated congressional hearings on Capitol Hill every time a catastrophic product defect or workplace disaster blows up in corporate America's face. What most people don't realize is that congressional action typically occurs only when the situation is severe enough to disrupt the relentless profitable growth and expansion of business and industry, or causes a hiccup in the surging Dow Jones average. Or if it so pervasively catches the fire of media attention that congressional leaders are *forced* to act.

THE ROLE OF CONSUMER COMMON SENSE IN HAZARD AVOIDANCE

Despite the "information underload" practiced by corporate entities and the often-lax regulatory oversight practiced by the government, most people would agree that consumers need to exercise a sufficient measure of common sense. This ought to be particularly true when it comes to operating potentially hazardous equipment like kitchen knives, ladders, or chainsaws, or when they find themselves in a dangerous environment, like a factory, or out on the highway in one's car, or … in the kitchen near the stove or the microwave!

Today many people probably still remember the case of Stella Liebeck, who in 1992, successfully sued McDonald's, which subsequently opened the floodgates for perhaps hundreds of thousands of personal injury lawsuits. We might dub Liebeck's action as "The Case That Launched a Thousand Frivolous Lawsuits." Of course, there are perhaps hundreds and hundreds of lawsuits that clearly qualify the hapless plaintiffs as finalists in the annual Darwin Awards for their comical ineptitude, poor judgment, or thoughtless behavior. But many of such lawsuits have not been quite so frivolous as they may have seemed on the surface—especially in the way they have been portrayed by sensational news media that typically plays up and slants quirky stories to achieve higher network viewer ratings. In fact, the Liebeck lawsuit was itself a case in point.

Undoubtedly, most people today who remember Liebeck's suit against the fast food giant believe that she got away with one. We all tend to remember the singular, simplistic premise of the lawsuit and might have remarked, "She spilled hot McDonald's coffee on herself. What a clumsy dope!" ABC News called it "the poster child of excessive lawsuits" when the case hit the airwaves. Yet, the facts brought up in court reveal that the decision really could have gone either way. More crucially, there was indeed some substantive merit to the plaintiff's claim.

In brief, Liebeck bought a cup of coffee through the drive-thru window at her local McDonald's. Her grandson was driving the pickup truck while Liebeck rode in the front passenger seat. After pulling out of the drive-thru, she asked her grandson to pull over to the side of the parking lot so that she could put creamer in the coffee. It was during that process that the coffee spilled into her lap and scalded her. In fact, she suffered serious third-degree burns over her pelvic area that put her in the hospital for eight days. She underwent skin grafting followed by two years of continuous medical treatment. Her injuries were real, excruciatingly painful, and—perhaps most importantly—they were debilitating.

Liebeck first requested that McDonald's simply cover her medical bills. They refused. So, she sued and ultimately won. A jury-awarded judgment in the amount of $2.86 million, though the award was reduced to $640,000 by the trial judge and, sometime later, the parties agreed to an undisclosed (and likely further reduced) settlement sum before a final appeal was decided. But neither did the severe extent of Liebeck's injuries nor her subsequent treatment tell the full story of this both celebrated and vilified court decision. The question might be asked, "How hot is hot enough?"

It turns out that McDonald's had conducted extensive market research that found that one of the main complaints people expressed about their coffee was it wasn't hot enough! While my company was not directly involved in any connection with the Liebeck lawsuit, several years earlier we had coincidently conducted some similar research that investigated this very same question. And, indeed, through a series of focus groups, our results found the same thing, which is to say that people complained that the coffee wasn't hot enough! Even more revealing, in its own customer survey data, McDonald's discovered that their customers were coming through the drive-thru window and getting a cup of coffee as part of their routine trip to work, and they wanted it to still be hot when they got there. Many of them didn't even open the cup until they got to their desks and, of course, they wanted it to still be hot even as they sat down to work.

For the purpose of argument, let's conjecture that—for the arguably well-intentioned reason that their customers wanted their coffee to still be piping hot when they got to the office—McDonald's deliberately juiced-up their percolators to overheat the coffee to temperatures that exceeded the industry norm. We might further conclude, based on the marketing data they had accumulated through their customer surveys, that their action in overheating the coffee was a legitimate and logical response to prevailing and perhaps overwhelming customer preferences. Now, with that customer-preference-oriented marketing rationale in mind, some people—whether business experts and entrepreneurs or just plain consumers—might be inclined to concede that McDonald's was only trying to do the right thing. They were only trying to give their customers exactly what they asked for. In other words, they were astutely listening to their customers.

But hold on for just a moment. Because it turns out that, as reported in *The Huffington Post* decades later,[10] McDonald's had already faced more than 700 hot beverage scalding claims *before* the Stella Liebeck case came to national prominence! Somehow, McDonald's had managed to keep those 700 previous complaints quiet until Liebeck caught the attention

---

[10] Weiman, "McDonald's."

of the media and the imagination of all the late-night talk show host comedians. Her story went viral before anyone knew what "going viral" actually meant! The point is that McDonald's flat-out knew—long before Liebeck was injured and before she brought her million-dollar lawsuit—that their overheated coffee posed a dangerous hazard to their customers. Yet, they did nothing about it. They didn't endeavor to find a way to eliminate the hazard. They took no actions to warn consumers about the safety hazard the overheated coffee posed to them.

And the thing of it is—and this is a major contention of this book—even if the decision to super-heat the coffee may have been ill-advised, the company's liability in the Liebeck case might have been minimized or even mitigated if only McDonald's had provided sufficient, highly visible warnings to their customers that the coffee they serve is super-hot. That certainly seems to have been warranted when you consider the testimony in the Liebeck trial, which revealed that, at 190 degrees, the coffee had been heated well beyond the temperature at which third-degree burns would be caused. They might even conceivably have turned it into a promotional marketing campaign: "McDonald's Coffee: The Coffee That Is Still Hot When You Get to The Office!" It is undoubtedly for all of these reasons and, in spite of the loud public outcry condemning the case as "frivolous litigation," that legal scholar Jonathan Turley argued that the claim represented "a meaningful and worthy lawsuit."[11]

In order to avoid liability, however, McDonald's product engineers or designers would have needed to perform a thorough hazard analysis to try to determine just how "hot" was sufficient and to identify how the super-heated coffee might pose a serious hazard risk to consumers, particularly those juggling the full cups as they receive them in the drive-thru window. Moreover, they could have easily done this astonishingly easily by simply observing their everyday customer behavior in action.

Think about it: Not every car has a convenient cup holder in which to place nuclear-strength coffee, and not every customer actually uses the

---

[11] Wikipedia, "Liebeck v. McDonald's."

cup holder at all. Instead, many people use one hand to drive and the other to sip the hot coffee they just bought. In other words, not *every* customer buys coffee at the drive-thru with the intention of *not* drinking it until they get to the office. Some people—heavens-to-Betsy!—place the coffee cup in their laps or slot it between their legs near their crotch! Had McDonald's product designers observed all of this very typical (albeit perhaps foolish) consumer behavior and been appropriately alarmed by it, they might have prominently featured in their stores and drive-thrus a large red-flag hazard warning, perhaps even printing it on the coffee cups themselves: **DANGER! EXTREMELY HOT COFFEE MAY CAUSE SCALDING! AVOID SPILLING CONTENTS UNTIL IT REACHES TEMPERATURE SAFE TO DRINK!** If they had done so then, McDonald's could conceivably have avoided literally hundreds of lawsuits and settlement costs, not to mention staying out of the spectacular media circus that ultimately surrounded the Liebeck trial and its aftermath. As a result, McDonald's coffee cups currently bear a warning that the contents within are hot.

And yet, this little exercise in the observation of unpredictable and sometimes head-scratching consumer behavior raises the question of how appropriately consumers will react to principled disclosure through such specific hazard warnings. That's because, of course, it is a matter of pure speculation as to whether Stella Liebeck would have exercised more caution in opening her cup of coffee had she received adequate *warning* of the *safety hazard* presented by the fact that the liquid contents were super-heated.

The point should be clear: the educated or informed consumer is much more likely to be a safe consumer. Regardless of our willingness or ability—or unwillingness, if you will—to engage in safer behaviors, we should have, at the very least, sufficient safety information and/or overtly communicated hazard warnings from product manufacturers, employers, and others. Only then may consumers *make informed decisions* regarding the risks we choose to take and the safety precautions or instructions we choose to follow. Or we can choose to ignore them at our own peril!

Finally, the Liebeck hot-coffee-spilling case may also offer a backend insight as an object lesson for consumers in terms of everyone's responsibility. Stella Liebeck did not know that the overheated coffee posed a significant risk to her health and safety because she was never properly informed of that risk. But maybe she would have been more careful if she had known the dangers. Consumers who are properly informed through principled disclosure have an inherent obligation to endeavor to only use hazardous products or operate in hazardous environments in strict accordance with the safety instructions, cautions, and warnings that are duly and effectively provided or communicated to them by product manufacturers, employers, government regulators, and others. As such, consumers and the general public at large form the third leg of a metaphorical stool—equally supported by business and industry and by government regulators, all doing their part to create safer circumstances across an array of activities and environments in which we live, work, and play every day.

In this book, I propose that what is needed going forward is the establishment of an acknowledged Principled Safety Disclosure Triad among three principal parties—companies, government regulators, and the general public—all of whose interests are at stake, respectively. Corporate America must provide safe and reliable products while earning profits for corporations, businesses, and shareholders. Government regulators must vigorously adopt and aggressively disseminate abundantly clear and proactively sufficient safety warnings and precautions where they are inevitably warranted. We must acknowledge that not all hazards can be completed fail-safe in this dangerous world. Finally, consumers must operate in reasonable accordance with product specifications or environmental constraints that will enable them to live happy, safe, and productive lives. You might say that we consumers need to "use as directed." However, in order to do that, we must be provided with principled disclosure by industry and competent oversight by government.

We will explore the Principled Safety Disclosure Triad in much greater detail in Part II of this book. First, however, I begin our investigation of hazards and warnings with a breakdown of the seven behaviors, or behavioral habitats, that, for the most part, define or underlie the range of activities and pastimes we typically engage in. This breakdown provides a convenient set of contexts for understanding the nature and sorts of hazards that lurk within each unique behavioral space.

THE SEVEN MOST COMMON BEHAVIORS AND THEIR HIDDEN HAZARDS

In the following chapters we explore the seven most common behaviors or "environments" that we essentially inhabit or operate within as we go through our daily routines. Particular attention is focused on the hidden safety hazards that exist in each environment. We will also examine what companies, product producers, and government regulatory agencies have done wrong—as well as what they have done right—with respect to informing consumers, workers, travelers, and the general public at large about those hazards. Have companies done everything they can to eliminate hidden hazards? Or, when that is simply not feasible, have they provided clear and sufficient hazard warnings and disclosures such that consumers may use them safely? We will look at whether those warnings and disclosures go far enough. And we will examine instances where companies and regulators both failed and succeeded in accomplishing the goal of principled disclosure that I advocate in this book.

Importantly, we will also cast a balanced and critical eye on the essential role of the general public—as the third leg of the safety triad—in taking personal responsibility when using hazardous products or operating in dangerous environments. Do consumers, in general, responsibly heed bona fide product and safety warnings? Or do they carelessly and recklessly ignore them at their own peril? The seven behavior habitats that I identify are as follows: residing, eating, working, playing, traveling, healing, and communicating. Here is a brief rundown:

Residing. Earlier in this chapter we learned that every year, 33 million Americans, roughly 10 percent of the total U.S. population, are seriously injured in their own homes. It may very well be the case that whatever else it certainly is, "Home is where the hazard is." When you take a moment to reflect, it may be shocking to realize how chock-full of potentially hazardous products and devices the average home or apartment typically is, from ladders, power tools, kitchen knives, chain saws, and firearms to appliances like stove tops, microwave ovens, space heaters, furnaces, wood stoves, and water heaters to cosmetics and powerful, chemical-based cleaning products and solvents to ambient environmental products like lead paint and polyurethane foam (which is essentially solid petroleum). As an example, consider the mildly unnerving prospect of so many "weekend warriors" who pull out the power tools to do projects around the home on their days off, with no more training than perhaps the shop class they took in high school or even eighth grade. Now there's a frightening prescription for disaster!

Furthermore, our homes and apartments literally have dangerous falling hazards built right into them, like a simple flight of stairs or an elevated deck, balconies, slippery bathroom tile floors, and so much more. Indeed, many typical home environments like bathrooms and kitchens or workshops and garages might merit the posting of hazard warning signs simply on the basis of the dangerous stuff we consumers store in those spaces!

Eating. Perhaps in no area of our lives is information obfuscation more ubiquitous and profligate than in the 600,000 processed food products (by some estimates) that line our supermarket shelves. The giant food companies that produce and aggressively market those foods use all manner of sometimes vacuous nutritional and health-conscious claims for their questionable food labeling practices. For example, we need only consider one very common commodity to illustrate the potential hazards with the issue of food additives and honest, transparent ingredient disclosure in food labeling: added processed sugar. Some nutritionists claim that over 80 percent of those 600,000 processed foods contain some quantity of added sugar. Yet, for decades, the FDA has allowed the megalopolis of the food industry to list added sugar not in ounces or teaspoons but in grams despite—or rather, because—virtually no Americans understand the metric system. As an added form of deception, the FDA allows those same food manufacturers to use terms like "high-fructose corn syrup" or "evaporated cane juice," which, by the way, means sugar cane that has been ground up, dried, and processed into—presto! you guessed it: granulated white sugar! Again, this is only one added ingredient among thousands, perhaps millions.

But that's not all. Hardly a day goes by when we aren't confronted with another challenge to our nation's food supply, once thought to be the safest in the world. Domestic food recalls seem to be on the rise, whether due to the efforts of manufacturers to produce larger and larger quantities economically and quickly, or possibly as a result of lax quality control resulting in food contamination and premature spoilage. Perhaps even more concerning, the burgeoning influx of imported foods makes Americans increasingly vulnerable to foods adulterated with chemicals like pesticides and potentially toxic fertilizers, some of which are actually banned for use on crops in the U.S. but not in their more lax countries of origin. The reverse is also true, by the way. Many European countries have banned the use of pesticides and herbicides that are used liberally in U.S. agriculture, particularly in conjunction with Genetically Modified Organisms (GMOs). Are we receiving adequate warnings and sufficiently explicit ingredient labeling from those who manufacture and distribute the food we eat or from the supermarkets that sell us our meat, produce, dry goods, and so on?

Even amid the increasing confusion across the broad spectrum of food safety, country of origin, chemical and nonorganic additives, herbicide and pesticide usage, and GMOs, the current administration under President Trump has already moved to delay or roll back a litany of food safety and labeling information guidelines. Among these roll backs and delays—quite alarmingly—are a number of guidelines that were only recently put in place by the previous administration in direct response to the new threats to the integrity and safety of our food supply from around the world. In light of this reversal, how strategically responsive and adaptable to new, as yet unknown threats may we expect the FDA and other government agencies to be in such an anti-regulatory administrative atmosphere? It's scary to think.

Working. It probably goes without saying that we could have a field day with this category! The Occupational Health and Safety Administration (OSHA) estimates that over 32 million workers in over 3.5 million workplaces are exposed to hazardous chemicals or substances, resulting in approximately 100,000 chemical illnesses and related injuries per year. Construction sites are especially dangerous. OSHA estimates that one in ten construction site workers are injured every year (about 150,000 injuries and 1,000 deaths per year), mostly due to falls or contact with construction equipment. These statistics make the construction industry the most dangerous industry in the United States, with 15 percent of all workers' compensation claims costs resulting from injuries at construction sites.

Mining and manufacturing sectors are not far behind when it comes to failing to ensure worker safety. Over the last two centuries, the history of the coal mining industry in America is one of staggering, arrogant, and blatant disregard for the health and safety of its workers. But as we will see, little has changed here in the 21st century, despite advances in the sophistication of mining machinery and technology that should all but eliminate the kinds of horrific fatalities and serious injuries that continue to make national headlines every few years.

From the manufacturing sector, we trace the history of a relatively high-tech and sole manufacturer of high-strength beryllium metal used in the fabrication of high-speed fighter planes and missiles. Our investigation reveals an allegation that the company may have engaged in a decades-long misrepresentation regarding the serious pulmonary dangers of inhaling excess amounts of beryllium dust. They apparently did so in conjunction with brokering a secret monopoly deal with the Department of Defense and the forerunner of the Atomic Energy Commission.[12]

In the *Working* chapter, I also present a case study of a foreign manufacturing company that successfully followed my simple formula for designing and displaying effective, litigation-proof warning labels. Moreover, this manufacturer of residential and industrial air conditioning equipment

---

[12] Chemical Industry Archives. "H.G. Piper."

engaged me to help them pursue principled disclosure to protect—not their own in-plant line workers—but the thousands of independent contractors and the employees of *those* independent companies' employees who would ultimately be the individuals installing the products in homes and offices across the U.S. What's even more remarkable about this story is that the company is based in a country, and more pointedly, in a culture in which injury liability lawsuits brought against employers by their employees are almost unheard of.

Playing. Americans love to portray themselves as competitive, sports-loving people who play as hard as they work. Certainly, the nation's play- and sports-related injury statistics bear out this claim. A recent report published by *USA Today* indicates that there are annually over 3.5 million sports-related injuries among America's youth.[13] This number represents only injuries that are serious enough to require a visit to a hospital emergency room. While adults and children enjoy everyday sporting and outdoor activities like hiking and swimming, traumatic brain injuries send over 500,000 people to hospital ERs every year.

The need for appropriate safety warnings involves everything from protective clothing and equipment to the design and sensible construction of outdoor ballfields with artificial turf, indoor hardwood courts and gymnasiums, and even the rules of play itself. In fact, the National Collegiate Athletic Association (NCAA) recently reached a settlement in a class action lawsuit that claimed that the NCAA was "negligent and breached its duty to protect all current and former student-athletes by failing to adopt appropriate rules regarding concussions."[14] The suit sought, "medical monitoring relief to diagnose possible long-term effects of concussions or the accumulation of sub-concussive hits for all current and former student athletes," which affects literally millions of collegiate student-athletes. Quite interestingly, this lawsuit demonstrates that nonprofit associations

---

[13] Mangan, "Youth sports injuries."

[14] National Collegiate Athletic Association Student-Athlete Concussion Injury Litigation.

are just as responsible as corporations and may be held equally accountable for providing transparent and effective safety warnings and protections to individuals who operate under its auspices.

Those who play organized sports aren't the only individuals who face risks of serious injury, as Americans vigorously pursue a myriad of outdoor activities in recreation and leisure. This chapter takes a hard look at the private swimming pool and the nation's theme and amusement parks. These present situations in which the hazards that would seem to be intuitively obvious turn out to not be nearly so, making effective warning signs and labels crucial for public awareness and safety.

Americans who notoriously love the great outdoors for fishing, hunting, and camping nevertheless all seem to like taking the conveniences of home along with them. Accordingly, this chapter examines the use of portable cook stoves and lanterns that burn fuels like propane, butane, and sometimes even gasoline. As useful as these products are, they are also prone to produce the highly dangerous by-product that might be described as the ultimate poster child of the hidden hazard: the silent and odorless killer, carbon monoxide.

Traveling. Americans have a love affair both with traveling and with their cars—the very vehicles that over 40,000 of us every year are driving or riding in when we take our last breath on Earth. We have already touched on a few of the most colossal automotive safety warning disclosure and regulatory failures in modern history. The advanced technology that is being packed into today's cars only serves to heighten the specter of increasing driver distraction, yet how safe and critically reliable will the fully computerized "autonomous vehicle" actually be?

Should we be alarmed that auto manufacturers are already racing to install fail-safe features to combat or compensate for driver distraction resulting from the use of mobile devices, texting while driving, and so on? Will innovations like automatic braking, lane-weave warnings, and accident anticipation—or ultimately the completely autonomous car itself—actually be successful in preventing accidents and saving lives and injuries? Or will they simply serve to even further elevate driver (or passenger) inattention to such dizzying and more perilous new heights that they create instead a whole new class of automotive hazards for motorists *and* pedestrians?

Another notoriously serious transportation issue that has been much in the news of late is with regard to railroads and the implementation—or the failure to implement—readily available technology like positive train control (PTC). The furor rages over implementing relatively inexpensive technology despite the fact that many experts believe that, in just the past three years, PTC could have prevented fatal crashes in Philadelphia, New York State, and the Hoboken terminal in New Jersey. But there's more with respect to the nation's rails. Specifically, questionable or misleading signage and faulty or nonworking drop-gates and flashing red warning lights at railroad crossings have contributed to a similarly recent rash of horrific automobile-train collisions. These have also resulted in numerous fatalities to drivers, motormen, and rail passengers. There is absolutely nothing high-tech or rocket-sciencey about designing common-sense railroad-grade crossing safety warnings and preventative equipment. Yet, in 2016, 232 people were tragically killed in the United States in accidents occurring at the places where the rails meet the roads.

Healing. In terms of the sheer breadth and magnitude of opportunity for unbridled exploitation, the medical-pharmaceutical health care industrial complex represents a virtual parallel universe of seemingly limitless possibilities. Today the sumptuous menu of available medications includes increasingly powerful prescription narcotics, painkillers, and psychotropics, as well as over-the-counter drugs and application remedies for just about every bodily ailment from headaches to knee pain. Then there is the mega-industry of vitamins and nutritional supplements, holistic and herbal home remedies, and prescription diet/weight loss pills or remedies. It quickly became clear that all of this offers an abundant fertile crescent for false or wildly exaggerated claims of miraculously effective cures for all of our ailments.

The health care industry aggressively markets these potions, procedures, and pharmacological remedies via a relentless barrage of television, radio, print, and internet advertisements extolling their amazing benefits to an unsuspecting and otherwise uninformed general public. Consumers, mostly through no fault of their own, are largely ignorant of precisely what these products actually do (and more importantly, perhaps, what deleterious side effects their use might entail). Perhaps understandably, consumers often desperately desire to believe the claims, often at the expense of common sense and logic.

Meanwhile, the enormity of the health care industry in its vastness, internal complexity, and political clout make it extremely difficult to comprehend the whole. For all practical purposes, it might convincingly be argued that the health care industry may well be infinitely beyond the scope of comprehensive and dutiful monitoring by government regulatory agencies, principally the FDA. This creates an untenable situation in which the FDA actually relies on the industry itself to author product safety warnings, proper usage instructions, ingredient identification, and most ominously of all, true and honest side-effect indications and precautions.

Case in point: In the *Healing* chapter we will undertake an extensive analysis of Direct to Consumer (DTC) television advertisements produced by the pharmaceutical industry and approved by the FDA. In this regard, we will explore the crucial question of whether these slick ads are delivering a mixed message created by eye-candy visuals that directly contradict the safety warnings presented in parallel within the ad itself. Such commercials also misleadingly encourage consumers to self-medicate by pressuring their doctors to prescribe the medications they see on DTC broadcast ads when safer or less expensive alternatives may be the better choice for them.

Communicating. The present era of human history that largely coincides with the onset of the 21st century has been dubbed "The Information Age." This is a term intended to describe an era characterized by a shift from an industrial-manufacturing economy to an information-computerization-digitization economy. Never before has the human race been able to communicate as fast and as far and as cost effectively as it can today. And never in human history has the creation of knowledge and information been more mind-bogglingly explosive to the point of being literally beyond comprehension. Computer engineers and technologists have for decades busied themselves with creating an unending cavalcade of smart communication, information processing, and sharing devices to try to help us assimilate, manage, store, and retrieve that knowledge and information at lightning speed.

While this chapter touches on the issue of the potential danger of radio wave radiation to our brains and bodies from the communications devices themselves (for which the presently available data are, at best, inconclusive), we focus primarily on a much more fundamental and somewhat philosophical question. Specifically: How does one warn about the hidden hazards of communication itself? Related questions include:

- How do/will companies and organizations use the personal data they acquire about individual consumers?
- How does the act of communicating in and of itself affect the conduct of our everyday lives?
- What happens when communication itself becomes "commoditized"?

Today's instantaneous electronic communication capability brings with it tremendous power for positive community building, or creating what Marshall McLuhan first described as the "global village." The research presented in this chapter also reveals a sinister side of internet-based mass communication: its ability to promote addictive behavior, for example, through online gaming that robs productivity, to outright online casino gambling that might rob some people of their wealth. The creation of the internet has also seen a significant and ominous rise in the relatively new phenomenon of cyberbullying that has been documented as the direct cause of an increasing number of fatalities and suicides—among both adults and children.

As McLuhan himself pointed out more than 60 years ago, "We're re-tribalizing. Involuntarily, we're getting rid of individualism."[15] No longer concerned with "finding our own individual way," we instead obsess over "what the group knows, feeling as it does, acting 'with it,' not apart from it." In our modern 21st-century information age, McLuhan's words certainly appear to explain the apparent, overpowering desire among the members of innumerable internet "communities" to think the same thoughts and act the same way. In some ways, this phenomenon may be the driving force behind the prevalence of misinformation and falsehood that we have come to call "fake news" today.

In this final and perhaps most omnipresent and ethereal behavioral habitat we examine the power of information itself—both good and bad. We look at the ability of instantaneous communication to rally support behind a common cause, but its power to also tear people apart from one another in very destructive ways. It is abundantly evident that we will need to make sense of what is clearly a whole new, unique, and uncharted panorama of technology, law, and social governance.

---

[15] Wikipedia, "Marshall McLuhan."

CHAPTER 2

RESIDING: DRIVEWAY TO THE DANGER ZONE

According to statistics compiled by the Consumer Product Safety Commission (CPSC), each year in America, "deaths, injuries, and property damage from consumer product incidents cost the nation more than $1 trillion annually," many of which occurs right in the familiar confines of our homes and apartments.[16] The CPSC data indicates that most of the people who are injured at home are over 55 years old, and that people over 65 account for over 10 percent of that trillion-dollar figure—or $100 billion. The numbers get worse as we get older. While people over 65 represent only 13 percent of the population, they make up 65 percent of all the fatalities of which the CPSC keeps records. Most of these fatalities and serious injuries are caused by falls, for example, by people falling off ladders or stepstools, down a flight of stairs, or simply from tripping on a rug, and people over 50 years of age account for 80 percent of all home-related accidents due to falls.

And yet, the CPSC's trillion-dollar estimate may be only the tip of the iceberg. Created by President Richard Nixon in 1962, the CPSC is charged with protecting the public against unreasonable risks of injuries and deaths associated with consumer products. They are responsible for compiling information on thousands of products from appliances like coffee makers, food processors, and microwave ovens to lawn mowers and all-terrain vehicles

---

[16] Consumer Product Safety Commission.

(ATVs), from toys, bicycles, and scooters to outdoor grills and smokers—the list goes on. A quick perusal of the CPSC's website reveals nearly 900 pages of product warnings and recalls dating back to 1973. Yet, despite this vast responsibility, the CPSC is very small, consisting of a Chairman, currently Robert Adler (Acting), and four other Commissioners.

However, it is the principal way that the CPSC obtains its information on product hazards that may be suspect, through its compilation and maintenance of a database known as the National Electronic Injury Surveillance System (NEISS). The NEISS database is compiled from a nationwide survey of emergency rooms across the U.S. Typically, whenever someone comes into one of the NEISS-sampled emergency rooms with an injury that is linked to a specific product, the hospital must report that data to the CPSC. The CPSC then extrapolates from this sample data to estimate the rates of similar injuries from the same products and issues reports estimating the total number of injuries, and profiling who was injured and what the typical type of injury was that resulted from the use of the product.

For example, in a report covering the year of 2015, the CPSC estimated that there were 94,524 injuries involving child nursery equipment, extrapolating that number from an NEISS count of 3,132 actual injuries based on a nationwide sampling of only 96 hospitals. The report broke down the number of injuries into age ranges and whether the injured persons were male or female. Finally, the report indicated that of the extrapolated numbers, the CPSC estimated that 89,993 of the ER patients were treated and released from the hospital, while 4,530 patients required a stay in the hospital or were fatalities.[17]

However, the problem is that while there were over 5,000 hospitals registered in the United States in 2017, the NEISS sampled only 96 hospital emergency rooms across the country. There are a number of flaws with this scheme, not the least of which is the fact that the sampling size is too small to be scientifically significant. Furthermore, there are hundreds of thousands of doctors across the country who are not part of this system, and not everybody who is injured using a product at home goes

---

[17] CPSC, "2015 Annual Report."

to the emergency room. Also, in response to the skyrocketing costs of health insurance (even with the Affordable Care Act in place), there are also thousands of urgent care facilities that have sprung up that are also not part of the NEISS database. The system may also be flawed along demographic lines, in particular with respect to socioeconomic status. For example, many poorer people who cannot afford health care premiums go directly to hospital emergency rooms as their primary source of treatment, whereas well-to-do individuals who do have insurance might simply go to their trusted family physician.

Finally, aside from the NEISS database and the accident and injury information that is reported from its sampling of hospital ERs, the expectations of the commission on the consumer products industry are largely voluntary. Companies are expected to report proactively product defects or safety concerns that arise from the products they sell to the general public. And while individual consumers may also report problems with specific products directly to the CPSC, there would appear to be little or no direct pressure on companies to report product defects to the commission—especially if they think they can get away by letting them slide. These lax standards also allow companies to write their own product safety warnings—not every company is willing to go to a safety warnings expert to obtain the kind of warnings language, graphics, and signage that might be required to adequately convey the danger to an unwary public.

THE COMPONENTS OF AN EFFECTIVE PRODUCT SAFETY WARNING

It will be most useful to begin by defining precisely what constitutes an effective and sufficient product or environmental safety warning. Specifically:

> *An effective product warning signals conspicuously a safety message about a hidden hazard, conveys the potential harmful consequences of that hazard, and provides instructions to follow that enable consumers to avoid these consequences.*

In the following example (Figure 2.1), note the signal word "Danger" is very large and stylized to make it highly visible. "Shallow water" is the hazard identified, "You can be paralyzed" is the harmful consequence, and "No diving," is the instruction. The accompanying graphic amply and very simply illustrates the danger in a way that most people should understand just by looking at it.

FIGURE 2.1

Courtesy of Dr. Gerald M. Goldhaber

However, product manufacturers often skimp on the safety warnings and user instructions they provide with their products. For example, a manufacturer of clothing dryers may include an instruction in the appliance's user manual to clean out the lint filter regularly without telling you why this is so critically important. Lint is highly flammable, and the superheated air produced by the dryer to quickly tumble-dry your clothing can easily cause a spark capable of igniting the accumulated lint, resulting in a house fire. But the instructions don't warn you about what may happen if you *don't* clean your lint filter regularly.

Often, the hazards posed by a product are not so obvious and intuitive as we might expect. Today, most people are probably aware of the choking or suffocation danger posed to infants and toddlers by bedrails on cribs or infant beds that are improperly spaced, allowing babies' heads to become lodged between them. But are you aware that the same hazard has been found to impact older people? In fact, the CPSC recently launched a voluntary recall of certain kinds of adult bedrails after its investigation revealed that, between the years 1985 to 2009, of 203 incidents of "entrapments, entanglements, or strangulations in bedrails," of which 155 resulted in fatalities, 123 incidents involved individuals older than 60, and another 31 involved individuals between the ages of five and 60.[18] Yet, previously there was no warning provided by manufacturers that the bedrails posed a danger to adults as well as children.

THE POWER IN YOUR MICROWAVE OVEN

Perhaps one of the most potentially hazardous items in your home is the microwave oven that millions upon millions of Americans use every day in their kitchens. But it's hazardous *only* when it is used incorrectly. When it is used properly, it may well be the safest appliance in your home. Here is, arguably, one on the most revolutionary home kitchen devices ever invented: a compact and easily portable counter-top oven that terrifically enables consumers to cook food and prepare hot meals in a fraction of the time it takes using conventional ovens or stove-top ranges. I want to emphasize: cook *food* and prepare *hot meals*. You will shortly learn why I provide that emphasis.

The microwave oven was invented by Percy Spencer, a self-taught orphan who never finished elementary school. But as head of the power tube division for Raytheon Corporation, he managed to become one of world's leading experts in radar tube design. Raytheon subsequently filed a patent for the microwave oven on October 8, 1945. The first commercially available microwave oven stood nearly 6 feet tall, weighed 750 pounds, and carried a list price of several thousand dollars. However, the first counter-top compact models began rolling off the assembly line in 1967 at a list price of just under $500.

---

[18] AARP, "Bed Rails."

While myths about leaking radiation around the doors or glass fronts of these devices have long been dispelled, the microwave oven offers unique insight into the ways in which all three parties to the safety triad often play a role in the hazardous misuse of a product. First, the manufacturer for failing to post safety warnings—or even important specifications that might be crucial to the safe and proper use of the product (like wattage output in the case of the microwave)—prominently enough; second, the regulators like the CPSC for failing to enforce stricter and more visible warnings that speak *directly* to the potential hazards; and third, the consumers who, truth be told, very often misuse the product in thoughtlessly foolish ways.

For example, the labels on many microwavable foods like frozen dinners instruct the consumer to heat the product for, say two and a half minutes in a high wattage (over 800 watts) microwave oven or for three minutes in a low wattage oven. However, most consumers have no idea what the precise wattage of their particular make and model actually is. Nor are the manufacturers of microwave appliances very much help since they typically put a small label on the back or the underside of the unit (where it generally cannot be seen when set up for use). However, this label usually does nothing more than indicate that the unit is 120 volts, which is mandated by Underwriters Laboratories. There is no requirement for them to disclose the so-called output wattage.

Even having this information proves to be of very little help at all. Bob Schiffmann is currently in his 17th year as President of the International Microwave Power Institute (IMPI) and is among the top microwave experts in the world. He has tested microwave ovens for decades and has found that most microwaves do not carry wattage labels at all. In a way, that's like selling you a car without telling you how many cylinders it has or the average gas mileage it gets. But Schiffmann points out that even if they did, his testing has discovered that the manufacturers' claimed wattage can actually vary widely, from 15 to 25 percent from the actual wattage. Not only that, but this so-called "output" wattage can vary several times over a few hours and from day to day (though usually not significantly) and differs more drastically with the type and quantity of food that is placed in the oven. To take this a step further, the exact same make and model of microwave oven designed and produced by the same manufacturer can vary widely in wattage from one unit to the other, and the heating characteristics of the internal space within each individual oven can vary, most typically with hotter regions being closer to the bottom—although that is not always the case.

The producers of microwavable foods aren't any more helpful than the appliance manufacturers, as we will shortly see. The problem of nonexistent, inaccurate, or confusing information with respect to the proper use of one category of products—thus opening the door to their inadvertent misuse due to hidden or unknown hazards—often has a diabolical way of spilling over to the concatenating misuse of other products that might be used in conjunction with the original products, resulting in exposure to even further potentially serious hazards. Let me back up a bit to explain what I mean.

Technological innovation, especially as it eventually finds practical use or becomes embodied in task-specific inventions or devices for general consumer use, has a way of spawning all sorts of further product innovation, as well as new assortments of hazards associated with them. So, for a very basic example, the discovery of how to harness electricity for home and commercial use inevitably led to the electrification of everything, from light bulbs, appliances, and vacuum cleaners to power drills, pencil sharpeners, and computers. Just think of the hundreds of thousands, perhaps millions of companies that exist today because they make and sell products that are capable of being powered by electricity.

Now this innovative technology itself creates a whole new class of safety hazards. One can, either by sheer accident or carelessness, be electrocuted, say by using an electric appliance like a hair curling wand or electric shaver in the bathroom that accidently comes in contact with your sink or bathwater. It's also a lot easier to slice off several of your fingers using an electric circular saw than it was when the only means of cutting a piece of lumber was by using a muscle-powered hand saw. How about the potential fate of a homeowner who tries to retrieve a slice of crispy pumpernickel by sticking a fork into a toaster that is still plugged into the wall socket? Faulty or improperly installed electrical wiring itself can result in house fires, which have even been shown to be caused by rodents gnawing on the insulation sheath surrounding electrical cables and exposing the "hot" wires to nearby combustible materials.

But new innovation and new products often create a kind of second generation of potential new hazards, some of which should be obvious, but many of which are, in fact, not so. We need only look at home electrical wiring itself to see what I mean. When the price of copper skyrocketed in the mid-1960s, many homebuilders began to substitute cheaper, single-strand aluminum wiring in homes built between 1965 and 1973. According to the International Association of Certified Home Inspectors, "After a decade of use by homeowners and electricians, inherent weaknesses were discovered in the metal that led to its disuse as a branch wiring material … aluminum wiring will generally become defective faster than copper due to certain qualities inherent in the metal. Neglected connections in outlets, switches, and light fixtures containing aluminum wiring become increasingly dangerous over time."[19]

Basically, aluminum wiring is not as ductile as copper, meaning that it is more prone to fatigue from bending and deforming, which is exactly what happens when your contractor installs electrical wires in your new home or addition. It turns out that this metal fatigue caused aluminum wiring to break down internally. When this happens, aluminum becomes increasingly resistant to electrical current, leading to a dangerous buildup of heat. Even more alarming, aluminum wiring exhibits excessive thermal expansion and contraction that make it an unacceptable substitute for more stable copper.

---

[19] Gromicko and Shepard, "Wiring."

Most homeowners know that electrical wires tend to heat up (within safe and acceptable limits) when the light switch or appliance is turned on and current is running through the wire. What many home buyers in the 60s and 70s did not know was that the excessive temperature-driven expansion and contraction of aluminum wiring, most critically at the point of connection either at the switch or device (say, your oven or kitchen range), or within the electrical circuit service box at the source, causes these connections to degrade rapidly. In simple terms, the constant expansion and contraction of the aluminum wires causes the connections to become loose over time, ultimately creating gaps between wire and connector. Electricity arcing across these gaps generates sparks that caused numerous house fires and resultant fatalities.

After its own investigation into the potential safety hazards surrounding the use of aluminum electrical wiring, the CPSC determined that, "Homes wired with aluminum wire manufactured before 1972 are 55 times more likely to have one or more connections reach 'Fire Hazard Conditions' than is a home wired with copper."[20] But here's the kicker. It is estimated that there may be as many as two million homes and office buildings in America that still have aluminum wiring as part of their electrical systems. And, while there is no way of knowing how many of these situations may have been remediated, to this day, in many states, there is no requirement that property owners must disclose the presence of aluminum wiring to potential buyers or to realtors representing those buyers.

Or think about what can happen when technologies collide. Like the first guy who tried to combine machine guns with aeronautics and presumed, rather incorrectly, that the nose propeller would spin so rapidly that the bullets fired from fuselage-mounted automatic weapons would rocket harmlessly past the whirring blades without shearing them off. Somewhat less humorously, electricity combined with and used to power automatic

---

[20] CPSC, "Wiring."

swimming pool water filtration and sanitizing systems resulted in many electrocution deaths until automatic short-circuit detection devices were added, which are capable of instantly shutting off the power to the system in split-second time to prevent disaster. Of course, it goes without saying that all of these "new" hazards can have equally serious consequences for our health and safety.

But let's get back to our discussion of the microwave oven.

It perhaps stands as compelling testimony to the unique and revolutionary nature of innovation represented by the microwave oven that, like electricity itself, the now ubiquitous device has spawned all sorts of product lines designed to be used in direct, presumably harmonious conjunction with the microwave. However, the crucial question is: Is it really safe to use all of those products with the microwave oven, or do some of these proposed uses represent cases of combining machine guns and airplane propellers?

Not surprisingly, one of the major industries or product innovations that quickly followed the convenience and popularity of the microwave oven was pre-prepared and frozen, instantly microwavable dinners and other food items for "people on the go." However, in October 2007, one of the largest food companies in the world, Conagra Foods, recalled all of its own "Banquet" brand as well as numerous customized store brand pot pies due to a potential link to an outbreak of *Salmonella*. Conagra's label called for the use of microwaves with at least 1100 watts and consumers were instructed to measure the internal temperature of the "not-ready-to-eat" products to be sure they were at least 165 degrees. This instruction, of course, presumes that consumers' microwave ovens have labeled the wattage, that the wattage is accurate and consistent during every use, and not only that the consumer has an accurate food thermometer to measure the internal temperature of the food, but also knows how and where to measure the food (in several locations).

But that only describes part of the difficulty. As we saw earlier, and based on the exhaustive research conducted by the International Microwave Power Institute (IMPI) and leading expert Bob Schiffmann, not only do most microwave ovens not have labels displaying their output wattage, there is no reasonable and easily accessible means by which consumers may accurately measure the precise wattage their individual ovens actually generate. And there is absolutely no guarantee that the output wattage claimed by the manufacturer is in any way accurate (regardless of whether they put it on a label or not). In fact, if Schiffmann's findings are correct, the only way that manufacturers would be able to ascertain this distinctly unit-specific wattage measurement would require testing every single microwave oven individually and creating a custom label for every unit tested and shipped!

Is there a solution to all of this?

Well, if the microwave oven manufacturers had done a better job with respect to principled disclosure of the inherent variability of the output wattage generated from one oven to the next, consumers would have had, at the very least, a somewhat better idea as to whether they might safely use Conagra's frozen, instantly microwavable dinners (as well as those produced and sold by dozens of other competitors in the lucrative frozen microwavable dinner market) in their respective units by matching up the unit output with the Conagra specifications on the package. Remember that this inherent variability by all appearances is really not the manufacturers' fault entirely: it appears rather to be an unavoidable artifact of the microwave technology itself. So for general consumers, a simple, properly designed and appropriately visible specifications label, complete with a disclaimer about the inherent variability of all microwave ovens, affixed to every unit and perhaps repeated on the outside of the boxes in which the units were sold, may very well have been sufficient as a viable consumer safety warning concerning the product's capabilities and limitations. In other words, the disclosure of this product specification information would have enabled consumers to make an informed decision about whether they chose to cook Conagra Banquet brand frozen dinners in their ovens. (Even before that, the unit specifications may have impacted their decision to buy this particular unit, or perhaps to select a different model entirely.)

As for Conagra, it seems clear that the company's product research and development (R&D) team failed miserably in its responsibility to perform aggressive and effective due diligence in researching the viability of producing and packaging complete, nutritious, and tasty instantly microwavable frozen dinners using uncooked, "not ready to eat" ingredients that could be fully cooked and safely eaten by consumers. You have to wonder. The company surely spent hundreds of thousands of dollars, perhaps much more, in the research and development of the Banquet frozen food line. Successful companies do not embark on creating such new product lines involving *major* investment of capital without doing at least *some* due diligence.

In writing the user directions for preparing the frozen dinners in the microwave ovens that were flooding the market at the time, it's virtually impossible to imagine that they did not first have to look at the output wattage for the typical oven. How else would Conagra's development experts know to specify the requirement of at least 1100 watts? And, while some might say it's a case of hindsight being 20-20, it honestly does not seem like much of a reasonable stretch to expect at least one of Conagra's researchers to ask, "Well, if 1100 watts is a critical specification, what other variabilities might impact the health risks associated with cooking instant frozen dinners in a typical microwave oven?" (Did any of their team try cooking this stuff in their home microwaves to see how well it worked?)

If they had asked this question, they would have undoubtedly discovered the highly significant, well-documented, and potentially dangerous anomaly of microwave output wattage variability and its unpredictable regional effect on temperature within each individual unit. Conceivably, that knowledge may (or may not, had Conagra hypothetically adopted the bull-headed, Ford Pinto damn-the-torpedoes mentality) have induced the food maker to rethink its product design with respect to the required food heating specifications, or abandon the proposed product line altogether. In either case, the company's costly recall would never have been necessary.

And, in fact, it is largely because of the unavoidable wattage variability inherent in every microwave oven—which represents a hazard that apparently cannot be designed out—that today most companies that continue to make microwavable frozen foods use ingredients that are fully cooked before they are packaged and sent to the supermarket. This effectively eliminates the threat of bacterial contamination of raw foods going to your plate after potentially remaining undercooked even after proper microwave preparation in accordance with the directions on the package.

Yet, in this instance, Conagra was at the very least attempting to manufacture and sell products designed specifically to meet what the microwave oven is supposed to be used for and—more strenuously in fact—what the Microwave Institute asserts and maintains is its only recommend use: the heating or cooking of food.

WHEN CONSUMER PRODUCT USAGE GOES ROGUE

Enter a microwaveable wax produced and marketed by a West Coast cosmetics company. This product is a facial hair remover wax designed, ostensibly, to be heated in the microwave and then applied using a provided plastic paddle to regions of the face plagued by unwanted hair, typically on the upper lip for some women. The instruction booklet (in the tiniest print you can imagine) tells consumers to heat the product right in its plastic jar for decreasing increments of 15 seconds as it is used, starting at one minute for a full jar (on first use), 45 seconds for a ¾-full jar, 30 seconds for a ½-full jar, and finally 15 seconds for a ¼-full jar. The jar has a small handle for conveniently removing it from the microwave.

The directions make no reference whatsoever to any required output wattage of the microwave one uses to heat the product. As for the variability of individual ovens, the instructions include only a very generic and nonspecific statement as follows: "NOTE: Microwaves and heating time vary. Therefore, 15-second heating times are suggested." In other words, if you heat the jar for the specified time and then find that the wax does not yet exhibit the "thick, creamy texture when it reaches the correct temperature for use" (again quoting directly from the directions), you are supposed to heat the jar again in 15-second intervals until the right consistency is achieved. Of course, these statements provided in the same print size and font as the rest of the instructions in the booklet are by no means adequate as recognizable and legitimate safety warning labels, and meet none of the required criteria for same.

By now, you can probably see where this is going. Recently, I was retained as a consultant in a case in which a female consumer, whom I shall refer to as Clare, attempted to use this microwaveable facial hair remover and did so by faithfully following the directions provided in the instruction book. However, when she opened it after heating the full jar for the prescribed 60 seconds, she found the wax inside to be very tacky and firm rather than "thick and creamy," and in no way ready for application. So, Clare proceeded to heat the jar for 15-second intervals until it did appear ready—again, as suggested in the product instructions.

However, at that point, when she picked up the plastic jar by the handle and removed it from her microwave for use, the bottom of the jar separated from the top, allegedly spilling a scalding mix of superheated wax and melted plastic all over her chest and causing extensive third-degree burns. Due to the inconsistent heating characteristics inside Clare's microwave oven, the very bottom of the jar and its contents became so superheated that it actually melted the jar, while the contents at the top of the jar remained so deceptively "undercooked" that it had not even reached the desired consistency for application.

The lesson that should be learned from this lawsuit, and the likely thousands of other cases just like it, is even more basic than the one that Conagra should have learned from its foray into leveraging microwave technology to launch a new frozen food product line. No one puts it more plainly or more categorically than Bob Schiffmann when he states: *Nothing should go into your microwave oven other than food.*[21]

Yet, most consumers simply don't know this simple but important rule. A quick search on the internet reveals a laundry list of "handy tips" for things you can do with your microwave that have nothing to do with

---

[21] Schiffmann.

preparing your dinner, ranging from the amusing to the idiotic. These include disinfecting and deodorizing sponges, disinfecting plastic cutting boards (we have already seen that microwaves are quite good at melting plastic), heating up health aids like headache gel packs, warming hair oil and other beauty products (I just recounted an example of how well that one works), sterilizing garden soil before planting seedlings, and, believe it or not, dyeing fabrics!

Here's one that probably 90 percent of microwave oven users routinely do without even thinking about it: Do you put a paper towel on the floor or turntable of your microwave? Because foods cooked in there tend to pop and spit, and you want to keep your unit clean, right? Are you aware that if you use recycled paper towels for this purpose, you are creating a fire hazard right in your kitchen? Recycled paper towels inevitably contain tiny shards of metal. That's because people don't take things like staples, paper clips, and spiral wire bindings out of the millions of tons of paper that are thrown into recycling bins across the country. These metals are ground into microscopic particles ingrained into the fibers of recycled paper towels and have been known to spark fires in microwaves.

The warning label on Bounty (Procter & Gamble) brand paper towels reads vaguely: CAUTION: ANY PAPER PRODUCT CAN BURN IF IMPROPERLY USED IN MICROWAVE OR CONVENTIONAL OVENS. However, the company states that its paper towels are made with all-virgin materials and contain no recycled materials. Marcal Paper Mills, on the other hand, advertises boldly on the package that its "Recycled fiber paper products save millions of trees annually." Marcal's warning label reads: CAUTION: IMPROPER MICROWAVE USE CAN CAUSE ANY PAPER PRODUCT TO BURN. OBSERVE PRECAUTIONS IN THE MICROWAVE OVEN OWNER'S MANUAL. Similar wording appears on packages of Brawny (Georgia-Pacific) and Scott paper towels (Kimberly-Clark). So, not only do the safety warnings posted by these three companies make no mention whatsoever of the increased risk of fire due to the potential for tiny metal shards in recycled materials, they astonishingly throw the issue back onto the microwave manufacturers!

Of course, this and similar cases raise serious questions for the manufacturers of the aforementioned microwaveable wax, questions that I must confess somewhat wickedly, am keenly interested in hearing what possible fanciful answers the company might come up with. Questions such as: In what universe did this manufacturer think that heating facial hair wax remover in microwave ovens was a good idea? Or, did the company do any substantive product research and testing whatsoever to try to predict any potential hazards that doing so might pose to consumers—whether the product was used strictly in accordance with the directions drawn up by the company, or even if it was accidently used improperly by unsuspecting consumers? Also, did the company's R&D researchers bother to consult with experts in the microwave industry to inquire about any possible drawbacks or hazards that might occur as a result of using the ovens in this "handy" and convenient nonfood application?

And, oh yes, I have a question for the microwave manufacturers, too: Why don't all microwave ovens that are sold to the general public have a highly visible warning label that states: "Warning: This microwave oven should be used for the cooking or heating of food only." Perhaps the warning should be even stronger: WARNING: PUTTING ANY NONFOOD ITEMS IN THIS MICROWAVE OVEN MAY CAUSE RISK FOR FIRES OR INJURIES. In fact, maybe putting anything into a microwave oven *other* than food should effectively void the warranty.

THE PASSIVE DANGERS IN YOUR BASEMENT AND WALLS

Most of the clear and present hazards in our homes involve things that we engage actively when we are using them; things like microwaves and lawn mowers, food processors and power tools, or kitchen knives and electric hair dryers or space heaters. But our homes are also full of things that are essentially noninteractive, or what we might call passive products, installations, or systems. Generally speaking, potentially hazardous passive products include things like lead paint in houses built before 1978 or insulated with toxic polyurethane foam blown or piped into the walls, or containing the potentially dangerous aluminum electrical wiring I discussed earlier in this chapter.

They also include certain appliance-driven systems like furnaces, central air conditioning, heat pumps, and water heaters that operate with such day-in and day-out unnoticeable automaticity from one season to the next that we hardly know these devices are even there, much less where they are located. But let's consider one such appliance that, remarkably as it may seem, enables me to relate the story of an American company that "did the right thing" with respect to providing principled disclosure to consumers. They did so specifically by creating and posting on their products a prominently displayed label fully meeting all of the component criteria requirements for an effective safety warning. The company is Rheem Manufacturing Company and the product is the gas-fired water heater.

We should begin by first considering what a water heater is and, very crucially, where it is usually located. The unit itself (in very simplistic terms) is basically a large tank filled with water and equipped with a very powerful heating element to provide hot water to the kitchen and baths throughout your home. The earliest gas-fired units manufactured by Rheem and several other companies required a pilot light as the source of the flame needed to fire up the unit whenever someone in the house used a hot water spigot at the kitchen sink to wash the dishes or fill up the bathtub to take a bath. To heat the water, the heating unit with its ever-present pilot light must be positioned at the very bottom of the unit below the tank, the flame itself only a few inches from the floor. Now, the fact that the pilot light needed to be designed in such a way that it could burn safely and unattended 24 hours a day, seven days a week was not a significant hazardous condition in and of itself. There are tens of millions of water heaters, furnaces, and gas or propane kitchen cook stoves all across the country that have pilot lights that present no danger whatsoever—barring other impinging circumstances of the sort I will describe shortly. However, this is where the actual physical location of the water heater unit within the home becomes the rub.

Unsightly passive systems like furnaces and water heaters are typically placed discretely and mostly out of sight in attached garages or home basements, or are often located in a utility room with the clothes washer and dryer, and quite possibly with the electric service circuit box that distributes power to the entire home. It makes perfect sense: natural gas, furnaces, water heaters, electricity—they're all "utilities," right? The uncanny thing is, quite logically, garages and basement utility rooms are also the prototypical places that unsuspecting homeowners store paints, flammable solvents like turpentine or mineral spirits, potent cleaning products, and, especially in the case of the garage, motor oils and gasoline. This disturbing juxtaposition is positively, potentially incendiary!

To illustrate, consider the fictitious story of hapless Harry the ambitious homeowner:

Harry is happily married to Marge and together they own a nice house in an upscale suburban neighborhood. Harry takes great, self-sufficient pride in keeping up his home and property primarily by himself, and he has all the tools and gadgets to prove it. His best work might be manifest in his meticulous maintenance of the parklike landscaping of the shrubs, trees, and expansive manicured lawns that surround the house. In support of that responsibility, however, Harry likes to store sufficient quantities of motor oil and gasoline for all of his power lawn equipment—lots of gasoline. He has a big, gas-powered riding lawnmower and a four-wheel ATV with a cart for hauling debris; he has a chain saw, rotor-tiller, power leafblower, string trimmer, and hedge clipper that all run on a gas-oil mix; and, for the winter, he has a state-of-the-art snowblower and a gas-powered generator, just in case the power goes out in a storm. He also feels he needs to store gasoline because, perhaps foolishly, occasionally he allows his kids to drive the ATV around the yard at breakneck speeds, and Marge has an absentminded tendency to forget to keep her car full of gas. So, he needs to add a couple of gallons from time to time just to ensure that she can make it to the gas station next time she goes out. Harry naturally stores the gasoline out in the garage with his arsenal of equipment and his automobiles, and right alongside his vast collection of paints and flammable solvents.

Yet, the garage is the same place where the home's water heater is located, right up against the back wall where the garage is adjoined to the house.

And while he is careful enough to store his five-gallon gas cans on the upper shelf of a steel rack, out there in the safety (so he thinks) of the garage, Harry didn't do so well in chemistry in high school. What he doesn't understand is those fumes and how they travel. Sometimes he fills the tanks of his machines right there on the floor of the garage, the fumes invisibly wafting along the floor. Sometimes he doesn't screw the caps tightly enough on the cans when he puts them back up for storage. More fumes escape. Harry doesn't understand that gasoline fumes are heavier than air, so just like a lead weight, fumes leaking from his array of fuel cans cascade to the floor like a silent, *flammable* Niagara Falls. The same is true for equally volatile fumes leaking from any improperly sealed paint cans or solvent containers.

Once those fumes hit the floor, they travel outward in all directions like an invisible fog, layering up along the floor, especially when the garage door is closed at night. Not only that, but the normal firing operation of the water heater creates carbon dioxide and some measure of excess heat that must be vented to the outside. That means it must draw air for combustion from—you guessed it—inside the garage and primarily the area around the base of the unit where the pilot light is located beneath the heating apparatus. This makes the pilot light a virtual vortex for any fumes lurking nearby at floor level. And, of course, when those volatile fumes eventually find the tiny but nonetheless open flame of the water heater's pilot light: **BOOM!** All of Harry's power equipment, his cars, and his ATV are in critical danger of going up in a massive explosion possibly destroying his home as well, not to mention endangering the life and limb of his family and even his neighbors. The water heater can be standing 20 to 30 feet away from those sturdy steel shelves on which the gas cans are stored, but it doesn't matter. Left unchecked, gasoline and other explosive fumes will seek their level, and will very likely ignite upon making contact with the pilot light flame. In point of fact, gas fumes are actually more volatile than liquid gasoline.

Lest we be too harsh on Harry for this potentially deadly oversight, this example demonstrates the very essence of a hidden hazard. The truth is, most homeowners don't spend too much time out of their day thinking about their water heaters. That, in turn, is the essence of a passive system from the consumer's point of view. You install it, you start it up, and you forget about it. Similarly, though admittedly somewhat less excusably, when those same homeowners store flammable products for routine home use, like gasoline and turpentine, they don't think about the heaviness of the fumes, or that they are heavier than air and apt to become more densely concentrated along the floor. They don't think about the hot water heater with a pilot light. Ninety-nine percent of the time, they've never even seen the pilot light, but it's there.

MITIGATING A HIDDEN HAZARD THROUGH WARNING LABEL RESEARCH AND DESIGN

While it was certainly true that lawsuits over exploding water heaters were beginning to mount up, when Rheem approached me as a consultant to create effective safety warnings for their products, their executives gave every indication that they wanted to do the right thing. Unfortunately, there was nothing that could be done about the pending lawsuits that would inevitably have to be adjudicated, and most likely settled out of court, but the Rheem executives sincerely wanted to do everything they could to avert future disasters among their customers. And the refreshing fact is that they admirably followed through on their intentions.

For example, Rheem understood that they really had only one opportunity to warn consumers of the danger posed by placing flammable liquids close to an appliance with a constant open-flame pilot light. That opportunity was upon installation of the unit. After that, no homeowner was likely to even look at the unit until perhaps it might need replacing 20 years later. So, they wanted to devise an easily understandable and highly communicative safety warning label to be placed so conspicuously on each unit that consumers could not miss it with their eyes shut.

Accordingly, we engaged in a process by which we did national studies to find out how many people were aware of this common hazard and we found out that, in fact, not a lot of people were. Next, we designed a number of warning label variations complete with demonstrative pictures and diagrams to try to illustrate the hazard graphically. The goal of any graphical depiction on a safety warning label is to make the nature of the potential hazard as instantly recognizable to the viewer as possible, even if that means evoking the horror that might result from failing to heed the warning. (*See Figure 2.2*)

FIGURE 2.2

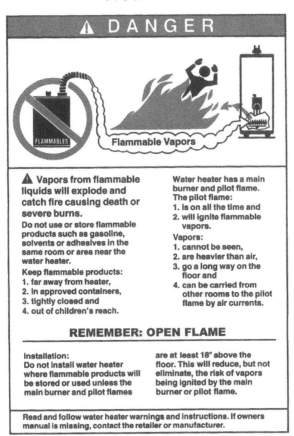

Courtesy of Dr. Gerald M. Goldhaber

We came up with different pictorials and tested them to see which achieved the highest recognition value. Additionally, we came up with differently worded statements of the hazard and tested those to see which of them were most effective in getting people's attention, but even more importantly, to determine the one that would be most easily understandable to the greatest number of people. In all of my experience, there is only one reliable way to test the effectiveness of a safety warning label design, and that is by showing it to as many unbiased people as possible, and carefully gauging their response. Next, we took our array of label design candidates and actually set up water heaters in a number of prominent malls across the United States. There, we randomly asked shoppers to look at the different units and give us their impressions. We specifically did not ask them to look at the warning labels, the crucial test being whether they noticed them at all, and, if so, how substantively did they "get the message."

As you can see from Figure 2.2, the final label design that we proposed, and which Rheem ultimately adopted, conspicuously signals a safety message about a hidden hazard, conveys the potentially harmful consequences of the hazard in highly understandable language accompanied by a fairly gruesome graphic depiction (including a guy on fire!), and provides equally understandable instructions to follow that enable consumers to avoid these dire consequences. The word "DANGER" in all caps appears in a red banner across the top. The graphic is transparently evocative of the potential peril, and the label itself is maximally designed to draw the attention of any responsible consumer buying or installing the unit. To the present day, these labels are placed prominently on each water heater unit right next to the utility hook-ups.

But the key takeaway here is that Rheem not only wanted to do the right thing in providing principled disclosure to consumers, it was also willing to do the due diligence necessary to see that commitment through. They accomplished this by retaining experts like myself to exhaustively test the effectiveness of various warning label designs, and by placing their safety warning labels in highly conspicuous locations on the physical units they sold to consumers and contractors, thus warning consumers even before they purchased and installed the product.

Here I want to state categorically that it is absolutely *not* my intention in this book to shill for the benefit of my own organization or interests. What I am suggesting—and in fact what I strongly advise and recommend—is that due diligence often, if not always, requires that companies seek out the advice and counsel of experts in whatever fields are pertinent to the products they manufacture as well as the circumstances under which these products are likely to be used. This is where Conagra and the cosmetic company went terribly wrong by apparently not consulting with experts in microwave technology or with the microwave oven manufacturing industry itself. Think of the troubles they could have avoided if they had!

And one more significant benefit accruing from Rheem's unilateral action requires mentioning here. Specifically, the company's willingness to proactively provide, of its own volition, principled disclosure to all consumers of the hazard associated with its products subsequently required *no government regulatory action whatsoever*. In other words, Rheem's actions represent a case of an industry policing itself. We hear a lot of argumentative rancor these days about government meddling in the affairs of business and screwing things up. Yet, it ought to be crystal clear that if more companies conducted themselves in the way that Rheem did in at least this one instance, *government would not be obliged to step in to protect consumers* from corporate nondisclosure (or outright deception). And in the end, American taxpayers might actually save a little money! It also is no surprise that today, Rheem enjoys a reputation for excellence that is unmatched by any other water heater manufacturer in the U.S. (a recent survey posted on the website waterheatergeek.com rated Rheem models first and second ahead of all other models made by their competitors).

An interesting postscript to our water heater parable is that modern versions of these units today are equipped with digital electronic spark ignition systems that eliminate the need for a continuously burning pilot light. This applies to units that are either gas- or oil-fired. However, this design change has nothing to do with eliminating the hazard, and everything to do with saving on the cost of today's very expensive fossil fuels. Of course, it should be obvious that wherever there's a spark, there's a potential for fire, and when gas or oil units are in operation producing hot water, those fuels are burning at high temperature in the heating chamber. The fact is that whether a pilot light or electronic spark generator is used as the "fuse" to fire up the unit, either one represents a potentially dangerous hidden hazard that simply cannot be engineered or designed out of the product. As such, it is incumbent upon manufacturers to provide principled disclosure. Where they fail to do so, it is subsequently the responsibility of the appropriate government regulatory body to force them to do so, or to adequately warn the public of the danger through its own media channels.

WATCH OUT: THAT LAST STEP IS A DOOZY!

One of the most common tools in any home is one type of ladder or another. In fact, it's hard to even imagine living in an apartment without having at least one step ladder around, or envisioning a single-family dwelling without a 6- or 8-foot ladder routinely used by the homeowner to perform household chores both indoor (like changing a light bulb) and outdoor (like cleaning out the gutters). Many homeowners have extension ladders that go precariously much higher, to reach the gutters on the second story, for instance.

Simple, practical device, the ladder: it's not a power tool, it has no sharp, dangerous cutting blades of any sort, and, if positioned properly (a big "if" indeed!), it has no moving parts (at least it's not supposed to). Yet, a recent report issued by the Consumer Product Safety Commission (CPSC) on ladder safety reveals some incredible statistics underscoring the frequency and severity of ladder-related accidents in the U.S. For example, the CPSC report states that more than 90,000 people receive emergency room treatment for ladder-related injuries every year, and that ladder-related injuries have increased by a factor of 50 percent over the last ten years.

Elevated falls account for almost 700 occupational deaths annually, and that figure accounts for 15 percent of all occupational deaths nationwide.[22]

The U.S. Bureau of Labor Statistics (BLS) estimates that as much as 50 percent of all ladder-related accidents are due to individuals attempting to carry items as they climbed. But what may be the most telling pronouncement issued by any government agency charged with monitoring the safety of consumers and workers comes from OSHA. OSHA eye-poppingly contends that fully *100 percent of all ladder accidents* could be prevented if proper attention to equipment integrity and climber training were provided. **One Hundred Percent.** This deserves exploring a bit more deeply.

First, let me state for the record: In my professional opinion, the common ladder is, for all practical purposes, a list of hazards looking for a purpose, or perhaps, a landing spot. It's just a matter of time. Think I'm exaggerating? Then consider this. The typical 6- or 8-foot folding ladder has no less than 21 warnings listed in tiny print on a label affixed discretely to one of the side supports. Here is a list of some of the more ridiculous warnings usually provided there:

- Never use a ladder with damaged or missing parts.
- Never use a ladder if you are not in good physical condition.
- Do not use a ladder in front of unlocked doors.
- Never place any object(s) under a ladder to gain height.
- Never use a ladder as a platform, plank, or brace.
- Use extreme caution getting on or off a ladder.
- Use caution when steps are being used to support other objects. You may trip and fall.
- Never overreach. Always keep belt buckle between side-rails when climbing or working. Overreaching can cause you to lose your balance or tip the ladder over.
- Windy conditions require extra caution.

[22] Westbend, "Ladder."

And then there's my personal favorite:

- Never walk, bounce, or try to move the ladder while you are standing on it.

You've heard of "jumping the shark"? I have come to calling the hare-brained maneuver suggested by that last warning, "jumping the ladder," and I can barely think of a more dangerous stunt one might attempt to pull while actually standing on a ladder! In any event, this veritable wash list of warnings-in-minutia trades upon a pronouncement issued by Supreme Court Justice Warren Burger in a speech given before the American Trial Lawyers Association back in the 1970s. Burger said essentially that when you warn about everything, you warn about nothing.[23]

I will have much more to say about the ramifications of excessive safety warnings to the point of plain absurdity—from the comical to the deadly—throughout the course of this book. But for now, the important thing to understand is that when warnings are extended to the most obvi-ous hazard factors—even beyond common sense and amounting to out-right (and often insulting) trivialization—people will simply shut down their brains and ignore them entirely. It's as if the manufacturer is mocking the consumer: "You want warnings? I've got your warnings right here!"

And yet, be that as it may, I submit that in a borderline wicked way this exhaustive list of 21 individual warnings may diabolically reveal some-thing very telling about the way people actually use ladders "out in the trenches." For some reason, the Three Stooges come to mind right about now. That is to say, we may rationally surmise that somebody somewhere in America has actually enacted every single one of these boneheaded, ladder-abusing behaviors, as well as probably many, many others that hav-en't made the warnings hit parade yet. The sorry truth is that thousands upon thousands of people are guilty of bad practical science when it comes to using their ladders, and probably multiple times over until they finally

---

[23] The Goldhaber Warnings Report.

experience an actual calamity as a result. Can there be a scintilla of doubt in anyone's mind that this is the reason why OSHA argues unequivocally that 100 percent of all ladder-related accidents are preventable? In the majority of these cases, it's not the ladder, it's the unwitting consumer who is at fault.

In this chapter I have argued that companies must engage more proactively and more responsibly in principled disclosure of the hidden hazards in their products as one leg in the Proactive Safety Triad. I have similarly argued that government regulators must do a much better job both of eliciting and enforcing principled disclosure by industry, and of informing the public about dangerous products or environments as the second leg in the triad. Yet, if the list of safety warnings is any indication of the common and apparently pervasive misuses of the household, it clearly points to a failure of the third leg of the Proactive Safety Triad, which, of course, is the consumer-public. Consumers are responsible for using products as safely as common sense permits in the first place. But they must also take responsible ownership for using them in accordance with safety warnings and user hazard-avoidance instructions that are duly and conspicuously provided through principled disclosure. Otherwise, principled disclosure by companies and consumer advisories issued by government regulators are useless and a waste of time and money.

Informed consumer behavior in essence completes the circle of responsibility among the three legs of the Proactive Safety Triad. But even when industry and government do their parts, badly behaving consumers are equally capable of creating a situation in which the safety triad becomes just as unstable as the two legs of the extension ladder they might be standing on as they reach out perilously to take down the Christmas lights!

CHAPTER 3

EATING: EAT, DRINK, AND BE DEAD

Hardly a day goes by when we aren't confronted with another challenge to our nation's food supply, which was once thought to be the safest in the world. More and more, in an age of remarkably efficient global commerce facilitated by improved shipping methods to prevent spoilage, and coupled with American consumers' relentless desire for foods new and exotic, the threat to food safety comes increasingly from foods produced in foreign countries imported into the U.S. Our grocery, supermarket, and big-box store shelves are loaded with a bewildering variety of fresh produce—from meats and fish to fruits and vegetables to prepackaged processed foods originating from dozens of countries whose laws, with respect to everything from product purity to hormone and pesticide use, may be alarmingly lax or simply nonexistent compared to strict U.S. standards as promulgated by the FDA and the USDA. Yet, we needn't go outside our borders to uncover urgent and significant threats to food safety or violations of principled disclosure of potential hazards.

The questions that must be asked are several. For one, are we receiving adequate, thorough information from those who manufacture and distribute the food we eat as well as the supermarkets and big-box stores that sell these products to us? This question applies especially to the freshness and wholesomeness of our poultry, fish and meats, fruits and vegetables, and other agricultural products. But it also applies to the ingredients and nutritional value (and advertising claims thereto) of the thousands of varieties of prepackaged processed foods that line our supermarket shelves.

The next logical question is, are we receiving, from those same food industry manufacturers, distributors, and packagers, adequate warnings when certain foods may contain significant hidden hazards, or even when some of their ingredients pose health risks either to people with certain allergic conditions or to the general consumer public at large? Because, as we all must know, certain foods, and more specifically certain ingredients in food, are just not good for your overall, long-term good health. Some of these are indeed "natural" in origin, like sugar and sodium. Yet many others are artificial, or chemical-based synthetic substances, including emulsifiers and preservatives, added to enhance the flavor or appearance of processed foods, or simply to increase their shelf-life at the supermarket.

A third question is, are the government agencies charged with protecting the healthiness and safety of our food supply, principally the FDA and USDA, doing enough to ensure that the food industry engages in the kind of sufficiently transparent principled disclosure that enables consumers to make informed choices about the foods they eat and provide to their children right from the day they are born? In fact, that's a good place to begin examining these crucial questions, by considering the case of American-made infant formula, thought to be among the safest and most regulated products in our food industry ... except that it may not be so.

INFANTS AT RISK

Hidden behind the typically warm and cuddly images on the front labels of various powdered infant formulas (PIF) may lurk the rare, but possibly deadly bacterium, *Cronobacter* (formerly known as *Enterobacter sakazakii* or *E. sakazakii*), which can cause severe brain damage or spinal meningitis in neonates (infants under 30 days old). There are no warnings about this risk because the PIF manufacturers have said that, among other reasons, the risk is too low (about 100,000 to one). I testified in two different PIF trials that the danger and more particularly the catastrophic nature of the consequences of exposure to this bacterium are so severe that the severity of the potential danger should, in all reason, trump *any* argument suggesting that the risk or likelihood of exposure is too remotely low to bother warning consumers against. Further, we have, as a nation, put warnings on a variety of products with risks (defined as "likelihood of occurrence") significantly less likely than the occurrence of meningitis from an obscure bacterium.

Yet, there is another unspoken and equally sinister reason why PIF manufacturers have resisted efforts to force them to come clean about the potential danger, as remote as it may be, of *Cronobacter*. Specifically, the formation of the bacteria has a peculiar tendency to occur in clusters. Imagine a huge silo filled with hundreds of tons of manufactured PIF before it is packed into individual cans for sale at supermarkets across the country. If there just happens to be any *Cronobacter* bacteria in this mountain of PIF, it is relegated to a few very discrete, microscopic clusters here and there throughout the stack. In other words, the presence of the bacteria is not in any manner spread evenly throughout the huge batch of powdered material. One couldn't reach in, grab a handful of the powder, and say with any assurance that they were holding some *Cronobacter* in their hot little hand. In fact, one could grab a million handfuls and never find any.

For this reason, the usual statistically valid methods for testing bulk material for purity or homogeneity simply will not work. In other words, the extreme randomness of these discrete microscopic clusters means that the standard testing methods, which really consist of nothing more scientifically exotic or mathematically sophisticated than physically taking random samples of the material from numerous locations throughout the entire batch and testing each sample individually for purity, or for whatever it is you are looking for. This, in turn, is yet another example of a hazard that cannot be fully eliminated from a given bulk product. In the end, *Cronobacter* is a naturally occurring bacterial contamination that, rare as it is, cannot be designed or engineered out of the PIF product. As such, the only reasonable alternative, and the imperative one in my view, is to warn consumers very effectively about it and let them (and their pediatricians) make an informed choice about whether to use it or not. This, again, is the essence of principled disclosure.

Nevertheless, under a mandate from the federal government, no PIF manufacturer, according to the FDA, is required to have a warning about meningitis on its packaging. However, by the same reasoning, the FDA doesn't prevent the industry from providing a warning. Yet, clearly this is a situation that further warrants that a warning is needed because numerous surveys have shown that large majorities of both pediatricians and parents of neonates were not aware of the possibility of this bacterium showing up in powdered formula—certainly they would be horrified if they knew this. Even more telling, most of the doctors and parents surveyed weren't even aware that PIF isn't even sterile to begin with.

Since the risk for the most part is to neonates for about the first 30 days of life, I recommended that—after discussing it with their pediatricians— mothers of neonates avoid PIF until at least the second month and to purchase (for a few pennies per serving more) a ready-to-feed sterilized version of the same product (sold already in liquid form ready for heating and serving) for children younger than two months. Yet, this "avoidance" strategy really isn't the issue, because the availability of the powdered form means some unwitting parents will opt to buy the PIF for their babies out of convenience (or perhaps based on their similarly uninformed pediatricians' unfortunate recommendations), and the absence of an adequate hazard warning means they will do so without any foreknowledge of the serious potential risk to their infants, as remote as it may be.

Accordingly, I also recommended that PIF manufacturers include a warning on the label that would read something along the lines as follows:

> **DANGER: This product is not sterile and may contain deadly bacteria that may cause brain damage or spinal meningitis in your infant.**

Without any orders issued by the FDA that would have required such a definitively clear and bluntly truthful warning (however appropriately alarming it truly is), the compromise wording that the industry settled on is this:

> **Powdered infant formulas are not sterile and *may be fed to premature infants or infants who might have immune problems* only as directed by your baby's doctor.**
> (emphasis mine)

The wording I've highlighted—"*may be fed to premature infants or infants who might have immune problems*"—sounds an awful lot like this so-called, watered-down "warning" is telling parents—and pediatricians—that it's *okay* to feed this formula not only to neonates, but also to premature infants and, even further, those most vulnerable individuals who may have confirmed immunological deficiencies. This "warning" is as unflinchingly cavalier as the suggestion voiced at the end of many a prescription drug commercial to, "Ask your doctor if _____ (*fill in the prescription drug*) is right for you." In fact, on the cans of one manufacturer's powdered infant formula, a banner placed right below the name reads: "For Babies Who Were Born Prematurely"! The very idea defies reason.

It's further ironic to note that the sterilized bottled form, which, by the way, is the exact same formula as the powdered form, is made by all of the major PIF manufacturers, meaning that they could just as easily recommend parents of neonates: (1) to feed only their liquid formula brands to neonates and premature infants until say, two months of age; (2) while strenuously and conspicuously warning in bold type against using the powdered formula for these infants; and (3) recommend in their advertising and promotions, as prominently as they wish, that parents may use the more "convenient" PIF for babies older than two months for whom the risk no longer exists. (By the way, PIF that has been mixed with water and ready for serving cannot be sterilized by giving it a good shot in the microwave oven, because doing so also destroys the nutritional value of the formula for your baby!)

So why don't the PIF manufacturers do this? It's very simple: Because they fear losing sales of their powdered infant formula. It's another clear and unequivocal case of putting profits ahead of consumer safety, even at the expense of the lives of the littlest and most vulnerable among us. One other telling observation must be made concerning the litigation surrounding the PIF safety issue, which stands out as a stark example of the "revolving door" in full swing. In one of the cases in which I was involved, one of the baby food industry's major experts hired to testify against my warnings recommendations was a former FDA employee involved in the regulatory decisions about PIF that had ultimately failed to impose stricter and more informative disclosure of the potential hazard to parent-consumers.

Of course, we needn't focus solely on potentially deadly renegade bacteria as the only source of hazards in our food. Many perfectly natural ingredients show up in them—regularly and in abundance—that can pose significant health risks, and we know all too well that they are often the things we most crave.

ONE SUGAR OR TWO?

Let's start with good, "clean," honest-to-goodness, "wholesome" plain white refined sugar. Yes, you probably think you've heard all you need to know about the "dark side" of the sugar you stir into your coffee or tea at the breakfast table every morning before you go to work, or relaxing with the newspaper on a warm Sunday afternoon. You know all about the huge amount of sugar that's contained in a single can or bottle of soda, because after all, it's been all over the news for years now, decades even. You've heard all about the diabolical interventionist governmental efforts, perhaps most notably former Mayor Michael Bloomberg's (dubbed the "Food Nanny of New York") effort to ban sugary drinks in excess of 16 ounces at restaurants, theaters, and food carts (an effort that was overturned by the courts) and more recently by the city of Philadelphia, where a controversial "soda tax" passed at the beginning of 2017 apparently remains enormously unpopular with consumers—and has also had a tremendous negative impact on some sectors of the local business economy.[24] (For a closer look at the legal issues surrounding New York City's efforts to ban large sugary drinks, see "Government Overreach or Hazard Warning Label? You Decide.")

GOVERNMENT OVERREACH OR HAZARD WARNING LABEL? YOU DECIDE

In March 2013, the New York State Supreme Court Justice Milton A. Tingling struck down Mayor Michael Bloomberg and the City of New York's proposed ban on large sugary drinks. Under the NYC Department of Health's (DOH) proposal, sugary soft drinks would have been limited to no more than 16 ounces per serving at restaurants, theaters, and food carts. Critics of the ban argued that anyone who wanted to drink more than 16 ounces could simply buy two (or more) of them, and that the ban would have been haphazardly enforced, allowing convenience stores such as 7-Eleven to continue to sell 32-ounce beverages while restricting restaurants and theaters.

The ruling, however, had nothing to do with those arguments, nor was it handed down because the judge himself has a penchant for consuming mass quantities of sugary drinks while contemplating case decisions in his chambers (He may or may not, for all we know!). Rather, Judge Tingling based his decision (as he should) on purely constitutional/legislative grounds, ruling that by independently seeking the ban, the mayor and DOH had improperly circumvented the City Council. The judge wrote, "One of the fundamental tenets of democratic governance … is the separation of powers. No one person, agency, department, or branch is above or beyond this."

Judge Tingling's ruling effectively sent the case on to New York State's highest court, the Court of Appeals, where the ruling was upheld in June 2014. Writing for the majority in a 4-to-2 decision, Judge Eugene F. Pigott Jr. of the New York State Court of Appeals reaffirmed that the city's Board of Health "exceeded the scope of its regulatory authority" in enacting the proposal, adding that the scope and complexity of the proposal and its reach into the everyday lives of millions of New Yorkers meant that the City Council ought to address it instead. However, in written dissent of the opinion, Judge

---

[24] Bomey, "Soda tax."

Susan Reed blasted the majority decision, arguing that it ignored decades of precedent that had allowed the NYC Board of Health broad powers to address public health issues such as regulating the city's water supply and banning lead paint in homes. Judge Reed strenuously charged that the court's decision "misapprehends, mischaracterizes, and thereby curtails the powers of the New York City Board of Health to address the public health threats of the early 21st century."

Indeed, at the same time, Judge Pigott apparently found himself able to draw a sharp and curious distinction between the sugary drinks proposal and other past—and successful—initiatives of the board, such as banning the use of trans-fat in restaurants. Banning trans-fat, the judge indicated rather bizarrely, had a more direct link to public health and represented, "minimal interference with the personal autonomy" of New Yorkers.

The issue of aggressive government regulatory intervention of this genre remains controversial. In New York City's case, for example Richard Briffault, a law professor at Columbia who filed a brief supporting the city's large sugary drink ban, stated that the Appellate Court's ruling, "Casts a cloud over the ability of administrative agencies to engage in innovative forms of regulation." By contrast, Robert Bookman, an attorney frequently at odds with the city over issues of government legislative overreach, had high praise for the ruling. "Under Mayor Bloomberg, the Board of Health seemed to feel that its power was unlimited," Bookman said. "Now they know they are no different than any other administrative agency."

Regardless of how you feel about the proposed ban, at about the same time of the judge's ruling, the American Heart Association happened to release more important news pertinent to the large sugary drinks debate. It cited a study conducted by the Harvard School of Public Health linking sugary drinks—alone—to 180,000 deaths worldwide and 25,000 deaths in the U.S. alone. Judge Pigott's majority opinion notwithstanding, it's hard to imagine a more alarming and detrimentally "direct link" to public health than that! On the other hand, of course, it remains an open question as to just how much power may be vested in federal, state, and city or local governments to regulate matters pertinent to the health of the general public health, while at the same time impinging on individual choice.

While former Mayor Bloomberg might have had the best interests of New York City citizens at heart (no pun intended), a warning label placed on all sugary drinks may be a better functional strategy to inform the general public about the serious role such drinks play in the obesity crisis we are now facing in America. We need to remember that it is not about restricting or controlling consumers with respect to what they eat or drink; rather, it is about making sure they know what exactly is *contained in* the stuff they eat or drink. This is the way that principled disclosure on the part of companies or government regulators enables or leads to informed consent exercised by the consumer.

So, you think, okay, given all of this mounting furor, maybe just to be on the safe side you'll limit the number of soft drinks you consume every day. That oughta do it, right?

Let's say you decide to take a seriously austere approach by allowing yourself to have just one, 20-ounce soft drink a day. And let's also say that you like variety, so in order to make your soft drink austerity program a little more bearable, you'll mix it up by drinking a different brand every day. Here are a few choices for you, conveniently listed with their added sugar content, as disclosed—by law—by the respective soft drink makers:

Coca Cola	65 grams
Pepsi	69 grams
Barq's Root Beer	74 grams
Mountain Dew	77 grams

The fact that the soda companies list added sugar in grams instead of teaspoons is an example of a deliberate and calculated attempt to deceive consumers that—even if today the deception has been to some degree unmasked through media stories and by health and nutrition gurus—nonetheless remains very effective in its power to obfuscate. That is, while it might be the case that many or even most consumers are in fact aware, however vaguely, that soft drink manufacturers use grams specifically to play down or hide the real amount of added sugar in their beverages, they really do not know what the numbers mean, and the natural tendency is to simply disregard them entirely. And, of course, the soda companies know this.

They know all too well that the metric system is simply not part of Americans' DNA and probably never will be. When we build houses, the wall studs are placed on *16-inch centers*; the football gridiron is measured in *yards*; every ardent baseball fan knows that it's *60 feet six inches* from home plate to the pitching rubber and 90 *feet* to first base, and we measure our submarine sandwiches by the *foot*. With the exception, perhaps, of a few exotic imported foods, virtually every product in the supermarket is measured and sold in pounds, ounces, gallons, quarts, or pints. Even our wine and liquor are doled out in fifths of a gallon. The very word *grams* sounds every bit to the American-English ear like something that is miniscule and therefore harmless.

However, take a look at the previous list of soft drinks and their added sugar content, only this time listed in teaspoons full:

Coca Cola	16.25 teaspoons
Pepsi	17.25 teaspoons
Barq's Root Beer	18.50 teaspoons
Mountain Dew	19.25 teaspoons

How healthy do those numbers sound to you?

So as you try to discipline yourself to consuming only one soft drink per day, I suggest a little thought experiment to help you grasp the full measure of the grams-to-teaspoons equation. The next time you have a Venti, 20-ounce serving of coffee or hot tea at Starbucks, imagine dumping 16 to 19 teaspoonsful of granulated white sugar into your cup! Then I suggest having a bottle of spring water instead.

However, the amount of sugar you choose to consume really isn't the issue here. Rather, the key takeaway from all of this is that listing ingredients including added sugar in grams is nothing short of a deliberate attempt on the part of soft drink makers to deceive consumers, plain and simple. In the narrowest of interpretations, it is "compliance" with legally required "disclosure" that immediately seeks to obfuscate or hide the vital information that is supposed to be disclosed. It certainly does not represent a warning on that bottle that you are about to consume an enormous amount of sugar in just one sitting. Yet, using the conveniently available metric system is only one tool in the food industry's bag of tricks, as we will shortly see.

WHY WARN ABOUT FOOD IN THE FIRST PLACE?

Before we go any deeper, however, let's back up a bit and examine the question: When and why should food labels contain a warning of any sort at all, assuming that a given product is not prone to be contaminated with something and, by all rights, should be suitable for human consumption? We have seen in the previous chapter that some foods do indeed require warnings when it comes to their methods of preparation for consumption, for example, to ensure they are cooked completely. The same obviously may be true, at least in terms of thorough, easily understandable instructions for proper handling and storage to avoid contamination and spoilage.

All of that seems to make intuitive sense, the same way that operating instructions provided on how to properly use a power tool (or a microwave oven) make intuitive sense. But warnings about hidden hazards in the "natural" food itself? Should it not be the case that we may reasonably expect people, when it comes to the type and quantity of the food they regularly eat, to live by provisos like, "Eat a balanced diet" and "All things in moderation"?

Well, the answer is that the criteria that other warnings experts and I use to determine the answer to these questions is quite the same as we apply to any other product or environment that might pose a risk to the health and safety of the consumer. To restate these criteria in brief, we try to: (1) identify the audience at risk; (2) determine the precise nature of the hazard and its concomitant risk; (3) determine whether codes and/or regulations suggest or require a warning; and finally (4) further determine whether the potential hazard is known or unknown by the typical product user or consumer at the time of use. Let's now apply this theory to food products with added sugar.

That added sugar is a national public health hazard has been widely accepted by the medical, nutritional, and scientific community, as well as by the general public for decades. However, most people are not aware of the severity and pervasiveness of the potential hazard, even among people who do know and understand that excessive sugar consumption can lead to weight gain and chronic obesity, as well as various long-term diseases like type 2 diabetes, heart disease, hypertension, liver disease, and certain forms of cancer and brain diseases. Recent studies even suggest a link between high-sugar diets and Alzheimer's disease.[25,26]

For example, just to cite some very broad statistics, one-third of all Americans are clinically obese, including 20 percent of children. Obesity is defined by the National Institutes of Health (the NIH) as a BMI (Body Mass Index) of 30 and above. (A BMI of 30 is about 30 pounds overweight.) Twenty-five million Americans are diabetic and another 80 million are prediabetic, while one-quarter million Americans die every year due to diabetes and diseases related to diabetes (about 10 percent of all annual U.S. deaths).[27]

Yet, we can go further. The risk of death from a heart attack or stroke is two to four times higher among diabetics. A recent Harvard study estimates that as many as 25,000 deaths each year alone are directly attributable to excessive consumption of sugary drinks.[28] In fact, there's a sign on the wall of my own primary physician's examination room that reads (rather accusatively, I would add): "Having just one 12-ounce can of sugary soda a day increases your risk of having a heart attack by 35%."

According to the website www.hungryforchange.tv, the average American consumes 64 pounds of sugar per year; the average teenage

---

[25] Moreira, "High-sugar diets."
[26] Franco, "Excess sugar."
[27] NIH, "Ideal body mass index."
[28] Feldscher, "Sickly sweet."

boy consumes a mind-blowing 109 pounds per year. Americans consume 22 teaspoons of added sugars per day, while teens consume 34 teaspoons per day. And per capita consumption of added sugars has risen by 28 percent since 1983. Those are staggering figures, especially when you consider that, according to nutrition experts, the empty calories in sugar do not provide any nutritional value to the body.

> Somewhat tangentially, the statistics presented really beg the question: Just how much added sugar should the average person consume each day? Here is the correct quiz show response, should you one day find yourself appearing on *Jeopardy!* and the category, "Things That Are Really Bad for You" comes up:
> *Answer:* Zero.
> *Question:* What is the FDA's minimum Recommended Daily Intake (RDI) for added sugar?

Now, before you break down in crocodile tears and start beating your breast, wailing imploringly in heart-wrenching lamentation that, saints preserve us, you *must* have *some* added sugar in your life and in your diet, let me quickly assure you I am not suggesting you should consume **NO** added sugar, nor is that the intent of this book. In point of fact, consuming no added sugar in today's world of prepackaged processed foods is practically, if not entirely, impossible unless you live on a farm and grow everything you ever eat.

But this fact itself speaks to the heart of the principled disclosure issue, because as we will shortly see, food manufacturers add sugar in various guises to over three-quarters of prepackaged processed foods that are the mainstay of the modern American diet. With that as backdrop, what we have established, however, is that consuming *excessive amounts* of added sugar is very likely to be very bad for you, and that Americans as a whole nevertheless consume entirely too much of it on a daily and yearly basis *without being aware that they are doing it.* And a large part of the blame for this is that American consumers are conspicuously unaware of the prevalence of added sugars in most of the foods they eat—and they are kept that way through the deliberate actions of the food and sugar industries. In essence, it is not enough for consumers to know vaguely that excessive sugar is a potential hazard to their health and safety: Point 4 of our warnings criteria cited earlier cannot truly be satisfied if consumers are not informed or are otherwise able to know exactly how much sugar they are getting in their daily diet. Let me state it plainly: the food and sugar industries do not want you to know this, and they spend millions of dollars to keep you ignorant—and overweight. Later in this chapter, we will look at how they do this.

But first, are you further aware that sugar may be one of the most addictive substances on Earth?

A recent study conducted by researchers at the Icahn School of Medicine at Mount Sinai and the University of Michigan[29] found that common sugar is eight times more addictive than cocaine, and that what many people may jokingly refer to as their "junk food addiction" ominously and perhaps alarmingly resembles drug addiction far more than researchers had previously thought. In issuing the study, Dr. Nicole Avena at the Icahn School of Medicine asserted, "Several studies ... suggest that highly palatable, highly processed foods can produce behaviors and changes in the brain that one would use to diagnose an addiction, like drugs and alcohol."

And some foods are loaded with sugar that most people, if asked, wouldn't think of in a million years. Do you love pizza? Avena explains that the tomato sauce in just one slice can contain as much sugar as several Oreo cookies, and studies have shown, not surprisingly, that pizza is one of the most addictive foods you can eat.

Once you understand this, it should not come as any surprise whatsoever that, by some estimates, up to 75 percent of prepackaged, processed multi-ingredient processed foods contain varying amounts of added sugar. The food industry is keenly aware that through manipulation of the addictive characteristics of sugar they can literally induce consumers to crave certain products, and to buy more of them in quantity to feed that craving.

---

[29] Schulte et al., "Foods."

They also know that sugar-rich snacks like cookies, chips, and nutrition bars—yes, I said *nutrition* bars—create an immediate "sugar high" that rapidly dissipates, which in turn only increases the craving for more of those snacks, so once again, you wind up eating more of them. So, they quite literally stick added sugar into just about everything they sell, especially when it comes to multi-ingredient processed foods. Let me state it with brutal bluntness: The process is precisely the same as that used by street drug dealers to get new users hooked to join the ranks of their loyal customers.

Let's take a moment to reflect on just exactly what this means. First, food companies do not warn or even make any attempt to inform consumers about the health risks of consuming excessive amounts of sugar. Second, they infuse many of their multi-ingredient packaged products with added sugar—often in amounts that obesity researchers and nutritionists deem excessive to the point of posing a health risk to unknowing consumers. And third, quite to the contrary of "informing" consumers about the amount of sugar contained in their products, food makers actively exploit the addictive properties of sugar to encourage (or induce) you to buy, and presumably consume, even more of their sugar-laden products. That, once again, sounds an awful lot like profits over safety, and a failure on the part of the food industry to uphold the principled disclosure leg of the safety triad. But wait; there's more.

A SUGAR BY ANY OTHER NAME ...

A Meeting between a Government "Health Inspector" and Mr. Milton, President and CEO of the "Whizzo Chocolate Company":

> Inspector: *Next we have number 4, "Crunchy Frog." Am I right in thinking there's a real frog in here?*
> CEO Milton: *Yes, a little one.*
> Inspector: *Is it cooked?*
> CEO Milton: *No.*

Inspector: *What, a raw frog?!*

CEO Milton: *We use only the finest baby frogs, dew picked and flown from Iraq, cleansed in the finest quality spring water, lightly killed, and then sealed in a succulent, Swiss-quintuple-smooth, treble-crème milk chocolate envelope, and lovingly frosted with glucose.*

Inspector: *Well don't you even take the bones out?*

CEO Milton: *If we took the bones out, it wouldn't be "crunchy," would it?... The label says "Crunchy Frog" quite clearly.*

Inspector: *Nevertheless, I must warn you that in the future you should delete the words "Crunchy Frog" and replace them with the legend, "Crunchy, Raw, Unboned, Real Dead Frog," if you want to avoid prosecution.*

CEO Milton: *Our sales would plummet!*

Inspector: *I'm not interested in your sales, I have to protect the general public!*

—Monty Python's Flying Circus[30]

As amusing as the above exchange is, as concocted by the devilishly fertile minds of the famous British comedy troupe, it also neatly frames the question of just what exactly constitutes principled disclosure on the part of food manufacturers when it comes to accurately identifying food ingredients on package labels. It also concisely identifies their greatest fear: "*Our sales would plummet!*"—a fear that I strongly maintain is illusory. And finally, it points to the related question of what role government regulators must play in ensuring that companies provide a reasonable measure of principled disclosure in order for such agencies to perform faithfully their function to "*protect the general public.*"

Because in order to hide just how much sugar consumers are putting into their mouths, as ingeniously defined and redefined by the food industry, refined sugar masquerades under a bewildering multitude of cryptic

---

[30] Chapman et al., Flying Circus.

terminological guises, semi-scientific names, and jargony euphemisms. Many of the names applied to these different variations do not sound even remotely like they have anything to do with sugar, such that even the most savvy, nutrition-conscious consumer is hard-pressed to know and understand exactly what they are.

The easiest ones to recognize on food labels, as a general rule, are any ingredients that end in the suffix -ose, and these alone are fairly numerous in their own right—sucrose, maltose, dextrose, fructose, glucose, galactose, lactose, high-fructose corn syrup, and glucose solids—yet it is highly questionable whether the average consumer knows or understands even this much. But as the website www.hungryforchange.tv points out, "Two really good ways [for food companies] to disguise sugar on food labels [are] to use a long, scientific-sounding word or to rename the sugar altogether." Table 3.1 provides a list of no less than 30 ingeniously creative names for sugar—though probably not an exhaustive one—that have been dreamed up by the food industry.

TABLE 3.1

Thirty Food Industry Names for Added Sugar

Cane juice	Corn syrup solids	Fruit juice concentrate
Dehydrated cane juice	Caramel	Dehydrated fruit juice
Cane juice solids	Buttered syrup	Fruit juice crystals
Cane juice crystals	Carob syrup	Golden syrup
Dextrin	Brown sugar	Turbinado
Maltodextrin	Date sugar	Sorghum syrup
Dextran	Malt syrup	Refiner's syrup
Barley malt	Diatase	Ethyl maltol
Beet sugar	Diatastic malt	Maple syrup
Corn syrup	Fruit juice	Yellow sugar

Here is where the complicity of government regulators comes into the picture, working hand-in-hand with the deceptive practices of the food makers. Because until May 2016, the FDA had refused to require food manufacturers to include an "Added Sugars" line (in grams, of course!) within the all-important "Nutrition Facts" section of the food label.

The Nutrition Facts section of the label does list "Sugars" under Total Carbohydrates. However, before the 2016 action by the FDA to change the labeling guidelines, food companies were not required to distinguish natural sugars from those specifically added to the product. Instead, added sugars needed only to be identified and listed in the ingredients list—and only in decreasing weight order, making it virtually impossible for consumers to determine what percentage of calories are directly contributed, specifically, by added sugars in packaged food products.

Food companies have exploited this glaring loophole by using several different types of sugars in each single product. By using a combined amount of three or four added sugars with different names instead of just one type, the food companies have been able to drop their added sugars further down on the ingredients list, because of course, the less the weight, the lower the rank on the list. The following example is from the www. hungryforchange.tv website:

> So … if a manufacturer wants to sweeten up a certain brand of crackers, it can either do this using 15 grams of "sugar" or, 5 grams of "malt syrup," 5 grams of "invert sugar," and 5 grams of "glucose." Some manufacturers [chose] this divide and masquerade method, placing these ingredients lower down on their products' lists, making us believe that the amount of sugar in the product is smaller than it actually is.[31]

And remember: the ingredients section lists only the names of the ingredients, not the quantity, so as a consumer looking at the package, you will see only the ingredient names, without any indication, in this example, that there are five grams each of three different sugars for a total of 15 grams, or nearly 4 teaspoons, of sugar.

Now, under the latest labeling guidelines issued by the FDA on May 20, 2016, this deceptive practice will no longer be permitted. Among

---

[31] Hungry for Change, "Sugar."

a number of other important new disclosure requirements, the directive that is most pertinent to the issue at hand states that the new Nutrition Facts label must include a "Declaration of grams and a percent daily value (%DV) for 'added sugars' to help consumers know how much sugar has been added to the product."[32]

It should be noted that the original initiative leading to the FDA's action included my recommendation, along with many others', that added sugars should be listed in TEASPOONS rather than continue to be listed in grams. The FDA refused, no doubt due to pressure from the sugar industry. So even as we consumers won one battle with the line item "declaration" of added sugars, we lost another. It is also worth explaining that "percent daily value (%DV)" is NOT the same as "Recommended Daily Intake (RDI)," which for added sugar, as I noted earlier, is still **ZERO**.

While this is a step in the right direction, given the epidemic proportions of the obesity problem among American consumers, as well as the severity of all the other chronic diseases linked to excessive sugar consumption, I believe it doesn't go nearly far enough. In 2013, I proposed essentially the following warning for foods containing large quantities of added sugar:

> **WARNING: This product contains a large amount of added TEASPOONS of sugar that studies have linked to Obesity, Type 2 Diabetes, Cardiovascular Diseases and certain Cancers. Consult your doctor about an appropriate diet with less added sugar.**

While such a warning label is unlikely to be mandated by the FDA any time soon—much less embraced by the food industry—there may be an ominously significant fly already in the ointment of the recent progress we have been able to make. As expected, Obama-era regulatory upgrades

---

[32] U.S. Food & Drug Administration, "Nutrition Facts."

were among the prime candidates facing immediate or eventual rollback, suspension, or outright cancellation by the Trump administration. Much of that occurred within the first two years under President Trump. Thus presently, it is highly unlikely that the 2016 regulatory changes enacted by President Obama will be fully implemented and enforced at all going forward, at least for the foreseeable future.

TAKING A PAGE FROM THE TOBACCO INDUSTRY

If this pattern of deceptive labeling practices wasn't enough, the food industry also has for many years engaged in what may be legitimately described as one aggressive disinformation campaign after another. Since as far back as the 1960s, food companies have spent millions of dollars paying scientists to conduct and write dubious studies casting doubt on the link between sugar and heart disease and the other serious, long-term illnesses noted earlier. They have even gone so far as to set up bogus nonprofit "institutes" or organizations that are merely fronts designed to promote the food industry's agenda. One such nonprofit formed in 2015 by the Coca-Cola Company was given the lofty, if somewhat enigmatic, name of "Global Energy Balance Network" (GEBN).

A *New York Times* editorial published on August 14, 2015 blasting this latest, entirely corporate-funded sham organization noted that, "beverage makers have long funneled money to industry-leaning scientists and formed innocent-sounding front groups to spread the message that sugary sodas have no deleterious effects on health," adding that the GEBN represented "the latest effort to put a 'science-based' gloss on industry positions." Even in acknowledging that the GEBN was, in fact, headed up by established and respected scientists—the group's president was prominent obesity researcher and University of Colorado Professor James. O. Hill—the *Times* editorial pointed out that corporate funding or sponsorship almost invariably have a powerfully biasing influence on research study results.[33]

---

[33] *New York Times*, "Coke."

And while Dr. Hill insisted, in a statement issued in August of that same year, that Coca-Cola had "no say in how these funds are spent" and that the beverage maker "does not have any input into our organization," the *Times* editorial cited an analysis published in PLOS Medicine that found that "studies financed by Coca-Cola, PepsiCo, the American Beverage Association, and the sugar industry were five times more likely to find no link between sugary drinks and weight gain than studies reporting no industry sponsorship or financial conflicts of interest."

So vehement and unrelenting was the universal criticism from public health authorities and medical nutrition experts across the country that the Global Energy Balance Network was disbanded in December 2015, after less than a year in existence, and directly after Coca-Cola was similarly forced by public pressure to withdraw its funding, which basically cut the legs out from under the group. A series of emails obtained by the *Associated Press* "suggested that Dr. Hill had allowed Coke to pick the group's leaders, create its mission statement, and design its website," according to an article by Anahad O'Connor published in the *New York Times* on December 2, 2015.[34]

In one such exchange, Coke's chief scientist, Rhona Applebaum, openly likened the establishment of the group and its purpose to "a political campaign" designed specifically to "develop, deploy and evolve a powerful and multifaceted strategy to counter *radical organizations and their proponents*" (emphasis mine). I guess those "radical organizations and their proponents" were the redoubtable public health authorities and legitimate obesity scientists who had vigilantly raised the red flag over the group's questionable funding source in addition to its questionable "science."

Upon the organization's ultimate demise, Dr. Yoni Freedhoff, the prominent University of Ottawa obesity expert who had helped to lead the charge against GEBN, said flatly that the organization was nothing more than a "megaphone for Coca-Cola," derisively adding, "Now that Coca-Cola is no longer providing the funds to support the megaphone, [GEBN]

---

[34] O'Connor, "Research Group."

is shutting down. That speaks to the purpose of the establishment of this group."[35] The University of Colorado School of Medicine announced sheepishly that it would return a $1 million grant it had received from Coke to help launch the organization.

You would think that such public repudiation ought to be enough to dissuade the food industry from continuing to engage in the commissioning of what is essentially fake, financially tainted, and discreditable scientific research. Yet, barely a year after the embarrassing disbanding of the GEBN, they were at it again. This time, the industry's disinformation effort came in the form of an article in a prominent medical journal in which the authors launch a withering attack on global health advice to reduce sugar consumption and claim that warnings linking sugar consumption to obesity, type 2 diabetes and other serious health problems are based on weak or conflicting evidence.[36]

Appearing in the February 2017 issue of the *Annals of Internal Medicine*, the study reviewed nine sets of previously published guidelines for reducing consumption of dietary sugar emanating from nine different worldwide health organizations, including the U.S. government, the World Health Organization (WHO), and Public Health England, and resulting in a total of 12 separate recommendations. The authors' conclusion is as elegantly simple as it is simplistically, diabolically calculated to deceive, insinuating that, because the guidelines are not all the same and their recommendations vary widely, they cannot be trusted. Their reasoning? That such variation "can result in confusion and raises concern about the quality of the guidelines and the underlying evidence." Never mind the fact that every single set of guidelines universally recommended that people reduce the amount of sugar they eat to prevent excessive weight gain and other serious health issues, as well as "nutrient displacement" (i.e., eating candy or sweets when you could be eating something with nutritional value, like fruits or vegetables), and that the guidelines differed only in degree.

---

[35] Ibid.
[36] Erickson et al., "Sugar Intake."

Yet, incredibly, that variation was enough for these authors to conclude that, "The quality of evidence supporting [the] recommendations was low to very low," and therefore the, "Guidelines on dietary sugar do not meet the criteria for trustworthy recommendations."[37]

Condemnation of the review was both sharp and swift, coming primarily from public health and obesity experts who immediately pointed out the study authors' close ties to the food and sugar industries, and with particular vigor, the glaring fact that the study was bought and paid for by the Washington, D.C.-based scientific group known as the International Life Sciences Institute (another lofty and inspiring name that would have made Ayn Rand proud, don't you think?). The International Life Sciences Institute (ILSI) is primarily funded by—and owes its very existence to—a phalanx of multinational food and agrochemical companies, including Coca-Cola, Monsanto, General Mills, Hershey, Mars, Nestle USA, Kellogg, PepsiCo, the Kraft-Heinz Company, and others. In addition, one of the study's authors, Joanne Slavin, sits on the scientific advisory board of Tate & Lyle, one of the world's largest suppliers of high-fructose corn syrup, and over the past three years her lab at the University of Minnesota has received funding from a dozen food and agriculture concerns or companies, from the Minnesota Beef Council to PepsiCo, Welch's, and Nestle.

In an editorial published in the same issue of the *Annals*, Drs. Dean Schillinger and Cristin Kearns, health experts and researchers at UC San Francisco condemned the Erickson study as the latest example of the "politicization of science" designed to "overly accentuate inherent uncertainties of science to cast doubt on the scientific consensus." Drs. Schillinger and Kearns rightly point out that the nine guidelines were written over a 21-year period from 1995 to 2016—an indisputably extended period of time for experts to conduct ongoing research, to develop new data findings, and during which one would naturally and very reasonably expect there to be revisions and refinements to scientific, evidence-based dietary

---

[37] Ibid.

recommendations. In other words, the "confusions" or variations among the nine sets of guideline recommendations that were of such vexing concern to Erikson and his colleagues in the industry-funded ILSI study.[38]

Schillinger, who is also chief of the UCAF division of internal medicine at San Francisco General Hospital, while acknowledging that questioning and persistently reviewing the quality of nutrition guidelines is highly appropriate—as well as is the need to hold them to the highest possible standards—nevertheless in this case accused the researchers and their "financial backers" with having an obvious agenda. Schillinger told the *New York Times*, "They're hijacking the scientific process in a disingenuous way to sow doubt and jeopardize public health."[39]

Dr. Marion Nestle was equally blunt. A professor of nutrition, food studies, and public health at New York University who also studies conflicts of interest in nutrition research, Nestle charged that the Erickson article, "comes right out of the tobacco industry's playbook: cast doubt on the science," adding, "This is a classic example of how industry funding biases opinion. It's shameful."

None of this is anything new. Documents recently uncovered by researchers at UCSF reveal that, as far back as the 1960s the sugar industry paid scientists to not only play down the link between sugar and heart disease, but to shift the blame to saturated fat as the culprit. According to a recent article in the *New York Times*:

> *The documents show that a trade group called the Sugar Research Foundation, known today as the Sugar Association, paid three Harvard scientists the equivalent of about $50,000 in today's dollars to publish a 1967 review of research on sugar, fat and heart disease. The studies used in the review were handpicked by the sugar group, and the article, which was published in the prestigious* New England Journal of Medicine,

---

[38] Kearns and Schillinger, "Guidelines."
[39] O'Connor, "Study."

minimized the link between sugar and heart health and cast aspersions on the role of saturated fat.[40]

Commenting on the newly released documents, Dr. Nestle wrote that they provide "compelling evidence" that the sugar industry conspired—for decades and quite successfully—to initiate research "expressly to exonerate sugar as a risk factor for coronary heart disease."

The *New York Times* article also mentions that while the Harvard researchers and the sugar industry executives with whom they collaborated are now deceased, a brief look at the career track of just one of the authors of the 1967 study provides an illuminating glimpse into the "revolving door" between government regulatory bodies and intimately vested industry, as well as the tragic legacy wrought by such a cozy and unrestricted relationship. The scientist was D. Mark Hegsted, who later rather incredibly became the head of nutrition at the U.S. Department of Agriculture. It was there, in 1977, that Hegsted was instrumental in creating the forerunner to the federal government's dietary guidelines. The fact that Hegsted used the power of his prominent position to influence the government's dietary recommendations is clearly evident in the fact that saturated fat warnings remain the cornerstone of U.S. dietary guidelines to this day, and that the health risks posed by excessive sugar consumption were largely ignored.

The result, according to Dr. Stanton Glantz, professor of medicine at UCSF, is that for many decades, public health officials encouraged Americans to reduce their fat intake, which in turn led many people to consume low-fat, high-sugar foods, a misguided and deeply flawed policy that many experts now blame for fueling the obesity crisis in our country today. "They [the sugar industry] were able to derail the discussion about sugar for decades," Glantz lamented.

And the tragic question, spanning the past half century and more, is how many people have died prematurely and how many billions of dollars

---

[40] O'Connor, "Blame."

have been squandered, as a direct result of just this one conspiratorial devil's pact between industry and government regulators?

And yet, as we have just read, that, apparently, is not a question that moves the food and sugar industries, whose agenda today remains one of obfuscation and deception.

YOU'RE GONNA TAKE SOMEONE'S EYE OUT WITH THAT!

Sometimes eating can pose a dangerous hazard even before you open the package or container that the food is sold in. In a 1984 lawsuit brought against PepsiCo, a Brownsville, Texas, jury awarded truck driver Rodolfo Leal $1 million after he was blinded by an exploding soft drink bottle cap made and distributed by the company. Before trial, Alcoa Corporation, which had bottled the beverage in question, along with two bottle manufacturers, had reached a relatively modest out-of-court settlement with the plaintiff of just over $200,000, though it should be kept in mind that this was only one case out of many hundreds.[41]

In bringing the suit against PepsiCo, Leal's attorney, Richard Roth, argued that the company should have warned the public about the dangers of its aluminum twist-off caps. Roth brought expert witnesses who testified that as many as 5,400 people were being injured each year when misapplied caps exploded under pressure when twisted off. That is, there was a manufacturing defect in that the caps prevented them from seating properly and securely on the bottle itself, thus making them prone to explode under pressure, prematurely flying off the top and into people's faces.

After the jury award, Attorney Roth stated, "I think this is just one of many kinds of lawsuits that will have to be won before PepsiCo will warn the public." Further noting that he alone had as many as ten other clients claiming similar injuries from exploding bottle caps, Roth added, "It will

---

[41] UPI, "Exploding."

take many of these types of judgments before they stop continuing on their present course of action."

The thing was, both PepsiCo and Alcoa knew about the bottle cap defect and chose not to warn consumers about it. Now, one may argue, quite reasonably in fact, that the ramifications of the exploding soda bottle cap defect certainly do not rise to the level of tragedy of infant fatalities from *Cronobacter* in powdered baby formula, and it may also be true that the number of serious eye injury cases resulting from exploding bottle caps pales in comparison to more serious and even deadly injuries resulting from hidden hazards stemming from many other dangerous or defective consumer products, from ladders to automobiles. Still, there are some revealing lessons to be learned from the way that different players in the soft drink industry responded to the problem. In particular, it provides another illuminating look into the way that the percentage size of a company's pre-existing market share can play an influential role in its leaders' decision-making process—specifically, whether in fact they do the right thing to warn consumers of hidden hazards in their products, or simply decide not to provide consumer safety warnings and take their chances in the courts [read: pay out a few million dollars in settlement costs in return for nondisclosure agreements signed by plaintiffs].

My recommendation, in this instance not to the FDA but to the Consumer Products Safety Commission (CPSC), was that the commission should require carbonated soft drink manufacturers to put a warning label on their soda bottles (worded slightly differently on either glass or plastic bottles) that would generally read as follows:

> **WARNING: Contents under pressure. Bottle may burst or cap may blow off causing eye or other serious injury. Point away from face and people, especially while opening.**

Smaller companies like 7-Up, Dr Pepper, and Schweppes actually agreed to adopt the warning and began printing it on their bottle labels.

However, this proposed warning simply enraged the larger companies like Coca-Cola and PepsiCo, who argued that the language was overblown and that such a warning would be seriously detrimental to their sales. We were ridiculed, with one industry-leaning organization going so far as to designate the proposed language dubiously as the "silly warning of the century." Accordingly, Coke and Pepsi categorically refused to print the warning, as proposed, on bottles of their carbonated soft drink products.

At a summit convened by the CPSC to discuss the exploding bottle cap issue, both major companies said, in effect, that rather than proactively warn consumers, or even alternatively, to try to fix the inherent manufacturing defect, they would simply raise the price of their products to cover the anticipated costs of litigation brought by injured consumers. And they, more than any of the other companies, had the power and might to do it: Collectively commanding somewhere between 80 and 90 percent of the soft drink market, Coke and Pepsi were the 900-pound gorillas who could do anything they damn well pleased, including putting profits over safety if they chose to. Which, of course, they did.

Eventually, the bottle cap seating defect was successfully engineered out, obviating any continued need for the hazard warning. Yet, one has to wonder: Would Coke and Pepsi eventually do enough soul-searching to finally step up and take proactive responsibly for correcting the defect? Not very likely, especially when you consider how cavalierly they reacted to calls for a proper warning label. Instead, they clearly regarded the lawsuits arising from bottle cap injuries as little more than nuisance litigation and as a routine part of the cost of doing business. Or should credit for finally fixing the problem more likely belong to Alcoa Corporation and the bottle makers, whom we might surmise simply wanted to make a better product for their corporate customers (and avoid further lawsuits against themselves)? We'll never know, of course, but you can bet that the Coke and Pepsi executives who made the decision not to warn feel themselves vindicated in protecting their companies' profits and market share.

EATING CAN BE HAZARDOUS EVEN BEFORE
YOUR FOOD IS GROWN!

A friend of mine who happens to be of Italian descent likes to talk about one of his favorite scenes in the classic Oscar-winning film, *The Godfather*. The scene, which vividly reminds this friend of his own father's (as well as several uncles') love of gardening, occurs when Vito Corleone, after being, shall we say, forcibly retired, is puttering around the tomato garden, pulling weeds, spraying noxious deadly poison on the insects, and playing hide-and-seek with his grandchild amid the vines (and also amid the mist from the toxic pesticide spray!). It is not without salient coincidence, to my way of thinking and if you'll forgive the darkly melodramatic irony of the metaphor, that it happens to be the scene in which the Don finally expires for good.

According to the National Gardening Market Research Company, the do-it-yourself home gardening market is currently a $36.9 billion industry. Further, industry expert Ian Baldwin estimates that 74 percent of American households participate in some form of lawn and gardening activities, noting quite interestingly that home food gardening by consumers along with increasing interest among millennials has led industry growth over the past three years. Of course, the bane of every home food gardener who desires high yields of fruits and vegetables is weeds.

Enter Monsanto company's new product called Roundup, a "revolutionary" new herbicide whose active ingredient is glyphosate, and which is designed to kill weeds without killing crops, especially when used by commercial farmers alongside Monsanto's brand-new line of glyphosate-resistant, genetically engineered (GE, also referred to today as Genetically Modified Organisms, or GMOs) "Roundup Ready crops". First introduced to the market in 1974, by 2007, glyphosate had become the most widely used herbicide in the U.S. agricultural sector and the second-most used one in the private consumer home and garden market, according to statistics compiled by the EPA.

The interconnected partnership of the two product lines has been staggeringly profitable for Monsanto, potentially creating a kind of "vertical" or cyclical monopoly for the company. Think about it: If you're a commercial farmer, you need Monsanto's Roundup herbicide formulations to effectively control weeds to protect your crops and successfully produce high yields for market; but you also need Monsanto's genetically engineered bulk crop seeds design to withstand those same powerful Monsanto herbicides and still thrive. As the old expression goes, Monsanto has got you "coming and going."

That being said, what made Monsanto's Roundup and its active ingredient glyphosate so "revolutionary" was the manufacturer's claim that, not only was it essentially nontoxic, but unlike previous poisonous weed killers that accumulate and linger in the soil for an indefinite period of time, glyphosate was also purported to be biodegradable, thus completely safe for consumers and the environment long term. The chemical was supposed to break down in the soil and disappear. This, of course, would have been a major breakthrough in the herbicide game. However, a growing and very alarming body of mounting scientific evidence appears to now show that none of this is even remotely true.

A March 2017 article published in *Rodale's Organic Life* asks the rather horrifying question, "How Much Toxic Roundup Are You Eating?" The article states that while glyphosate "has been marketed as safe and even 'biodegradable,' the science is pouring in, and the [evidence] will make you sick."

"Roundup," the article's author, Leah Zerbe, reveals is a "systemic chemical," meaning that it is taken up into the food crops that are consumed by both people and farm animals, some of which, of course, become food on our dinner tables. Zerbe cites studies by Norwegian researchers that found "excessive" levels of glyphosate inside American food crops such as soy beans and genetically modified corn, two products that show up in hundreds of processed foods under dozens of different ingredient names, such as mono-diglyceride, soya, lecithin, and textured vegetable proteins, just to name a few. We may summarize Zerbe's investigative findings as follows:

- **Roundup Doubles Your Risk of Lymphoma:** A major new review of 44 scientific studies found that glyphosate exposure doubles farmers' risk of developing non-Hodgkin's lymphoma.
- **It's Raining Roundup:** Each year, nonorganic farmers dump millions of pounds of Roundup on food crops. The levels are so excessive that federal scientists recently detected the weed killer in the air and rain.
- **Roundup Flat-Out Kills Human Cells:** In 2009, French researchers published a scientific paper in the journal *Chemical Research in Toxicology* showing that low levels of four glyphosate formulations used in Roundup—levels that are far below what's allowed in agriculture, but that are right on par with the amount of the chemical found to be in our food—all kill human umbilical, embryonic, and placental cells within 24 hours.
- **Roundup Is Detrimental to Human Digestive Health:** Glyphosate isn't just an herbicide; it's also registered as an antimicrobial agent in the U.S. thanks to its ability to wipe out a wide variety of pathogenic organisms. The problem is harmful pathogens like *Clostridium botulinum*, *Salmonella*, and *E. coli* are able to survive in the gut, but the "good guys" in your digestive tract, protective microorganisms, *bacillus* and *lactobacillus*, for instance, are killed off. This could set your digestive tract up for a nightmarish situation, including "leaky gut," where the protective gut lining is compromised, allowing bacteria and toxins to escape into your bloodstream and make you sick.[42]

But the news on Roundup only gets worse, because numerous scientific studies have shown a potential link between exposure to glyphosate

---

[42] Zerbe, "Roundup."

and development of non-Hodgkin's lymphoma. The latest study conducted in 2019 by researchers at the University of California, Berkeley, the University of Washington, Seattle, and the Icahn School of Medicine at Mount Sinai, New York, found that glyphosate raises the cancer risk of those exposed to it by as much as 41 percent.[43]

HERE WE GO AGAIN

Monsanto was dealt its first major blow over glyphosate in its Roundup products when a San Francisco Federal Court ordered the company to pay $289 million in damages to Dewayne Johnson, a 46-year-old and terminally ill former groundskeeper, in a landmark and precedent-setting case. However, not only did the jury determine that Monsanto's Roundup had caused Johnson's cancer, it also found that the company was responsible for "negligent failure" to warn him of the health hazards from exposure; and furthermore it had acted "with malice or oppression."[44]

However, if the verdict itself and the pronouncements of the jury weren't disturbing enough, the federal trial also revealed an all too familiar pattern of deception precisely like that perpetrated by the sugar industry. Among the documents brought to light during the proceedings were hundreds of internal Monsanto emails, including one written by Monsanto executive William F. Heydens and sent to a number of other company officials indicating that they could ghostwrite favorable research on glyphosate and pay established academics to sign their names to the published papers.

Further displaying his admirable devotion to Monsanto's bottom line, Heydens wrote, "We would be keeping the cost down by us doing the writing and they would just edit & sign their names so to speak," and actually revealed that the company had engaged in precisely this tactic before.[45] And so, once again, it seems clear that Monsanto has been lying all along about

---

[43] Zhang et al., "Exposure."
[44] Levin, "Monsanto."
[45] Rosenblatt et al., "EPA."

the alleged safety and biodegradability of its Roundup herbicidal products and has known all along that neither of these specious claims are true.

Does any of this sound familiar?

At this point, you may be asking, where were U.S. government regulators, in this case the EPA, while all of this was going on? The question is even more troublingly poignant when you consider that Monsanto's consistently deliberate deception has been "going on" right into the 21st century and some 50 years since the tragic aftermath of the recklessly indiscriminate and widespread use of DDT (a dangerous and deadly pesticide) so eloquently indicted by Rachel Carson's landmark book *Silent Spring*. Well, as far as can be determined from the available evidence, the EPA appears to have been looking the other way or operating on radio silence through the 1970s, 1980s, 1990s, and right on into the new millennium.

That was until as late as 2015, when the International Agency for Research on Cancer (IARC), a branch of the World Health Organization, was preparing to announce its determination to label glyphosate a probable carcinogen based on a growing body of research linking exposure to the chemical to the development of non-Hodgkin's lymphoma. At about the same time, the U.S. Department of Health and Human Services (DHHS) was considering undertaking its own independent review of research on glyphosate; perhaps in part because no other government regulatory agency—including the EPA—seemed to have any interest in doing so.

And that is when the EPA sprang into immediate action.

Email traffic among numerous Monsanto executives indicates that EPA Deputy Director Jess Rowland promised them that he would do everything in his power to quash DHHS' plans for conducting the independent review it was considering.[46] In an email to Monsanto executive Dan Jenkins and in reference to that effort, Rowland brashly wrote, "If I can kill this, I should get a medal." Rowland must have had some potent political juice, because the proposed independent DHHS review never happened.

---

[46] Ibid.

As a postscript to the whole Roundup-glyphosate affair, even as liability litigation continues (and will likely do so for years to come), according to Rodale's, there is growing scientific research evidence that the technological model underlying Roundup and other organism-selective herbicidal agents, used liberally in "partnership" with genetically engineered crops, simply does not work, particularly in the long term.

Likening the approach to the overuse of antibiotics in humans and animals that leads only to the creation of hard-to-kill, antibiotic-resistant bacteria or "superbugs," Leah Zerbe writes, "Genetically engineering crop seeds to live through herbicide sprayings that would normally kill the crop is a failed technology and a losing battle." Instead, she continues, "abusing Roundup has fueled the emergence of nearly impossible-to-kill super-weeds."[47] Moreover, one of the alleged major advantages of genetically engineered crops or GMOs, highly touted and promoted by Monsanto and the other chemical companies, was that their widespread use in commercial farming would significantly *reduce* the need for chemical herbicides and pesticides to protect crops. However, quite disturbingly, the exact opposite has overwhelmingly proved to be the case. In evidence, a recent study conducted by Dr. Chuck Benbrook, a researcher at Washington State University, found that between 1996 and 2011 GMO technology actually *increased* herbicide use by 527 million pounds; an 11 percent increase over 15 years.[48]

Zerbe concludes by describing an alarming prospect for the potential future safety of farm-grown produce in America and around the world—a prospect that will be made even more frightening should scientific research ultimately conclude that glyphosate and other similarly selective herbicides are, in fact, dangerously carcinogenic. She writes:

> *Because glyphosate-resistant GE crops are failing misera-*
> *bly, the Environmental Protection Agency (EPA)—right*

---

[47] Zerbe, "Roundup."
[48] Benbrook, "Crops."

*now—is considering the approval of an even nastier GE seed designed to survive dousing of glyphosate **and** the highly toxic, older 2,4-D weed killer. This is called "stacking," and it's expected to dramatically increase the amount of 2,4-D used on our food. In fact, approving crops genetically engineered to survive repeated dousings of 2,4-D will likely **quadruple** pesticide use, according to Dave Mortensen, PhD, weed scientist at Penn State University. That's bad news, considering 2,4-D has been linked to hypothyroidism, suppressed immune function, Parkinson's disease, among other ills.[49]* (emphasis mine).

There is a great irony here in the current public outcry and concern over the increasing prevalence of GMOs in our everyday diets. The fear and resistance to GMOs is quite evident in the increasing array of "organic" food products that are being advertised—by companies no doubt interested in capitalizing on that fear—as being completely "non-GMOs." Yet, that public health concern may be disastrously misplaced. The truth is that the human race has been genetically modifying crops and animals since long before Gregor Mendel was playing with peas and the ancient Egyptians and Chinese were breeding new species of cats and dogs. However, today, the threat to human health and safety comes not from GMOs but from the frighteningly excessive overuse of the potentially carcinogenic herbicides they have been engineered to withstand.

All I can say is: Bon Appétit!

---

[49] Zerbe, "Roundup."

CHAPTER 4

WORKING: HI HO, HI HO, IT'S OFF TO DEATH WE GO!

We don't often think of Richard Nixon as the "consumer advocate" president, yet it was Nixon who, in 1970, signed into law the Occupational Safety and Health Act, creating, as of January 1, 1971, the Occupational Safety and Health Administration (OSHA), whose main goal, according to its website is "to assure safe and healthful working conditions for working men and women by setting and enforcing standards and by providing training, outreach, education and assistance." Nixon was also responsible for signing into law the Highway Safety Act of 1970, which created the National Highway Traffic Safety Administration (NHTSA). Although, as we have already seen, the impetus to form that organization began much earlier with the publication of Ralph Nader's landmark book *Unsafe at Any Speed* and the highly publicized congressional hearings in the mid-1960s that led to the passage of the first seat belt laws in America.

On its website, OSHA states that, on average, 4,500 workers are killed on the job each year. OSHA also estimates that over 32 million workers in over 3.5 million workplaces are exposed to hazardous chemicals, resulting in approximately 100,000 chemical illnesses and related injuries each year. As we might imagine, construction sites are particularly dangerous, and OSHA estimates that one out of ten construction site workers are injured every year, or about 150,000 injuries and 1,000 fatalities every year in the construction industry alone. In terms of sheer numbers, these statistics make the construction industry the most dangerous industry in the United States, comprising 15 percent of all workers' compensation claims nationally.

According to the latest figures available from the U.S. Bureau of Labor Statistics, there were 4,821 fatal occupational injuries in 2014. That's 239 more than the previous year, or an increase of 5 percent over 2013.

Clearly, working can be dangerous to your health, yet at the same time, perhaps in no other area of the seven behaviors identified in this book is the issue of human health and safety more complicated, more contentious, and more controversial than in connection with worker on-the-job safety. This is likely because in none of the other areas do more separate, vested interests seem to intersect, or collide if you will, wherein those differing interests appear to be at obvious odds with one another.

That is to say, when we look at the different, competing interests on a purely surface level, we have employers who want to make as much profit as possible for themselves and their stakeholders without the encumbrance of government intervention through "onerous" regulatory oversight. This is juxtaposed with employees who are in need of steady, reliable, gainful employment yielding respectable wages and ideally affording an ever-improving standard of living. And, while workers generally also want safe working conditions, they are often willing (or forced) to accept certain risks in exchange for reliable employment. How many times, for example, after a serious fatal incident like an oil rig platform fire or a chemical plant explosion, have we seen workers on the evening news calmly acknowledging that the danger "comes with the job"? For their part, federal regulators may be pushed in conflicting directions as well. For example, by powerful and monied corporate businesses and industries that want government to "get out of their hair" or by partisan politician office holders who want to foster high employment and job growth among their loyal constituencies (and to improve their chances of being re-elected), versus union and other independent public interest advocates wanting better working conditions and higher safety standards for workers. When it comes to the nature and extent of effective workplace safety warnings about hazardous materials, equipment, and job-site conditions, government regulators are often obliged to balance it all, the fundamental question being, "How much is enough?" What must companies do to meet a high standard of principled disclosure? What must employees do to take responsibility for their own actions working with dangerous equipment or within hazardous environments?

Viewed this way, all of these competing interests might appear to be inherently incompatible. After all, many occupations are inherently dangerous, yet as the cliché goes, "somebody's got to do them." But I believe these three components are not incompatible at all. The great equalizer among these parties lies in each holding up their end of the bargain as legs of the Proactive Safety Triad, and it all begins with principled disclosure. So, in the first example presented in this chapter, we'll look at a company that did the right thing, and which—even more remarkably—had to cross a cultural divide in order to do it.

A TUTORIAL IN PURSUING PRINCIPLED DISCLOSURE

Based in Japan, Daikin Industries, Ltd. is one of the world's largest air conditioning manufacturers with over $15 billion in annual sales and operating in 140 countries. They also hold the distinction, to the best of my knowledge, of having never been sued in the United States for failure to warn about the potential hazards of their products. So, with respect to Daikin, there are no court cases to talk about and no internal, "smoking gun" emails revealing any deceptive practices, or deliberate cover-ups, or any wrongdoing at all. Anecdotally, however, there is much that can be learned about this company's approach to the issue of principled disclosure that has enabled it to remain lawsuit-free. Their story reveals how the process works well when it is done right. The first thing they did was to hire an expert in the field of safety warnings.

When they were preparing to enter the U.S. market, around 2004, they called me in as a consultant to help them design the kind of safety warnings their product line would need to effectively avoid liability. In fact, their top management people flew from the company headquarters in Osaka to New York, where I met with them along with their U.S. attorney. First, however, I asked them to show me exactly what a commercial air conditioner unit is. I wanted to see the actual beast for myself. They took me to a warehouse and showed me various units. These are massive pieces of machinery, the kind of units that you see being hoisted to the roofs of commercial buildings by huge cranes. As such, they are generally not something that would in any way endanger the general public—unless of course the crane cable snapped and the unit came crashing down onto the city street when it's being installed. But that's a different story.

And, of course, that was my next question: Who specifically is at risk to get hurt? The simple answer was two people: the worker (or workers) who installs the units and the person (or persons) who maintains them going forward. Sometimes that can be the same person because companies often hire outside contractors to do both the installation and long-term routine maintenance. Having now established that there are two types of people at risk, I asked pointedly how these individuals who are either installing or maintaining the unit are apt to be hurt. What can happen or go wrong? Where do the potential dangers lurk? It is important to bear in mind that a proper safety warning label or sign must clearly identify any hazardous conditions at the point of use of the product that, if not addressed, can hurt, injure, or kill a person—particularly those conditions that may not be obvious to the product user or worker. This invariably requires a little bit (or a lot) of brainstorming.

Ideally, this is best done at the design stage. In Daikin's case, they had already designed the many types of air conditioner units they planned to bring to the U.S. market, but they hadn't gone into mass manufacture yet. So, theoretically, there was ample time to make production-line adjustments and, at minimum, to design warning labels to go on the individual units themselves before they were to be shipped and installed. The key is that company officials approached me at the right time—when it was still possible to make those adjustments. So, the first thing I did was lead a six-hour brainstorming session with company executives and engineers to map out all of the potential hazards posed by the units in terms of installation and maintenance.

We identified three hazards that were hidden from the worker that I felt strongly needed to be addressed with individual, specific warning labels. The most obvious one was electrocution, the second involved rotating parts, and the third was a burn hazard.

As you would expect, the amount of electricity running through these giant commercial air conditioning units is enormous. That should be obvious, though this fact—in and of itself—does not really represent the greatest danger. A worker touching the wrong thing inside the unit while the unit is running will be electrocuted instantly. Where the hidden hazard comes in is in the amount of time involved in turning the units off—completely—and then the amount of time it takes the units to wind back up to full operational power. Because of the time it takes, workers anxious to get their jobs done oftentimes do not like to shut the units off while they work on them, which, of course, is as infinitely dangerous as it sounds. Not only that, but even after the units have been shut off, it takes a certain amount of time for the electrical "juice" to fully drain from the internal systems. Consequently, the electricity amounts remain potentially lethal until that surge of power completely dissipates.

The second major hazard is also a function of the failure to shut the unit off completely before working or performing maintenance. It involves rotating parts, mostly huge and powerful ventilating fans. In this case, a worker who sticks a hand into the wrong place while the unit is running could easily lose a couple of fingers or perhaps the whole hand. However, here again, the fans on these units can spin quite silently for several minutes after they have been shut off at the electrical switch. The instant, do-it-yourself amputation danger isn't over until the fan has completely stopped. An aversion to turning the air conditioning unit completely off is, again, a crucial factor, whether it's a worker who simply wants to get a job done as quickly as possible or—it is entirely fair to speculate the possibility that occasionally—a worker may just be too lazy to take the time to shut the unit off or a worker is too impatient to wait for the damn fan to stop spinning. (We should remember that being careless or lazy never stopped an injured worker from suing a company for failure to warn.)

In both of these cases, the danger posed by electric shock or rotating parts is immediate, so the warning labels I designed for Daiken addressing these two separate hazards both have the word "DANGER" written in red, white, and black (*See Figure 4.1*).

FIGURE 4.1

Courtesy of Dr. Gerald M. Goldhaber

Both labels clearly identify the particular hazard in capital letters with an exclamation point in a warning triangle—ELECTRIC SHOCK HAZARD! and ROTATING PARTS HAZARD! Both also describe starkly and succinctly what can happen as a result of worker mishandling of the equipment: Death or dismemberment. Just as importantly, both provide ample instruction to turn the power off; "ALL POWER" in the case of the electric shock warning, and to "make sure fan has completely stopped" in the case of the rotating parts warning.

The electric shock warning label goes a bit further (and appropriately so, on a scale of magnitude) by indicating that, "Only a qualified service technician should install or service" the unit, and, for workers who may not understand English, it includes the international graphic code for electrocution hazard. This is a stick figure symbol that has already been developed and tested to prove that over 90 percent of people can interpret the graphic to understand what it means. This meets the criterion set by the American National Standards Institute that has gained worldwide acceptance.

The third safety concern surrounding Daikin's air conditioning systems is a burn hazard from inadvertent exposure to the refrigerant R410A used in the units and sealed under pressure. Because the danger is not immediate in the same way as that posed by high voltage or moving machinery, it does not require a red, white, and black "DANGER" warning. It is, however, serious enough to warrant an orange and black "WARNING" label and the words "BURN HAZARD!" in capital letters (*See Figure 4.2*).

FIGURE 4.2

Courtesy of Dr. Gerald M. Goldhaber

HOW WARNING LABELS ARE DESIGNED, TESTED, AND CHOSEN

The warning labels shown in these two figures were the winners of a fairly intensive experimental testing procedure, and one that is important to understand.

Once we had established the three major hazards presented by Daikin's products and the specific people who might be hurt by them—in this case a very small universe—the next step in the process of principled disclosure is to discover what warning label designs will work the best at informing that universe of users quickly and as understandably as possible. You begin by working up a series of different candidate designs, combinations of words, warnings, and graphics, and then you test them on people. I took a bunch of different safety label designs for all three hazards to Daikin's commercial trade showrooms in three states, New Jersey, New York, and Texas, where I recruited about 50 people in each location. These were industry people specifically working or employed as installers or service maintenance of large-scale air conditioning and other office and some residential infrastructure systems. I bought them into a room under the guise that I was going to use them for half a day and give them each a couple hundred bucks for their trouble, as simple as that. In fact, I wouldn't be surprised if that was the single most expensive part of the test phase, paying the workers a total of roughly $10,000 in cash across the three locations. But I made lots of friends! Basically, and in very brief terms, this kind of field testing works this way:

First and foremost, in order for your study to be empirically valid, you cannot tell your survey participants that you specifically want them to look at or evaluate the safety warning labels. In essence, you are trying to establish how easily people see and understand them when they are actually *not* looking for them. So you can't clue them in.

Instead, they were told that Daikin wanted them to check out their new equipment line and was interested in their impression and opinions. However, I divided our participants into groups that would each see a different version of the warnings label designs, exposing them to a variety of versions and different sizes, using different language, depicting different graphics or pictograms, and placed on and around the equipment where, ideally in a real workplace setting, the manufacturer would most want the signs to be *seen*, read, and heeded! It's truly amazing what you can learn from this simple blind procedure. Sometimes the placement of a warning label two inches up or down, or to the left or the right, can mean the difference between being immediately seen and recognized or completely missed and disregarded! In any case, the trick is to try to determine as accurately as possible: When asked, which labels did the majority of people report seeing and which locations seemed to be the most advantageous in terms of ensuring that the labels were in fact seen? At the end of the session, I typically hold up different versions of the language or terminology used in the various label designs and I pointedly ask the participants to describe individually what their understanding is of what the words actually mean. In the end, the language, graphics, and design arrangements that were most easily understood are the features that wound up being incorporated into the final design of each label.

THE ESSENTIAL COMPONENTS OF AN EFFECTIVE WARNING MESSAGE

In the field of communication, there are always two crucial variables that determine whether a particular communication is effective or, stated differently, to determine that the particular communication was accurately received and understood to mean what it is supposed to mean. Phrased as questions specifically with respect to safety warnings, the first variable is, "Did you see the warning?" (Was the message quickly and easily noticed?) The second is, "Do you know what the words mean?" (Was the message understandable to the person receiving it?) The same criteria apply for both words and pictures or graphics. So, my questions to my panel of participants in the second part of the test session are as basic as, "What does the picture mean? Tell me in your own language."

And the goal is to devise warning labels that 90 percent of people see and understand immediately. Yet, in the most fundamentally practical terms, the acid test for companies willing to embark on this process is how well warning labels designed and tested in this fashion stand up in court. No one can guarantee that a worker will not simply ignore warning signs or won't perform their on-the-job duties in a reckless fashion that endangers themselves and others. Nor can anyone guarantee that workers who fail to heed hazard warnings or who circumvent designed-in safety equipment (like metal bars or containments around moving parts) won't wind up suing the company or the manufacturer—or both. But the standard in court concerns whether the warning properly described the hazard and its potential consequences and gave adequate instructions for avoiding the hazard, and concerns the question of whether injured workers reasonably should have been expected to know, understand, and heed the stated warnings and then act with an appropriate measure of caution.

The point is that I have never had a warning message that I have field tested in the manner I have just described that was not accepted as valid and adequate in a court case. Not only have I never had a warning that I tested and designed thrown out of court as inadequate, but I've also never had anyone succeed in countering my warnings as inferior in comparison with a "better" or allegedly more effective one. In fact, the opposite has been true. In many instances, litigation disappeared. For example, the soft drink exploding bottle cap litigation described in Chapter 3 disappeared once the explicit warnings I designed were printed on the bottle labels.

Whenever I tell the Daikin story to a corporate executive who seems reluctant to embark on the inherently simple process of principled disclosure, I feel like ending it by asking, "Now, does that sound so difficult? Or onerous? Just think of the legal headaches (and legal fees) you'll save! Not to mention the potential payout in out-of-court settlement monies!" Yet, this emphasis on worker safety and effective warnings communications cannot happen without the full commitment of the entire management team. It cannot happen when company executives or officers wrongly believe that principled disclosure is too costly to implement. Because it is almost never more costly than the legal alternatives and, let's face it, it very often saves lives.

By hiring a warnings expert and engaging in the necessary due diligence to devise effective safety warnings for their products, Daikin amply demonstrated to OSHA their willingness to do exactly what OSHA asks for: to design or create a safe work environment. If your task is to provide air conditioning for huge business offices or residential complexes, you can't design out electricity. You can't design out moveable parts. You can't design out having a cooling agent. Those are three things you have to have. You can try to protect danger points with circuit breakers or guards around moving parts or sophisticated valves to seal in the refrigerant, but the fact is that you have these really creative, ingenious people maintaining these units and fixing them when they break down. They are individuals who are abundantly capable of circumventing any safety features you might be able to devise.

From the company's liability standpoint, as harsh as it may sound, the issue is not really about trying to prevent mechanics, in fail-safe fashion, from engaging in potentially dangerous behaviors in the conduct of their job responsibilities. It's about a practical and defensive legal strategy of adequately warning them that they do so at their own risk. And we must not forget that workers have their own responsibilities to operate professionally and with due caution as part of the safety triad.

Finally, what makes the Daikin example so remarkable is that you must bear in mind that this is a Japanese-managed company. Japan's social and corporate culture is vastly different than the one we have in the U.S. today. In fact, the difference is like night and day. In Japan, by comparison, there are no lawsuits. It is virtually an insult to sue somebody. They don't even strike.

In Japan, a worker who gets injured on the job—even seriously injured—is more likely to apologize to his or her superiors for their own ignorance or incompetence than they are to drag the corporate executives (shackled in handcuffs with raincoats over their heads) into court on charges they failed to warn about the hazards of the job. They are not a "sue first and ask questions later" crazy culture like in the United States. It is almost inconceivable, based on the culture they came from, to think that Daikin executives would have had even the slightest prerequisite incentive to engage in, much less embrace, principled disclosure in the way that they did.

When I worked with their management people, I could not help but think about the fact that I was working with good people who probably, deep down, didn't even fundamentally understand why we in America are so obliged to put safety warnings on products and in workplaces to avoid lawsuits. Even if there were some respects in which I had to judiciously explain the "why" behind my safety recommendations, it took very little convincing to have them accepted by the company's executive management. The result, as I alluded to earlier, is that Daikin Industries has never been sued for failure to warn. It would certainly seem that their investment in principled disclosure was well worth it—for everyone concerned.

And yet, here we must go from the bright, edifying light of principled disclosure into the dark, subterranean depths of corporate criminality.

SAFETY LAST

At 3:27 p.m. on April 5, 2010, a massive explosion ripped through the Upper Big Branch (UBB) coal mine near the little town of Montcoal and about 30 miles south of Charleston, West Virginia, killing 29 of the 31 workers who were in the mine at the time. What sounded like a single horrific explosion was actually even more terrifying. A mile-long chain-reactive series of explosions milliseconds apart were fueled by a deadly buildup of methane gas and the heavy presence of highly flammable airborne coal dust. Intense fireballs rocketed through mineshafts in every direction from the blast epicenter, creating a rapidly spreading inferno that instantly incinerated some of the men and simply crushed others with the sheer force of the concussion.

One miner who survived the conflagration was 18-year-old Jason Stanley, who that day was working with a crew assigned to pumping water out of the mine. Having just finished his shift for the day and riding on a transport known as a mantrip, Stanley was about a thousand feet from an exit and more than a mile from the explosion. Yet, even that far away, he would later report that the air suddenly became a white fog of dust so thick he could not see his outstretched hand. The pulverized flying debris from the explosion, he said, "felt like a swarm of yellow jackets stinging me," adding, "I remember just trying to find a way out."[50] It was the deadliest disaster in the U.S. coal mining industry in nearly 40 years—and utterly preventable.

At the time of the tragedy, the Upper Big Branch mine was owned by Massey Energy Company, led by iron-fisted CEO Donald Blankenship and the sixth-largest coal producer in the U.S. In 2009, Massey took in over $100 million in profit, while Blankenship received over $17 million in combined salary and bonuses. The UBB complex was Massey's most profitable mine, shipping coal worth more than $300 million in 2009. The longwall section alone (longwall is a form of coal mining in which a long, continuous wall of coal—typically 3 to 4 kilometers long and 250 to 400 meters wide—is mined in a single slice) could produce more than $600,000 worth of coal every day. Furthermore, CEO Blankenship retained extensive holdings in the company—more than a quarter of his wealth was bound up in Massey stock and, therefore, tied directly to the company's bottom line.

Concluding that Blankenship was behind what they described as "misconduct" (an exceedingly blithe descriptor, when you consider the magnitude of the tragedy), in November 2014 federal prosecutors indicted the CEO on four criminal counts, including three felony counts of conspiracy to violate mine safety standards, conspiracy to impede federal mine safety officials, and making false statements to the Securities and Exchange Commission (SEC). He could have faced 31 years in federal prison if convicted on all counts. That last charge involved lies Blankenship told to investors and SEC authorities after the disaster in an effort to stop the free fall of Massey Energy stock and, of course, to try to preserve his own plummeting wealth.

It borders on the absurd to say that the findings of the government task force that investigated the deadly incident shortly after its occurrence would ultimately "reveal" that corners had been cut on important safety

---

[50] Segal, "Coal Baron."

measures, especially when you consider that the Upper Big Branch mine had been cited for serious safety violations over 500 times by the federal Mine Safety and Health Administration (MSHA) in just the year leading up to the catastrophe.

At trial, MSHA data analyst Tyler Childress testified that between January 2008 and April 2010, UBB was cited by MSHA for federal health and safety violations 836 times, 311 of which were classified as "significant and substantial," which the agency defines as "reasonably likely to result in serious injury or illness." Over the same period, Childress indicated that UBB was issued 59 unwarrantable failure orders where sections of the mine were shut due to "aggravated conduct constituting more than ordinary negligence."

The faulty ventilation systems alone—critical systems essential to keeping the air clear of combustible gases and a key contributing factor in the UBB explosion—had received 61 citations in the two years prior to the incident. In one test performed in June 2009, for example, MSHA inspectors found downright anemic airflow of 147 cubic feet per minute in a section of the mine in which federal regulations called for 9,000 cubic feet per minute. Moreover, poor ventilation contributed to the excessive buildup of highly volatile coal dust and was another serious violation of federal regulations.

Another method that is used to tamp down and control the buildup of coal dust on the mine floor, commonly referred to as "rock dusting," consists of spreading pulverized limestone dust, which forms a protective, stabilizing layer over the coal dust and prevents explosions. However, Gary Young, a miner who worked the overnight shift at UBB as a rock duster, testified at trial that his equipment was often broken or unusable, his shifts regularly truncated. Worried and frustrated about not being able to do the job properly, Young began to keep a journal to record the problems and to try to communicate the seriousness of the situation with his manager. His last journal entry reads: "I am being set up to fail." It was written two weeks before the fatal blast.

The final MSHA report left mine safety experts both in and out of government utterly astonished by the magnitude of willful negligence and deception practiced by Massey's executives and managers and stupefied at a modern-day catastrophe having all the ancient earmarks of many such horrific tragedies from a bygone and less technologically enlightened era. (Some might also want to say, a less morally and ethically enlightened era. However, the UBB tragedy certainly and disturbingly calls that notion into serious question.) As former MSHA safety inspector, now a professor at George Washington University, Celeste Monforton assessed the incident, "We haven't had a coal dust explosion in 20 years," adding emphatically, "They are completely preventable, and everybody knows it. Coal dust explosions happen in Ukraine and China, not in the United States."[51]

Even a very brief rundown of the general categories of Massey Energy's programmatic safety violations contained in the ten-page "Executive Summary" of the MSHA report (the full document runs nearly 1,000 pages) is frightening in its own right.[52] A review of the summary also highlights, about as abundantly as one could possibly imagine, the extreme emphasis of profits over safety openly displayed by Massey Energy and particularly by its CEO Don Blankenship. Among the MSHA findings:

Massey failed to perform required mine examinations adequately and also repeatedly and consistently failed to remedy known hazards and violations of laws related to worker safety. MSHA regulations require mine operators to examine certain areas of the mine on a weekly basis, as well as before and during each shift, to identify hazardous conditions. At UBB, Massey examiners often failed to even bother to travel to areas they were required to inspect or, in some cases, travelled to the areas but did not perform the required inspections and measurements. For example, in the weeks prior to the explosion, company inspectors conducted no methane examinations at all on the longwall tailgate. The tailgate is an area directly behind the coal-cutting or excavating operation and, consequently, is a prime area for methane gas to build up as it is released from the breaking coal. It is not surprising that the tailgate is where the explosion began.

---

[51] Ibid.
[52] Mine Safety and Health Administration.

Even when Massey performed inspections and identified hazards, it rarely corrected them.

In addition to methane buildup, these grossly negligent inspection practices allowed loose coal, coal dust on the floor of the mine, and float coal dust accumulation in the air in dangerous levels over days, weeks, and months, which in turn provided a deadly volatile mix of fuels for the explosion that killed 29 men.

In spite of all this, in one terse memo issued to all of the deep mine foremen at UBB in 2005, Blankenship directly instructed them to ignore calls for remediating hazardous conditions or making essential safety repairs and demanding that they concentrate solely on coal production. He stated flatly, "If any of you have been asked by your group presidents, your supervisors, engineers, or anyone else to do anything other than run coal (i.e., build overcasts, do construction jobs, or whatever), you need to ignore them and run coal. This memo is necessary only because we seem not to understand that the coal pays the bills."

Massey kept two sets of books specifically for concealing hazardous conditions from federal inspectors and the workers themselves. At UBB, Massey maintained one set of production and maintenance books for internal use only and another set that they provided, as required under the Mine Act, for examination and review by MSHA and the rank-and-file miners themselves. While keeping two sets of financial books might be the hallmark of organized crime, in the case of the mining industry, MSHA regulations require these vital examination books to contain complete records of all known hazards. Federal and state agency enforcement personnel must rely on their accuracy and completeness to guide them in conducting their safety inspections to protect the lives of the miners. It is difficult, if not impossible, to imagine a work environment in which full and uncompromising principled disclosure could be more critical than one, such as in coal mining, in which ignorance or simple unawareness of a hidden hazard may more directly result in immediate death or serious injury to workers. Yet, regardless, numerous hazards that the company recorded in its internal production and maintenance books were not recorded in the required open examination books provided to federal and state enforcement personnel to review.

Even when Massey did record specific hazards in the examination copy, it nevertheless often failed to correct those dangerous conditions. A glaring example: In longwall mining, a huge circular device known as a shearer is used to chew off the continuous slice of coal. As the shearer moves along the coal face, each of its numerous tungsten carbide drill bits or "teeth" must be continuously sprayed with water to keep the bits cool and to immediately douse any sparks that are given off. The MSHA investigation of UBB revealed that many of the water sprayers on the shearer were missing or not working, and some had been deliberately plugged. It was a spark from the shearer mechanism scraping the sandstone roof of the mine shaft that is believed to have ignited the catastrophic April 5th explosion.

Massey intimidated miners to prevent MSHA from receiving evidence of safety and health violations and hazards. The Mine Act provides whistleblower protections for rank-and-file miners if, for example, they are fired or subjected to other adverse employment actions because they reported a safety or health hazard. Such protections are designed to give miners a voice in the workplace and an avenue to protect themselves when mine operators engage in illegal or dangerous practices or fail to correct hazardous conditions. The MSHA investigation revealed a pattern of intimidation by Massey executives and managers to prevent workers from exercising their whistleblower rights.

The Executive Summary states that, "Production delays to resolve safety-related issues often were met by UBB officials with threats of retaliation and illegal disciplinary actions. On one occasion when a foreman stopped production to fix ventilation problems, Chris Blanchard [President of Performance Coal Company (PCC) the Massey subsidiary that ran UBB)], was overheard saying: 'If you don't start running coal up there, I'm going to bring the whole crew outside and get rid of every one of you.'" In another incident later reported at trial, former miner Brent Racer testified that Blanchard rebuked a mine boss who had halted production to try to correct a poor ventilation problem, insisting the mine workers "would get more air soon, [but] we needed to worry about running coal." And in at least one instance revealed in the MSHA report, a section foreman who also delayed production for no more than one or two hours to make needed safety corrections was later suspended for his actions by a top Massey official.

As further evidence of such intimidation, it is also quite revealing that, for a period of approximately four years prior to the explosion, MSHA did not receive a single safety or health complaint relating to underground conditions at UBB, this even though MSHA offers a toll-free hotline for miners to report anonymously operational safety and health violations or complaints. Given the company's utter disregard for safety concerns, not to mention its policy of intimidating or reprimanding anyone who voiced such concerns, it seems wryly absurd that Massey actually had its own toll-free number for occupational safety and health complaints. What's not surprising, in contrast, is that several miners testified that they were reluctant or simply refused to use it for fear of retaliation.

Massey failed to provide adequate training for its workers. The MSHA report found that the company failed to adequately train their workers in mine health and safety from top to bottom; that is, from examiners, supervisors, and foremen right down to the rank-and-file miners. This was especially true within the critical areas of hazard recognition and remediation, and the MSHA report pointedly concluded that lack of safety training in particular left miners unequipped to identify and correct life-threatening hazards at UBB.

Massey established a regular practice of giving advance notice of inspections to hide violations and hazards from enforcement personnel. The Mine Act expressly prohibits mine operators or their employees from giving advance notice of an inspection by MSHA enforcement personnel. However, internal company documents and the testimony of miners and others indicate that the practice of illegally warning underground miners of the presence of inspectors became institutionalized at UBB.

All told, the Upper Big Branch mine complex was enormous and deep. In his opening remarks at Don Blankenship's trial, prosecuting Assistant

U.S. Attorney Steve Ruby explained that it could take inspectors more than an hour and a half to travel from the entry portal to the deepest sections of the mine. That allowed ample time for the miners below to either correct, or in most cases, to simply cover up chronically hazardous conditions after being tipped off by managers or other workers on the surface. "There was almost never a time," Ruby told jurors, "when safety inspectors were able to see what the mine truly looked like when they weren't there."

Gary May, a supervisor at UBB, told investigators that PCC president Chris Blanchard had instructed him in no uncertain terms, "I don't want no inspectors going to the working sections unannounced," and admitted to routinely covering up hazardous conditions in advance of approaching safety inspectors. May further revealed that more than 100 employees were in on the sophisticated advance warning system that included code words ("It's a cloudy day," meant that surprise inspectors were on their way), and was routinely set into motion by none other than the security guards at the Massey property entry gates. May was eventually sentenced to 21 months in prison on federal conspiracy charges for his role in the April 5th disaster.

Of course, MSHA was far from blameless in the disaster. A 2012 report conducted by an independent panel of the National Institute for Occupational Safety and Health (NIOSH) at the request of then Labor Secretary Hilda Solis blasted federal regulators for failing to take steps that might have prevented the tragedy. The 26-page report charged that MSHA failed to heed warning signs or implement the agency's own regulations, leaving in place conditions that led to the explosion and fire that swept through the mine that terrible day.

The NIOSH report concludes: "If MSHA had engaged in timely enforcement of the Mine Act and applicable standards and regulations, it ... possibly could have prevented the UBB explosion." The panel was also critical of the MSHA's own report, stating that its "characterization of the facts ... understates the role that MSHA's enforcement could have had in preventing the explosion." When you unearth (no pun intended) the serious health and safety threats that the miners at UBB and other Massey mines were faced with day after day, even that statement by the

NIOSH panel sounds like the motherlode of all understatements, again, no pun intended.

PROFIT OVER LOSS: A CASE OF EXTREME DEPRAVITY

In many respects, the trial of Blankenship, whom the media often took to calling a "Coal Baron" (*Rolling Stone* alternatively dubbed him the "Dark Lord of Coal Country"), only served to provide a grotesque open window into the workings of an industry with a long and sordid history of coal mine tragedies dating back to the mid- to late-1800s, and one that historically has scoffed at the very idea of worker health and safety. Tragically and deplorably, it displayed quite publicly that things haven't gotten much better in the 21st century. And while the Charleston (WVA) Gazette hailed the politically powerful CEO's indictment as a "breakthrough," it might easily have never been brought if it wasn't for two of Blankenship's own compulsive obsessions, which ultimately may have proved to be his undoing.

The first of these was his almost manic insistence on receiving production updates on Massey mines every 30 minutes, a torrent of continuous information that he pored over like a stockbroker watching a market ticker. When he learned of coal production slowdowns as a result of the miner's efforts to do necessary construction to mitigate hazardous situations, he would characteristically launch a barrage of memos to both surface and below-ground managers demanding to know what the hold-up was and ordering them to focus strictly on producing coal. According to an extensive article published in the *New York Times*, in one 2008 memo to a UBB executive, Blankenship wrote, "We'll worry about ventilation issues or other issues at another time," in reference to two sections of the mine experiencing dangerously poor air flow, adding, "Now is not the time."[53]

---

[53] Segal, "Coal Baron."

However, and to his own peril, this kind of obsessive micromanagement would later serve to substantially undercut his defense counsel's claim, commonly invoked in negligence cases involving CEOs and other high-level executives, that Blankenship was far removed from the everyday workings at UBB. Those continuous production reports provided a highly detailed, real time, tell-tale record not simply of coal production rates, but also of hazards directly encountered by the workers involved in the mining operations, and thus, of course, the CEO knew about each and every one of them—in minute detail, it might be added. In point of fact, he frequently countermanded the efforts of miners and their managers to remediate them.

According to Patrick McGinley, one of the authors of the state's report on the disaster and a professor at West Virginia University College of Law, "One reason that Blankenship [was] prosecuted is that he was different than other top coal executives. Most CEOs don't get production records every half hour by fax. That places him right in the mine, hands on. That [made] him vulnerable."[54]

Blankenship's other bizarre obsession appears to have been an almost Nixonian penchant for secretly recording his own conversations with other executives and staff right in his own workspace. The recordings reveal a man intensely consumed with furthering his own wealth, obsessed with maximizing at all costs the daily production or "running" of coal, and deeply frustrated by federal regulators and Massey's own officials who pushed for greater attention to safety.

For example, in reference to his constant clashes with Massey's compensation committee in 2008 to 2009 over his $12 million pay package that included an additional $6 million in stock options, Blankenship is heard on the tapes as saying, "You can't go to the grocery store and buy groceries with options." By contrast, Massey's rank-and-file mine workers earned an average of $60 an hour toiling in deplorable and dangerous conditions. In another recording, Blankenship lambastes Massey's top safety

---

[54] Ibid.

official for being too concerned with the "social aspects" of her job, later telling another official, "You've got to have someone [in that position] who understands this game is all about money."

Other recordings capture deliberate deception perpetrated by Blankenship and his management team. In one conversation, Blankenship expresses concern over a confidential internal safety memo warning of serious ventilation problems at UBB and other Massey mines and stating that Massey was "plainly cheating" in the rigged sampling procedures it was routinely using to measure coal dust accumulation. However, his concern was not over the serious safety issues or the cheating on ventilation testing procedures. Not at all. Rather, his only concern was how it would look if Massey was sued over a deadly mine accident and the internal document ever got out. Blankenship is heard to say, somewhat prophetically I might add, "If [there] was a fatal, or if we had one, that would be a terrible document to be in discovery." That indeed turned out to be true.

Finally, a number of the recordings vividly display the CEO's utter contempt for some of the mining industry's most firmly established and long-standing hazard safety issues—and, once again, largely preventable ones. In yet another damning conversation caught on the tapes and in direct reference to MSHA inspectors' concerns about operations at UBB, Blankenship says, "The truth of the matter is that black lung is not an issue in this industry that is worth the effort they put into it." Autopsies of the 29 miners killed in the UBB explosion revealed that 71 percent of them suffered from black lung disease. The industry average for black lung disease in 2010 was 3.2 percent of all workers nationwide.

AFTERMATH

There is much, much more to the story of Massey Energy and the underlying practices that led to the tragedy at the Upper Big Branch mine that is beyond the scope of this book. In the aftermath, several revealing books have been written both about the disaster itself and shedding light on the corruption within the coal industry as a whole, including its historically cozy relationship with federal regulators that looked the other way.

In the end, the MSHA completed its investigation on December 6, 2011, concluding that the disaster was an entirely preventable coal dust explosion and stating that "the root cause of the tragedy" was the "unlawful policies and practices of the company." In conjunction with the release of the final report, MSHA issued 369 safety violation citations. Even that number, in my opinion, was a matter of too little too late. Earlier that same year, Massey Energy was acquired by Alpha Natural Resources, which subsequently agreed to pay a civil fine of $10.8 million to MSHA plus $209 million in settlement with the Department of Justice. The settlement allocated $46.5 million for restitution payments ($1.5 million to each of the two survivors and the families of each of the 29 fatal casualties), $34.8 million in fines for safety citations, $48 million for a health and safety research and development trust fund, and $80 million for safety improvements to be made over a two-year period. The civil fine was nearly five times bigger than the previous largest fine ever levied by a court in a mining disaster.

And as I so often do as a safety warnings expert, the fundamentally practical question I want to ask corporate executives like CEO Don Blankenship is: Was it worth it? But, of course, and far, far more importantly, what must not be forgotten is that 29 men lost their lives because the company they worked for put profit ahead of safety, plain and simple. Twenty-nine families were destroyed, and an entire community, or perhaps several of them, was ripped apart.

Blankenship became the most prominent American coal executive ever convicted of a crime involving deaths due to a mining accident. Even with all that, he was convicted only on a single misdemeanor charge of conspiring to violate federal safety standards, which carried a maximum prison sentence of one year and a fine of $250,000. And if you think he was the least bit sorrowful or repentant for what he had done, think again.

While in prison, Blankenship authored and self-published a bizarre book titled and portraying himself as *An American Political Prisoner*.

After serving his one-year sentence, the disgraced CEO emerged from prison in May 2017 like a man on fire, raging against those whom he still claims conspired against him. Immediately upon his release, Blankenship launched a torrent of tweets that would have made President Trump proud. Among them, he persisted in blaming regulators and federal prosecutors, tweeting, "Again, one or the other lied. MSHA or prosecution witnesses. Which one is it?" In several others, he took on Senator Joe Manchin III (D-W.Va), who had incurred an especially epic level of Blankenship's wrath when he told ABC News in 2014 that the CEO of Massey "has blood on his hands." In separate tweets Blankenship wrote that Manchin "said I conspired to commit safety violations that caused the death of 29 miners. Not true. He needs to apologize now," and threatening, "A U.S. senator who says I have 'blood on my hands' should be man enough to face me in public."

Blankenship went so far as to write an open letter of appeal directly to President Trump for help in overturning his conviction, pleading, "You and I ... share relentless and false attacks on our reputation by the liberal media ... I am hopeful that ... you will put aside the media's false claims about me and help me expose the truth of what happened at the Upper Big Branch (UBB) coal mine in West Virginia on April 5, 2010."[55]

Blankenship's letter may also have been prompted by recent efforts led by Virginia Representative Bobby Scott, a ranking member of the House Education and the Workforce Committee, to impose harsher criminal penalties for the violation of federal mine safety laws. Rep. Scott and others argue persuasively that the willful and wanton violation of critical mine safety rules should be a felony offense carrying up to a maximum five-year sentence, and obviously a far stiffer penalty than the slap-on-the-wrist misdemeanor conviction, with a maximum of only one year in prison, which Blankenship received for killing 29 men.

Upon reintroducing the Robert C. Byrd Mine Safety Protection Act in April 2017, Rep. Scott had written:

---

[55] Jervey, "Blankenship."

*The release of the former Massey CEO who served the maxi-
mum possible sentence of only one year for willfully violating
mine safety standards that led to the Upper Big Branch Mine
disaster should serve as a reminder that the criminal provisions
in the Federal Mine Safety and Health Act of 1977 remain
woefully inadequate … The maximum penalty for the willful
violation of a mandatory health and safety standard is a mere
misdemeanor—rather than a felony—regardless of the number of miners killed because of criminally reckless conduct.[56]*

Yet it remains to be seen whether anything will really change in the
corporate culture of coal country as a result of the UBB tragedy. One
thing is certain: Blankenship has never apologized to the families of the
29 coal miners who perished violently—and needlessly—in his Upper Big
Branch mine.

COAL DUST AIN'T THE ONLY THING IN THE AIR:
THE BERYLLIUM STORY

Admittedly, in the context of the modern-day workplace, coal mining is
something of an anachronism, and an inherently dangerous occupation
even when the most innovative of safety precautions are strictly adhered
to by truly safety-minded owner-operators, mine managers, and foremen.
Yet, at least one other example taken from what is by and large a much
more technologically advanced industry clearly reveals that modern companies may be no less willing to put corporate profits ahead of worker
health and safety.

In connection with a series of legal cases from roughly 2003 to 2006,
I was called to provide expert testimony for a company named Brush
Wellman, Inc. (BWI). Originally founded in 1931 as the Brush Beryllium
Company, BWI remains today the only U.S. supplier of beryllium metal,

---

[56] National Safety Council, "Blankenship."

oxides, alloys, and ceramics that have a range of uses from computer and electronic circuitry to automotive air bags and telecommunications technology applications. In its early years, however, the company concentrated on producing pure beryllium. Blue-gray in color, the metal's unique characteristics of extreme strength and reliability made it a prime candidate for military applications.

After an aggressive and unrelenting acquisitions spree spanning nearly three decades from 1982 to 2011, during which BWI picked up more than a dozen high-tech companies including Technical Materials, Inc. of Lincoln, Rhode Island; Williams Gold Refining Company in Buffalo, New York; Electrofusion Corporation in Fremont, California; PureTech Inc. in Brewster, New York; OMC Scientific Holdings in Ireland; Thin Film Technology, Inc. in Buellton, California; CERAC of Milwaukee, Wisconsin; Techni-Met in Windsor, Connecticut; Barr Associates Inc. in Westford, Massachusetts; Academy Corporation in Albuquerque, New Mexico; and Shanghai-based EIS Optics, BWI filed corporate papers with the SEC reunifying all of its subsidiaries under the curiously 1950s space-age-sounding name of Materion Corporation.

For example, beryllium is 30 percent lighter than aluminum, but is stronger (by weight) than steel. Because it maintains integrity of shape and strength over extremes of heat and cold, coupled with a high capacity for heat absorption, it became the material of choice for high-speed, high-altitude, military jet fighters up to the present day. Brush Beryllium Company also made significant contributions to the development of atomic energy, and while it has never affirmed it publicly, there is good evidence to suggest that the company produced crucial components used in the manufacture of the atomic bombs that were dropped on Hiroshima and Nagasaki in 1945. Previously, with the advent of the war, the company had been instrumental in the development of missiles, aircraft, and rockets to support the war effort. In light of all this, it should come as no surprise that BWI has long been one of the darlings of the U.S. Department of Defense (DOD).

However, the problem with beryllium is not with the exotic metal itself; rather, it originates with the toxic dust that is created when the metal is cut, drilled, sanded, and shaped into the forms and parts that go into the fabrication of things like jet fighters and missiles. Beryllium dust is highly carcinogenic. This time around, I'll start by immediately deflating the suspense you might be already anticipating: Yes, BWI knew very well that inhaled beryllium dust can cause lung and other cancers. There is even a name for it: berylliosis, or chronic beryllium disease (CBD), defined as "a chronic allergic-type lung response and chronic lung disease caused by exposure to beryllium and its compounds, a form of beryllium poisoning." According to the Cleveland Clinic, people exposed to breathing unsafe levels of beryllium dust develop collections of cells called granulomas that may eventually cause scarring within the lungs.[57] Beryllium disease erodes the lungs, making it very difficult for a victim to even walk across a room without severe chest pain and exhaustion, and usually results in a slow, painful death by suffocation. The Cleveland Clinic also reports that lung cancer rates are significantly higher among people exposed to beryllium dust.[58]

BWI even warned workers and major contract customers like the DOD about it … sort of.

Accordingly, when BWI was multiply sued in the early 2000s by workers who had contracted CBD, as an expert witness for the defense, my job specifically was to examine and evaluate whether the company's overall program of safety warnings issued to its employees as well as its outside contractor-customers met the rigorous standard of principled disclosure. It was not to investigate the medical science underlying berylliosis or CBD, nor to examine the maximum exposure limits beyond which workers would become susceptible to these terrible diseases. And in all candor, my extensive research into the company's hazard warnings and related safety communications led unwaveringly to the strong conclusion

---

[57] The Cleveland Clinic, "Beryllium Disease."
[58] Ibid.

that they had done, in fact, nothing less than a stellar job of warning contractor-clients and workers alike about the health hazard posed by beryllium exposure. Even a brief summation of the company's disclosure efforts sounds impressive.

Specifically, the company conducted initial worker orientation and continued beryllium safety training programs for its employees complete with literature handouts and quiz item questionnaires; it administered annual physical examinations including chest X-rays and a breathing test along with respiratory training; it provided specific hygiene instructions, mandatory protective clothing, and a shower procedure for eliminating beryllium dust transmission. BWI posted explicit warning signs in prominent locations throughout its production plant and regularly posted air sampling data it had gathered from discrete locations in and around the plant, including downwind from its factory smokestacks. It published and disseminated the Brush Wellman Code for Safe Working Practices for Contractor Personnel as well as providing instructional videotapes for its customers, and it provided an Industrial Hygiene Personal Protection Equipment Guide for its workers. It held daily and weekly safety meetings where, unlike Massey Energy, questions and feedback from employees were encouraged.

In light of these facts, to briefly summarize the findings from my final report, I wrote with definitive certainty:

- Brush Wellman's warnings and safety communications were more than adequate and the company's message was clear, repetitive, and consistent;
- BWI's communication strategy to inform employees included, in the best traditions of effective organizational communication, the use of credible information sources, multiple channels (e.g., oral, written, and mediated), and ample opportunities for feedback;
- BWI's overall warnings and safety communication program for its contractors was well planned and also combined written, oral, and mediated (e.g., videotapes) channels of communication to deliver

a consistent message that workers exposed to airborne beryllium were at risk of contracting CBD, a serious and potentially fatal lung disease.

In my conclusion for the court, I could not have been more emphatic, arguing that it was "highly likely that plaintiffs were or should have been exposed to the information about beryllium hazards" communicated by Brush Wellman and further declaring, "as a communication expert and consultant to some of the largest companies both in the United States and abroad, I would rate Brush Wellman's overall safety communications program for its contractors, from inception to the present, as exemplary and among the best that I have ever evaluated."

In terms of the nuts-and-bolts *process* of what an effective and dedicated program of principled disclosure should be, I maintain with all the power of my most deeply held convictions that these statements in my report remain absolutely true. BWI had indeed done all the right things. Yet, viewed as a function of the fundamental principles of logical reasoning, while my conclusion was sound, it was the foundational premises I had been provided by the company that, according to information later made public by the Chemical Industry Archives, would turn out to be inaccurate and misleading. And indeed, the problem was that the company's program of "disclosure" had been based on a false premise, and a significant one at that.

That false premise originated out of the purely arbitrary determination that established in the first place the federal standard for the "safe" level of exposure to beryllium dust at 2.0 micrograms per cubic meter of air—and thus, of course, the standard duly and openly disclosed across all of BWI's informational warnings, instructional training, and industry literature. But the 2.0 micrograms standard was not firmly grounded upon any medical scientific research studies specifically designed to determine exactly *what level of beryllium dust exposure (if any) would be reasonably "safe."* I call it the taxi cab standard, because the number is actually believed to have been created somewhere in the early 1950s by a scientist working with the

Atomic Energy Commission, whose name is now lost to history, but who, according to the legend, wrote it on a paper restaurant napkin in the back of a taxicab and handed it to a prominent and powerful executive in the beryllium industry.

As early as 1975, however, alarmed once again, this time by studies revealing the highly carcinogenic characteristics of ambient beryllium dust, OSHA began pushing for lowering the artificially conceived "standard" from 2.0 micrograms to a scientifically based 0.2 micrograms per cubic meter of air, a whopping reduction of 90 percent! That alone gives you some idea of how serious OSHA scientists had come to believe the threat to BWI's plant workers and its contractors from inhaling beryllium dust truly is. Consequently, the government agency began to focus more energy and resources on research into berylliosis and CBD.

And here, unfortunately, was when BWI ceased to live up to the high standards of health hazard warnings and transparent safety communications that I had extolled in my consultative report. Because shortly after OSHA began sounding the alarm about the significant dangers of beryllium workers developing CBD, BWI's only market competitor-producer announced, in 1979, that it was going out of the metallic beryllium business entirely. That left BWI as one of only two metallic beryllium producers in the world, the other plant being, not surprisingly and rather ominously in particular to the Department of Defense, in the Soviet Union. And so, like any good sharks that smell blood in the water, BWI executives immediately leveraged the company's newly achieved monopoly status to cut a secret backroom deal with the military atomic scientists at the DOE as well as with, to a lesser extent, the generals at the DOD, both of which desperately wanted to secure a reliable and plentiful continuing supply of weapons- and armament-grade metallic beryllium. Quite naturally, both DOE and DOD very willingly signed on to the deal in the sacred name of "national security" or national defense, and to support the ongoing concerted effort to win the Cold War.

An internal memo to company executives written and signed by then Chairman and CEO H.G. Piper in 1983 reveals that the covert deal stipulated that, for its part, BWI "agreed to a long-term commitment to remain" the government's sole metallic beryllium supplier. Even further under the agreement, BWI guaranteed that it would abundantly supply all of the beryllium that DOE and DOD wanted to meet their needs, as long as those agencies acted to protect BWI's monopoly status through proactive "Oversight of Government facilities contractors to *avoid unfair competition* under the guise of research" (emphasis mine). But above and beyond the effort to set in irrevocable stone BWI's determination to corner the metallic beryllium market indefinitely, there was one more condition in the covert agreement, and in point of fact, it significantly came ahead of all the others.

Further, in the 1983 memo, Piper derided an OSHA proposal calling for "drastic reductions in the already extremely stringent allowable concentrations of airborne beryllium in the workplace" that he claimed were "technologically unattainable, no matter how much money was expended to achieve them." Subsequently, BWI threatened both DOE and DOD with the impending potential specter of a complete and total shutdown of all beryllium metal production as a result of an anticipated "prolonged and highly expensive period of litigation" to fight any newly proposed OSHA regulations. Thus, the very first condition embodied in the backroom agreement called for the "Satisfactory resolution of the OSHA problem." That, arguably, may be most politely described as industrial code-speak for "Make the OSHA regulatory meddling go away or else."[59]

A slew of previously classified government documents and secret internal industry memoranda released by the Chemical Industry Archives in July 2006 prove that BWI had very much to fear from OSHA's deepening investigations into berylliosis and CBD over the last quarter of the 20th century. These documents also chillingly reveal a clear and definite pattern of suppression of the medical research evidence that would have exposed the serious health risk, not simply to plant workers and contractors, but to spouses, families, and community members as well. For example,

---

[59] Piper, "Beryllium."

a damaging study conducted in 1997 in BWI's Elmore, Ohio, processing plant confirmed what both government and industry had known since the 1940s. The study's researchers, including two medical scientists from the famed Cleveland Clinic, found that 59 workers, some 9.4 percent of the plant workforce, showed abnormal blood tests indicating early stages of beryllium disease and further discovered that 29 employees, nearly 5 percent out of a total of 632 workers at the plant, were suffering from chronic, incurable, and most likely fatal forms of the disease. Previously, the company had acknowledged that less than 2 percent of its employees had shown symptoms of the disease.[60]

Yet, BWI knew far more than this, and much sooner than 1997.

A medical symposium convened in Saranac Lake, New York, in 1947 inaugurated the first scientific review of beryllium disease and its related cancers. The collective data showed that, up to that point, some 40 cases of the chronic form of the disease, including at least seven deaths and a disturbing 500 cases of acute beryllium disease resulting in over a dozen deaths, had been reported in the United States. But that was only the tip of the iceberg. Also presented at the conference were newly developed scientific processes that effectively enabled much more accurate chemical analyses of beryllium in air and human tissue samples, and that made it possible to begin quantitative investigations in both the field and laboratory. Almost immediately, these new techniques would lead to an alarmingly significant spike in the verified number of diagnosed cases going forward.

In fact, in the very next year of 1948, a comprehensive study discovered at least 11 non-occupational cases among local residents living mostly within a mile downwind of BWI's plant in Lorain, Ohio. Referred to as "neighborhood cases," ten of these were people who were not employees at the plant but who were believed to have become seriously ill with CBD as a result of constantly breathing factory-belching smokestack emissions laced with excessive amounts of beryllium dust. The eleventh victim of the

---

[60] Kreiss et al., "Risks."

disease, also not an employee, was actually the wife of a plant employee who dubiously became the first documented case (to be followed by many more) of a spouse contracting the disease from laundering her husband's beryllium-contaminated work clothes. Shockingly, the stricken woman's husband had worked at the plant for only three months prior to when she became ill.[61]

Despite all of this knowledge and documented evidence of the incidence of beryllium disease among both its workers and residents living near its manufacturing and processing plants, BWI continued for over five decades to deny that a serious problem existed and further, insisted that its safety measures were adequate. In an open letter to concerned residents living near the Elmore, Ohio, plant and dated July 11, 2001, BWI's Vice President for Environmental Health and Safety, Marc E. Kolenz wrote that the company, "has and will continue to work diligently to protect the health of our neighbors," and claimed that, "for more than 40 years ... no neighbor has ever been harmed by our emissions."

In the letter, Kolenz criticized a Columbus-based environmental activist group, known as Ohio Citizen Action for its "effort to discredit our company's good name and spread inaccurate and misleading information regarding the health effects of beryllium and about our operations," adding rather outrageously:

> *CBD is not a community health issue. It is a work place occupational disease that is to this day not fully understood, despite our efforts to find answers. No one sees the tragedy of this disease more than we do and nothing is more important to us than preventing CBD among our workers. Our energy, our financial resources, and a huge amount of time are focused on ending it forever.[62]*

---

[61] Eisenbud, "Origins."
[62] Kolenz, "Beryllium."

While for BWI this was yet another case of an American industry putting corporate profits over safety, we might easily conjecture that officials of both DOE and DOD would have eagerly rationalized (and rather loftily at that) that it was rather a critical matter of national defense over public safety, and that sacrifices had to be made. In one document and in reference to BWI's Elmore, Ohio, manufacturing and processing facility, an AEC official by the name of E. Velten made the glaring statement that "… there is only one reason for this plant, and that is because I have been instructed to get beryllium. Unless [I am] instructed otherwise, production comes first and then health."

Oh, what we do for our country!

POSTSCRIPT TO THE BERYLLIUM SAGA

On May 20, 2017, OSHA at long last issued new rules in connection with exposure to beryllium. It is perhaps worth noting that under the heading "Compliance Schedule," OSHA stated the following: All three standards contained in the final rule took effect on May 20, 2017. On December 12, 2018, OSHA began enforcing most provisions of the beryllium standard for general industry, except for change rooms and showers (March 11, 2019) and engineering controls (March 10, 2020).[63] Among its key provisions, the rule reduces the permissible exposure limit (PEL) for beryllium to 0.2 micrograms per cubic meter of air, averaged over eight hours: precisely the same level the agency sought to impose some 42 years earlier in 1975. The rule also establishes a new, short-term exposure limit for beryllium of 2.0 micrograms per cubic meter of air over a 15-minute sampling period and requires employers to: use engineering and work practice controls (such as ventilation or enclosure) to limit worker exposure to beryllium; provide respirators when controls cannot adequately limit exposure; limit worker access to high-exposure areas; develop a written exposure control plan; and train workers on beryllium hazards. Finally, the

---

[63] OSHA, "Final Rule."

new standard also requires employers to make available medical exams to monitor exposed workers and provides medical removal protection benefits to workers identified with a beryllium-related disease. All good stuff.

Yet, achieving this was not as simple and straightforward as it might seem on the surface. In order to fully understand the underlying circumstances leading to the adoption of the new rule by OSHA, and its even more remarkable acceptance by industry after decades of political delay, deflection, and deception, we are obliged to take a closer, deeper look at the forces that were at work in finally exerting what amounts to a veritable sea change in the regulatory environment. To begin with, we need to take into account that it took two years of intensive negotiations between Materion Corporation and the steelworkers union that represents the beryllium plant workers to hammer out the final wording of the new rule, and to agree on all of its provisions. But then, what might appear to be the biggest mystery of all, and one taken perhaps from the "what's wrong with this picture?" file, it was the monopoly industry, specifically Materion, that first approached the steelworkers union with an offer to work together to develop a recommendation for a new beryllium exposure standard to OSHA!

So what happened here that would cause such a monumental reversal? Had all the executives at Materion been visited by the ghost of Jacob Marley and the Three Spirits?

Actually, the answer is neither mysterious nor miraculous at all. Because when we look closely, we see that Materion initiated the collaborative gesture in around 2010, only four short years after the Chemical Industry Archives released the damaging documents we reviewed previously. Industry insiders were quick to point out that, largely as a result of that information becoming public and much as we might expect, the company very quickly began to face an escalating number of lawsuits from employees and residents living near its one remaining processing plant, and who began to put the pieces together and realize they were suffering from berylliosis or CBD.

So here again, we have the simple financial mathematical equation of a company embarking on a long overdue program of principled disclosure only after it has become clear that the amount of money it anticipates it will have to pay out to settle mounting court claims is likely to surpass the amount of money it will take to fix the problem, or at least establish a more correct exposure standard and warn employees about it. And we have a federal regulatory agency in OSHA that, it turns out, could be effectively shut down by other, more powerful departmental interests of the federal government.

CHAPTER 5

PLAYING: STICKS AND STONES WILL BREAK YOUR BONES

David Goldberg didn't know that he only had one hour to live. On May 5, 2015, at about 4:00 in the afternoon, Goldberg, the CEO of Survey Monkey and husband of Facebook top executive, Sheryl Sandberg, left his room at a vacation resort in Puerto Vallarta, Mexico, and proceeded to the state-of-the art exercise room and spa to do a routine workout on a treadmill. He fell on the treadmill, struck his head, and suffered a traumatic brain injury and hypovolemic shock resulting in severe blood loss. He was not alone. According to the Consumer Products Safety Commission (CPSC), treadmill-related injuries are responsible for more than 24,000 emergency room visits every year. CPSC statistics also reveal that over the ten-year period from 2003 to 2012, some 30 deaths from treadmill-related accidents have been reported, an average of three fatalities per year. The agency's records indicate that no other single piece of exercise equipment causes more accidents than treadmills. Overall, almost half a million Americans are injured annually using exercise equipment and 32,000 of these injuries are very serious or deadly.[64]

---

[64] Madhani, "Treadmill."

The typical warning that is placed on treadmills today reads as follows (this one appears on machines made by NordicTrack):

> *To reduce risk of serious injury, stand on foot rails before starting treadmill, read and understand the user's manual, all instructions, and the warnings before use. Heart rate monitoring systems may be inaccurate. Over-exercising may result in serious injury or death. If you feel faint, stop exercising immediately.*

Does this warning appear adequate for the safe use of the machine? There may be as many as a half-million Americans who would say "no." Right off the bat, I see a number of issues with it. First, it tells us what to do when we start up the machine, but nothing about proper use once it is running. Also, I wonder what other specific warnings and/or instructions might be outlined in the user's manual that one is supposed to read. Everyone—and that includes NordicTrack and the other manufacturers of exercise equipment—knows that consumers don't read instruction manuals. More pointedly, it is doubtful that the printed manual was present and available in the exercise room at the Mexican vacation resort for David Goldberg to consult before using the machine, any more than it is at any of the thousands of gyms or fitness clubs across the United States. It is worth noting that the International Health, Racquet and Sportsclub Association, a trade association for the health club industry, estimates that more than 63 million. Americans used a health club in 2014, and about 54 million Americans have health club memberships. That's a lot of folks using machines they may not be totally familiar with.

Second, nothing in the safety warning tells us anything about any hazardous conditions that might attend the machine when we are actually using it, other than that the heart rate monitoring system may be inaccurate (one wonders: is it faulty or something?). We may reasonably conjecture that Goldberg wasn't killed in the act of starting the machine up, but in the act of running on it.

And finally, the "medical" aspect of the warning label, far from being simply inadequate, tells us absolutely nothing that we don't already know. If fact, the last line, "*If you feel faint, stop exercising immediately,*" puts me in mind of the old joke about the guy who goes to his physician and says, "It hurts when I do this," and the brilliant doctor astutely counsels, "Then don't do that." Two of the main reasons that people become seriously injured when exercising on a treadmill are due to the dizzying effect on some people of the moving tread in an otherwise stationary device, and distractions from simultaneously watching television or talking, texting, or otherwise concentrating on an iPhone, iPad, or other mobile device. Yet, the warning label says nothing about these hidden hazards.

AMERICANS AT PLAY: RISKING LIFE AND LIMB

A long popular theme in American culture is the idea that Americans like to "play as hard as they work." While that may be true, it also seems clear that it is in playing, perhaps more so than in any of the other six activities, that Americans are most likely to behave recklessly, or at least carelessly, in ways that jeopardize their own safety as well as that of others. Many of our cherished leisurely activities ranging from competitive and individual sports, to cycling and swimming, to hiking, camping, fishing, and hunting involve a very real component of unavoidable personal risk-taking and the often ever-present possibility of injury. At the same time, thrill-seeking attractions like high-speed roller coasters, mammoth water slides and dozens of other hair-raising rides and activities at amusement and water parks are often designed to simulate extreme danger while in reality posing none, yet amusement park rides cause thousands of injuries every year, not all of which are due solely to riders behaving badly.

Perhaps no other leisure activity illustrates more clearly—and more starkly—the risk-taking propensity of Americans at play than swimming. In the summer season, we flock to pools, lakes and rivers, and the beaches of the oceans, and what better way is there to get into the water than just diving in? You would think that most people know that diving into shallow water is potentially very dangerous and likely to result in serious head and spinal injury, and according to numerous surveys that were taken some years ago, you would be correct. What will surprise you is how many people are willing to dive in anyway, ignoring their own fundamental knowledge of the hazards.

For example, in 1986, Robert Weiner and Associates, in cooperation with survey expert Alphonse Chapanis from Johns Hopkins University, conducted a survey in which they randomly interviewed 316 people who were using public swimming pools in Maryland, Virginia, Florida, and California. They specifically asked the respondents about their knowledge of shallow water diving risks. The results indicated that the overwhelming majority—91 percent—were aware that diving into shallow water could result in a broken neck. Notwithstanding this knowledge, 60 percent of the people interviewed admitted that they themselves had dived into shallow water and, even more shockingly, some 25 percent of those who indicated that they had dived into shallow water admitted to doing so after *witnessing another person* sustain an injury as a result of shallow water diving.

Not long after the Weiner survey, I conducted my own research into this. My team and I interviewed by telephone 600 adults aged 18 years or older and randomly selected from households across the U.S. to determine, in part, their awareness of and belief in the potential dangers of diving into waters that were too shallow, including the risk of spinal injury and paralysis associated with such dives. Our results indicated that most adults were indeed aware of and believed that it is dangerous to dive into either an above-ground or in-ground pool specifically due to the risk of suffering an injury resulting in paralysis—even though, as with the respondents to Weiner's survey—many had done it regardless. In fact, 91 percent of those who had dived into the shallow end of an in-ground pool had heard of the hazard and 93 percent who had done so understood that their own behavior (of diving into the shallow end) was very dangerous. Somewhat oddly, only 80 percent of those who indicated they had dived into an above-ground pool believed that they could become paralyzed as a result. But still … 80 percent! And they, too, had done it anyway!

Thus, both studies provided empirical evidence strongly indicating that most adults are aware of the potentially very serious hazard of diving into shallow water, including the risk of a broken neck or paralysis—and yet as many as 60 to 93 percent of them engaged in this dangerous activity regardless, with predictable results. For example, according to Baylor Scott & White Health of Texas, there are approximately 1,000 spinal cord injuries each year in the U.S. due to shallow water diving, a profoundly sobering 90 percent of which result in paralysis. Baylor Scott & White also found that most of these injuries occur to males aged from 15 to 25, most occur while diving into water 6-feet deep or less, and three out of four shallow-dive injuries occur in lakes, rivers, oceans, and other natural bodies of water.

However, when we undertake a deeper analysis of the statistics, it turns out that they point to the very specific population that is by far most at risk for diving-related injuries. That is, the statistics show that 6,500 adolescents each year are brought to the hospital for diving-related injuries. On average, two-thirds (64 percent) of these injuries occur in in-ground pools, while one-third (36 percent) occur in above-ground pools. About half of these took place during swimming pool parties where alcohol or drugs were involved. Seventy percent of these injuries were directly caused by head-first dives, and of those, 80 percent took place in shallow water 4-feet deep or less. Finally, 80 percent of all diving accidents took place at a swimming pool that had no warning signs posted.

In the interest of examining how both private and commercial swimming pool owners might endeavor to make these leisure facilities safer, it is fair to make some presumptive observations about the characteristics of this most vulnerable population, as the statistics clearly show, and the kinds of behaviors they typically engage in. So for example, while our surveys indicate that the vast majority of adults over the age of 18 are aware of the risks of permanent injury from diving into shallow water, it is reasonable to conjecture that adolescents, especially those under age 18, are likely to be far less aware of the danger, and even less mindful of the horrifically disastrous consequences that might result from a serious error in juvenile judgment.

Next, the fact that roughly half of adolescent diving-related injuries occurred at pool parties suggests rather convincingly that the kids who are injured in this fashion are likely guests unfamiliar with the design dimensions and depth characteristics of the swimming pool itself. It also suggests a lack of parental or adult supervision, particularly if underage drinking is involved. Even setting aside for the moment the influence of alcohol or drugs, we might easily conclude that many teenagers who sustain serious injuries under these circumstances simply do not realize that they are diving into water that is just too shallow to do so safely. When you add in both mental and physical impairment due to alcohol consumption or drug use, you have a recipe for disaster. And, while the statistical fact that 80 percent of all diving accidents took place at swimming pools without prominently posted warning signs, any sincere and dispassionate effort to try to prevent shallow diving accidents among any population cohort—and in this case, adolescents in particular—demands similarly dispassionate honesty in assessing the mindset and behavior characteristics typical of that population.

So let's imagine a typical scenario. The average guy, and according to the statistics it is predominantly a guy, who dives recklessly into shallow water might look something like one of these dudes.

Jack Armstrong and his cronies are all 17 to 18 years old and about to graduate high school in June. They've all just completed that revered adolescent rite-of-passage in getting their drivers licenses, and a couple of them have even managed to buy cars that they've subsequently tricked out as hot rods with money they've saved up from their summer jobs over the past three or four years. They're feeling pretty good, virile, and cocky about themselves—invincible as they say—even calling their inner circle of comrades the "Young Turks." (Not very original, perhaps, but you get the idea!) They're reasonably athletic, a mix of football, soccer, and baseball lettermen at their school.

In May, just as the weather is getting delightfully warm, the boys get wind of a swimming pool party at Staci Skidmore's house. Staci is on the cheerleading squad and well connected with all of the "hot" girls at the high school. And her parents are going out of town for the upcoming weekend. When the Young Turks learn of this exciting opportunity, you can almost smell the testosterone. The boys have never been to Staci's house before, but there's a first time for everything.

Fast forward to the Saturday night party. There is, practically as a matter of adolescent principle, no parental supervision whatsoever for the nearly 100 teenagers who mass together for the festivities. Let's assume also that there is no safety warning signage around the Skidmore's swimming pool, on the one hand, because it is not required by law, and on the other hand, because Staci's parents simply do not think it necessary—even believing that warning signage is ugly and detracts from the beauty of their professionally designed and landscaped pool environment.

Some of the underage but entrepreneurially resourceful partygoers have supplied, to the undying admiration of all their peers, at least a half-dozen kegs of beer as well as some wine and hard liquor to more than abundantly fuel the all-night bacchanal. The food, on the other hand, consists sparsely of a dozen or so bags of chips and pretzels and a few large pizzas that somebody sprang for, but which quickly disappear. But, hey, who needs food when you've got beer?

You can easily imagine the potential, perilous outcome of this very typical scenario. A prodigious amount of beer and spirits is consumed in a very short time, accompanied by very little food, thus accelerating the head-long rush to inebriation. Perhaps also some marijuana is smoked and more ominously an assortment of mind-altering drugs is passed around. Before long, dozens of drunken kids are jumping in and out of the pool, diving, cannon-balling, or simply flopping in at every access point along the perimeter with no regard to the depth of the water or even who they might land on; any semblance of caution tossed to the wind. It's dark, after all, so who can tell how deep the water is?

Quite clearly, this is a hazardous perfect storm for our primary at-risk population of young adolescent males: alcohol and possibly drugs, little or no food, girls to impress, no adult supervision, and no residential signage (for those who might have actually read it). And of course, this is a population that all manner of statistics show is prone to ignore warning signs with impunity anyway, or even to do so out of a self-styled principle of rebellion against the "authority" that put the signs there in the first place.

Late in the evening, the Young Turks become engaged in a friendly but fiercely competitive diving contest to see who can do the most awesome jackknife from the toughest angle or corner of the swimming pool—or maybe by leaping from the roof of the nearby cabana—largely to impress the cheering girls in the skimpiest bikinis at poolside. It's enough to make a parent shudder to think about the potential consequences.

Maybe—hopefully—no one gets hurt, and the only residual damage from this whole affair is that a hundred or so kids have terrible hangovers just in time for repentance at Sunday services the following morning. But there is an even chance or better that one of these guys will plunge head-first into shallow water in the quest to perform the ultimate awsome-est dive of all, crashing his head against the floor of the pool with tremendous g-force sustaining serious head, neck, and spinal injuries resulting in per-manent paralysis or brain trauma. All too often, he will consequently face the grim prospect of a lifetime of pain, regret, and anguish. It is an all too common occurrence.

WHEN SAFETY WARNING SIGNS ARE NOT ENOUGH

In my view as a safety warnings expert and advisor, it goes without saying that I believe all swimming facilities must have, and should be required by law to have, prominently posted warning signs prohibiting users from diving in shallow areas, as well as effectively communicating the extreme dangers of doing so. This applies equally to both commercial and residen-tial pool owners. In Chapter 2, I used my "Shallow Water—No Diving" warning sign (Figure 2.1) as an example in precisely describing what spe-cific components are necessary in the design and wording of an effective warning message. (For convenience, Figure 2.1 is reprinted as Figure 5.1.) You should recall that I said that *"An effective product warning signals con-spicuously a safety message about a hidden hazard, conveys the potential harmful*

consequences of that hazard, and provides instructions to follow that enable con-
sumers to avoid these consequences."

FIGURE 5.1

Courtesy of Dr. Gerald M. Goldhaber.

My "No Diving" sign accomplishes these requirements. As I noted in Chapter 2, the word "DANGER" appears in capital letters in red and white to indicate an immediate and serious, possibly life-threatening hazard, and the words "SHALLOW WATER" succinctly define the nature of the hazard. Further, the words "YOU CAN BE PARALYZED" state pretty definitively the potential consequences of diving at this particular location, and "NO DIVING," rather unequivocally, tells pool enthusiasts in two words all that one needs to do in order to avoid the potential consequences of the hazard at hand.

However, as I have described, the population we are attempting to warn in this case presents a unique and formidable challenge, especially to the millions of residential swimming pool owners across the country. Because this is a case in which posting the signage alone is simply not enough. Remember that, as I stated in Chapter 4, there are always two crucial variables that determine whether a particular communication is effective, meaning that first, it is accurately transmitted by the sender and received by the target audience, and second, that it is categorically understood by that audience to mean what it is supposed to mean. In point of fact, the posting of the signage alone—however strategically effective the message itself—in this case may fail on both counts.

Given the fact that most shallow diving injuries occur among the population most likely to ignore posted safety warnings, as well as one that may not be fully cognizant of the potential consequences of their own actions, the role of the pool owners becomes a vital component of any safety warning system. Swimming pool owners must not only post No Diving warning signs along with depth markers running the sides and both ends of the pool, but they must institute a policy of orally warning all pool users, especially the friends of their children who might be using the pool for the first time and are unfamiliar with its depth dimensions. This should include, for example, specific, expressed oral warnings that there must be absolutely no diving in the shallow water areas of the pool. In this way, parents or guardians who, as consumers, technically comprise the third leg of the safety triad, are also called upon to act as proponents of the second leg. That is, they are obliged to provide as well an authoritative regulatory function over their children's poolside behavior.

If this sounds like good, old-fashioned parental or adult supervision, well, it is. Yet, few would argue that private swimming pool owners must take responsibility for ensuring that such facilities are used safely, that users are permitted into the water only when they know the "rules of the pool," and that reckless—and unsupervised—behavior will not be tolerated. All of this must be effectively communicated to anyone even entering the pool enclosure. However, while this and other examples we will examine in this chapter serve to underscore the crucial, collaborative role that must be played by all parties in the safety triad, such examples also make clear that the realm of responsibility at, let's call it the "interface" of the three legs of the triad, is not always a clear and distinct line. Oftentimes, for the safety triad to work effectively and seamlessly, the responsibilities of the parties must necessarily overlap, which is to say, at a minimum, they each must serve to reinforce the others.

For example, I have advised swimming pool manufacturers and install-ers to permanently print my warning signs on the vinyl liners for both in-ground and above-ground pools, even though this is not generally man-dated by law in most jurisdictions. Depending on the overall dimensions of the pool, I generally recommend imprinting eight to ten of them at intervals around the perimeter so that they cannot be missed. I also rec-ommend affixing larger versions of the warning signs to the entry gates of swimming pool enclosures, as well as at intervals along the fences around them (fences are mandated in many jurisdictions even if warning signs are not). Aesthetics be damned; we are talking about serious, debilitating inju-ries here. And it is simply not enough for swimming pool contractor-in-stallers to cavalierly hand the homeowner-consumer a bunch of properly designed warning signs and expect them to do the right thing by posting them prominently in critical areas around and inside the pool enclosure. Because they won't. Nor, in many jurisdictions, are they required to do so by law (as I believe they should be).

It should be noted that automatically printing the warnings on pools can get very complicated because different, discrete components of today's sophis-ticated swimming pool installations—from liners and pool covers to diving boards and waterslides to hot tubs and Jacuzzis—are often made or con-structed by different, specialized companies or suppliers. Component manu-facturers are likely to be unrelated to the contractors or companies that do the actual installation. For example, if a company only manufactures vinyl pool liners, that entity would be the one responsible for imprinting my warning sign into the liner itself, but not for providing (and installing) the signage to be installed on gates and fences. That responsibility might reasonably fall to the contractor.

I do not think the responsibility of manufacturer-installers to do their part to ensure the safe and enjoyable use of their product should end sim-ply with providing the necessary hazard warning signage. Because I believe that the contractor who does the actual installation of the pool, and who presumably is the individual (or individuals) who deals directly with the homeowner literally at the homeowner's place of residence, also should be required to provide an oral tutorial of safety guidelines in the use of the pool to as many members of the household as possible, but at a minimum, to the parents or guardians. Installers should also be required to hand the customer a printed version of those guidelines for future reference. It might be a colorfully printed pamphlet with a title like, "Sensible Ways to SAFELY Enjoy Your Swimming Pool." In theory at least, such practices in aggregate would be sufficient to meet a high standard of principled disclosure for the industry leg of the safety triad by fully informing consumers of the hidden hazards of pool ownership. In doing so, we might reasonably conclude that the consumer "has been warned."

Here again, you may find yourself asking, why should pool manufacturers and installers be the ones saddled with the lion's share of the onerous burden to provide safety instructions and to warn consumers exhaustively about what is by any measurable standard an inherently hazardous environment, the clear and present dangers of which ought to be intuitively obvious? The short answer is that, should something go seriously wrong due to anything that might be viewed as a hidden hazard, such as an accident resulting in one of the kids being paralyzed or killed, you can bet the homeowner is going to sue the construction company for failure to warn. The hard truth is that there will always be cases in which no measure of principled disclosure will prevent consumers from filing lawsuits that, however flawed plaintiff's claims may be, are so highly emotionally charged that they will stand an excellent chance of winning a favorable judgment in open court.

THE "DEEP POCKETS" PRODUCT LIABILITY SETTLEMENT: WHEN THE FACTS DON'T MATTER

I was sitting in the only available restaurant, just off the hotel lobby somewhere in Ohio. It has a large tree growing in the middle of it. It is not exactly Buddha's Bodhi-Tree of Enlightenment, but sitting beneath it did have a relaxing effect. I had stayed an extra day, after having done a mountain of research, and completed my expert testimony in court on behalf of my clients, a major swimming pool components manufacturer and industry supplier. When circumstances allow, I like to stick around for the verdict. Call it my own personal "Yelp!" review—I do my homework and I want to see the review. I want to know that the message of my testimony has been received by the jury or judge.

The case was an all too familiar one: A wild, out of control pool party at a private residence, dozens of underage teenagers consuming alcohol and who knows what else, all while the homeowner parents were away. In this case, there had been proper warnings signage around the pool. However, one of the things the plaintiff's attorney latched on to was the pool company's advertising logo, which depicts a person diving into one of their pools. It was something of a reach, to put it mildly.

Because what had happened was classic. One of the boys, a guest at the party, had gotten himself so drunk that he decided to dive from the roof of the house, bringing all the inertia of that one-story-plus plunge into the shallow end of the pool. As tragic as the end result was, the liability for the ensuing injury was about as one-sided as it could conceivably be.

Shortly, my client's attorney walked into the restaurant with the big tree in the middle of it and sat down at my table. "Sorry, Gerry, no Yelp review this time," he said, "He [plaintiff] took a $1 million settlement while the jury was deliberating." It did not come as a surprise.

Later, we polled the jury to determine which way they were leaning before their judgment had been preempted by the settlement agreement. I still wanted my Yelp! review, even if it was now moot.

They were in unanimous agreement and intent on awarding $30 million to the plaintiff. At the same time, they acknowledged that my testimony had been spot on; my client had done everything they could to help avoid such a horrific tragedy. They acknowledged the impaired kid had done a terribly foolish thing while ignoring clearly worded warnings that were properly placed in sufficient locations. When gently pressed by the attorney as to why, then, were they all prepared to make this prodigious $30 million award, their answer was simple. In so many words, they said, "The kid's a quadriplegic. He's going to need intensive care around the clock for the rest of his life." And then the hammer: "Someone needs to pay for all of that and they [the pool company] are the only ones with *deep pockets in product liability insurance* to do it." Bingo.

The sobering fact of the matter is that nearly 95 percent of all product liability lawsuits settle rather than are decided by a jury, and settlement negotiations have nothing whatsoever to do with experts or the letter of the law, or who did the right thing versus who did the wrong thing. It's all about dollars and who can go higher, or conversely, who can be induced to go lower. Neither plaintiff's attorneys nor the lawyers for the defense want to roll the dice with an emotionally sympathetic jury that might, as in the case described here, rule in direct contravention to the painfully inescapable facts of the case.

But to look at this more circumspectly, just as with the food warnings we discussed in Chapter 3, the meaningful question becomes: Should we require companies or individuals—or anyone—to put a warning on what many courts have called an open and obvious hazard? Many summary judgments have been issued in federal courts stating that the extreme danger of shallow diving should be obvious to anyone who enters a pool. Except that it isn't; not in actual practice. Those judgments aren't always right. At dusk you can't tell; at night you can't tell even if there are underwater spotlights illuminating the depths. Even in daylight, you often can't tell with any certainty due to optical illusion. Or at the time of the incident, there's no one standing in the water by which the luckless diver may judge the depth of the water he or she is about to plunge into.

In other words, it isn't enough to know that diving into shallow water is mortifyingly dangerous if you don't also know exactly where the water is deep enough to make it safe for diving or where it is simply too shallow to do so. And even if the Weiner and Associates' as well as my own similar survey results reveal that in fact, most adults do understand the risks, thus tending to support the court rulings. In this chapter, we have explored extensively a specific consumer segment and very predominant user of swimming pools that is prone to ignore safety warnings altogether, not to mention also being prone to naively reckless or careless behavior.

As I am obliged to reiterate often in this book, this is the dark side of principled disclosure for the business and industry leg of the safety triad. It is when I must recommend a heightened emphasis on full disclosure that really does go above and beyond what "a reasonable person" should know and understand about an "open and obvious hazard" in stressing that companies must do whatever they can to protect themselves from the bad judgment and bad behavior of the consumers who buy and use their products. Fortunately, in this case, the swimming pool industry apparently agrees.

Because, perhaps recognizing that it was indeed dealing with a product that unavoidably represents a potentially deadly hazard—a hole in the ground (or above ground, if you will allow) filled with water (what could possibly go wrong?), almost 50 years ago in 1968, the swimming pool industry formed an organization known as the Association of Pool & Spa Professionals (APSP). As an industry-focused organization, of course, APSP's mission is to promote the economic growth and development of its members' businesses and the recreational pool and spa industry as a whole. But what is most interesting and relevant to our purposes is that APSP assumes a proactive, forward-thinking, and industry-specific self-regulatory function to ensure, as its website suggests, the safety and enjoyment of pools and spas for consumers.

Business and corporate industry leaders of every stripe are inclined to complain loud and long about interventionist government regulation impinging on their various enterprises. And as we have already seen (with yet more examples to follow), government regulation of industry hasn't always worked very well, or it's become corrupted or subverted by the very industries it is supposed to be regulating. At the very least, government oversight of industry has a tendency to cause friction between those two legs of the safety triad while causing confusion to the third leg, namely consumers. By contrast, here we have an industry making an apparently serious and sincere effort to responsibly and proactively regulate itself. According to its website, the services provided by APSP include:

- Setting and advocating industry standards that serve the interests of the consumer and the industry
- Advancing technical competence

- Convening leaders around important industry issues
- Promoting professionalism
- Serving consumer interests and public safety
- Protecting the interests of the pool, spa, and hot tub industry[65]

Earlier, I alluded to the fact that there is some necessary and quite useful degree of safety-responsibility overlap among the three legs of the safety triad, nor must their responsibilities be mutually exclusive. As the APSP example demonstrates, the regulatory function may ideally include a mix of federal, state, and industry or trade organizations devoted to meeting the challenge of making sure their products are enjoyed safely by consumers. Perhaps if more industries did what the pool and spa industry has done, the U.S. might have less need for government-based regulatory agencies and the American taxpayer might actually save a little money.

GUARDS AT THE GATE: ACHILLES HEEL OF AMERICA'S THEME AND AMUSEMENT PARKS

One area where you might intuitively expect there to be a strong regulatory presence would be at America's amusement and entertainment theme parks, especially those featuring all those scary thrill rides of every sort. Yet, here again, you would be mistaken.

The International Association of Amusement Parks and Attractions (IAAPA) lists approximately 400 amusement parks and attractions currently operating in the United States and another 300 throughout Europe. All told, when one adds in all theme and amusement parks, attractions, water parks, family entertainment centers, zoos, aquariums, science centers, museums, and resorts, the total comes to some 30,000 attractions that produce a total nationwide economic impact of over $220 billion annually. In the United States, the attractions industry is a perennial leader in the creation of nonexportable jobs, directly employing 1.3 million people

---

[65] Association of Pool and Spa Professionals.

and indirectly generating another one million additional support jobs across the hundreds of cities and towns where they are located. Theme and amusement parks create 500,000 seasonal jobs every year. According to IAAPA statistics, some 375 million Americans visit theme and amusement parks annually.

And while most of these amusement parks are highly reputable and take very seriously their responsibility to protect the safety of their throngs of consumer guests, you may be surprised to learn that the theme and amusement park industry is not federally regulated. With respect to thrill rides, for example, only roller coasters are subject to regulation and regular inspection by government public safety agencies or authorities.

The result is that the first line of defense in the interest of promoting safe enjoyment of amusement park attractions—and avoiding serious injuries to park patrons—lies with the operators of the various rides and attractions and their ability to enforce the rules. We may joke all we want about fuzzy caricatured warning signs that say things like, "You must be this tall to go on this ride," but the truth is that such warnings are generally vitally important attempts to convey a serious safety message in a "feel good" way that fits within the intended park-friendly atmosphere, in which everyone is supposed to simply be having fun. Bluntly, such signs are a way of saying "No"—in the land of "Yes!"—without actually saying the ugly word itself. Moreover, the primary restrictions that apply to whether certain individuals may go on various rides involve issues that may intimately affect the sensitivities of those particular individuals, such as height, age, and, in particular, weight. Further, while in many cases the rules of allowable ridership are reinforced audibly by a continuously running pronouncement over public address systems, the communication effectiveness of that message is highly debatable. Amid the ambient cacophony of sounds from blaring music, the screams, shouts and conversations of dozens of patrons rushing around in close proximity, and the mechanical noises emanating from the amusement ride machinery itself, it is doubtful that anyone actually hears such audio warnings, much less pays them any heed.

This is serious stuff, because the prototypical accident at amusement parks is someone falling or being thrown out of a rollercoaster or some other rapidly moving ride due to the failure to follow the safety rules associated with the attraction. Injuries due to ride malfunctions are far fewer in number, although failure of restraint bars, harnesses, and seat belts do occasionally occur. Examples may include small children for whom seatbelts or locking bars may be insufficient to secure them in their seats or overweight adults who cannot fully close the locking bar due to their girth. In both cases, the riders are at serious risk of being ejected violently while the ride is in motion. In fact, in all of the legal cases involving injuries or fatalities resulting from amusement park rides in which I have been called to testify, every one of the injured parties was well beyond the standards that were clearly posted as to who may go on the ride and who may not.

In point of fact, the fixed-site rides at amusement and theme parks are remarkably safe. The IAAPA points out that Americans enjoyed some 1.6 billion rides in 2015, and it estimates that the chance of being seriously injured in a fixed-site amusement park ride is one in 16 million (IAAPA likes to add, comparatively, that the National Weather Service estimates the chance of being struck by lightning in the U.S. is 1 in 775,000). Further, the total of 1,500 injuries suffered by ridership patrons in 2015 actually represents a 20 percent reduction from 2003, according to a Ride Incident Survey Report issued by the National Safety Council. These figures would appear to indicate that the amusement park industry's efforts to police itself with respect to overall ride safety have been largely and admirably successful. And yet, where it may be most lacking comes down to enforcement of its own rules.

Because far too often, the typical amusement park's weakest link in assuring the safety of its thrill rides lies in the people they hire to operate them. Think about it: These operators are the people on the front lines most able to observe first-hand the consumer-patrons entering the rides. Consequently, they are also the park personnel in the best position to ensure compliance by patrons with the rules of the ride; and conversely, they are the employees most likely to be faced with confronting would-be ride-goers intent on ignoring the rules. So who do amusement parks typically hire as ride operators?

Kids.

They often hire high-school students in their mid-teens who are off from school for the summer—predominantly, we may conjecture—to fill those half-million seasonal jobs. They receive very little, if any, formal training with respect to the potentially hazardous aspects of the ride or in the safety features or protocols designed to avoid those hazards—what training they do get presumably covers only how to take those tickets (i.e., collect the fare) from the gleeful riders. They are not paid very well—which, of course, is the reason they were hired for this job in the first place. And they are … KIDS! Teenagers charged with the responsibility of adults. Yet, against all logic, these are the people placed as the gatekeepers at the precise point of risk.

This scene is easy to imagine, whether it's Benny from Brooklyn taking his family to Coney Island, or Dan from Dallas bringing his brood to Six Flags Over Texas. Benny loves his breakfasts of scrambled eggs and potato pancakes topped with sour cream and lots of powdered sugar. Dan is definitely a bacon, ham, and egger with maybe a slice of apple pie on the side. Neither of these fun-loving dads is familiar with the concept of a healthy Body-Mass Index. As they approach the entrance to the roller coaster ride at their respective amusement parks, they encounter this 15-year-old kid who says, "I'm sorry, sir, but I can't allow you to go on this ride."

"Say what?!" Benny and Dan might bellow simultaneously from different time zones.

"Sir, you have to be able to close the safety bar in order to go on this ride."

"Are you saying I'm too FAT to go on this ride?!!!" Now Benny and Dan are indignant—insulted by a teenager right in front of their families, right in front of their own adoring kids, mind you!

"Listen, young man [or "lady," or some similar euphemism thereof], I'm going on that ride with my kids. You let me worry about my 'safety'. Come on, kids."

Intimidated and afraid of these big, overbearing adults, the ticket-taking teenager at the gate relents, as Benny and Dan push past triumphantly to take their seats along with their kids in the roller coaster car of their choice. Maybe they will be able to suck their formidable guts in far enough to secure the locking bar; maybe they won't. If not, maybe they will, nonetheless, be able to hang on for dear life during the ride or, what may be more likely, somewhere down the rails they will be launched into the air like luckless human cannonballs without a net.

In virtually every court case in which I have been called upon as an expert witness for the defense, the amusement owners' attorneys have wanted to make the case that the proper warning signage was there in place. And while occasionally some judge or jury might agree, I insist that this is yet another case in which the signage is simply not enough. Blaring warnings over public address loudspeakers is not enough. At Disney Parks, for example, because of their international appeal and attendance by people from many different countries speaking many different tongues, they make such announcements continuously in as many as five or six different languages. It's almost academic that the running drone of the message quickly becomes part of the background white noise that patrons quickly cease to hear anymore. Excited kids and parents are running up to the entry gates of rides they've been waiting to get on all day. Their minds are not focused on signs or audio broadcasts; it's on being the first to get a seat!

Park operators need to take into account the frenzied, noisy, even chaotic information environment in which they are trying to communicate a sobering safety warnings message. Doing so is made all the more difficult by the way in which amusement parks routinely and aggressively market danger and high-risk adventure in their hyped-up television, radio, internet, and print advertising. Such ads for roller coasters and other thrill rides tout frightening, death-defying features like "the steepest vertical drop" or "greatest G-force" ("fastest" and "tallest" and "longest" are *soooo 20th century*!). They have names like "Intimidator 305" at King's Dominion in Virginia or "Zumanjaro: Drop of Doom" and "Nitro" at Six Flags in New Jersey or "Fury 325" at Carowoods in North Carolina. So when you consider that patrons come to the amusement park literally *expecting* danger, how else would you imagine they are going to react to signage that warns of danger or that indicates rider restrictions that only further add to the perception of imminent peril? They're going to tend to ignore them; that's what.

Thus, in an ironic way, the marketing and advertising strategies that promote the perception of danger and risk-taking are the dark enemy of an effective warnings program. "Of course it's dangerous," consumer-patrons might say, "It's supposed to be thrilling and exciting and risky." But, of course, they don't expect to be killed by it either.

There is nothing in principle that is wrong with amusement parks hiring high-school teenagers as seasonal employees, and the last thing I would want to do would be to make any kinds of recommendations that would result in denying summer jobs to a population that sorely needs them and has few alternative opportunities. However, I have advised theme and amusement park operators that, one way or another, they must fully empower the gatekeepers—whoever they are—to be able to prevent a ride from being started if there is even one single individual who insists on boarding and who will not be safe because of the failure or inability to comply with the rules of the ride.

It means giving the gatekeepers proper training, but it also may mean creating some mechanism for teenage employees to contact authorities, including uniformed police officers if necessary, should they be confronted with an intimidating or surly patron who tries to bully his way onto a ride and into a potentially dangerous situation. In my view, it is quite the same as the pilot and crew of a commercial airliner refusing to fly the plane until an unruly passenger is removed from the aircraft. And it is that important if the amusement park operator wants to avoid being sued for failure to warn after a serious injury or fatality as a result of someone being on that ride who shouldn't have been.

THE SPECIAL CASE OF DISNEY RESORTS AS "THE HAPPIEST PLACE(S) ON EARTH"

"We know you'll enjoy your stay in Westworld, the ultimate resort where nothing—nothing—can possibly go wrong …
… go wrong …
… go wrong …
… go—"

—From the movie trailer for *Westworld*, 1973[66]

Not all serious injuries or fatalities at theme and amusement parks are the result of accidents on high-speed or intense-action thrill rides, however. One of the most talked about incidents in just the last year was the tragic death of two-year-old Lane Graves, who was snatched by an alligator while picnicking with his parents on the beach of the Seven Seas Lagoon at Disney World in Lake Buena Vista, Florida. Not surprisingly, the incident gained worldwide media attention. What few people realize, however, is that in some respects, Disney became an unwitting victim of its own extensive and strategically calculated public relations campaign and the brand identity that it has striven to promote for many decades.

In the fictional movie *Westworld*, guests visiting a fantasy resort are treated to a completely computerized recreation of the Wild West of the 1800s populated with robotic gunslingers, bar tenders, bar maids, a sheriff, and a full complement of townspeople and villains—all fantastically life-like automatons in a kind of electronic dude ranch. Here the guests are encouraged to play out their fantasies of rugged frontier life in the Old West, including bar brawls, gambling, and gunfights, and even one-on-one pistol duels with outlaws. At night, technicians in white lab coats roll in quietly to collect all the shot-up automatons, repair them, and put them back into the town for the next day's fun. It's all a simulation of course, and no one is supposed to get hurt. That is, until the mechanical gunslingers

---

[66] Crichton, *Westworld*.

get ahold of live ammunition and go haywire, and all of a sudden some very real, very unsimulated mayhem takes place as the human guests must defend themselves from annihilation by renegade robots gone rogue.

In a peculiarly similar way, at its multimillion dollar entertainment properties around the world, the Disney franchise has extensively branded itself as the "Happiest Place on Earth," essentially promoting each of its fabulously lavish resorts as the ultimate pinnacle of the family-friendly vacation destination, devoted entirely to fun, fantasy, and flights of child-like imagination for all. Only good, wholesome things are to be enjoyed by guests staying at Disney Worlds around the globe and, much like *Westworld*, absolutely nothing bad can happen to kids and their families here; nothing—*nothing*—is supposed to go wrong. Parents and their children may completely relax, because all of the evils of the world are locked outside the gates of The Magic Kingdom.

And that is precisely why the signage on the shores of the Seven Seas Lagoon and perhaps dozens or other bodies of water on Disney entertainment properties failed to warn that they are inhabited by potentially dangerous alligators and snakes. In the weeks and months after the terrible, heart-wrenching death of the boy from Nebraska, whose family had likely never in their lives seen an alligator prior to the tragic incident, numerous former guests of the resort came forward, revealing that they had seen alligators lurking in the reedy waters of the lagoon. At least two of those guests even indicated that they had reported their sightings to Disney employees within less than two hours of the incident, yet evidently nothing was subsequently done to warn or protect the people relaxing on the beach.

After the attack, however, officials from the Florida Fish and Wildlife Conservation Commission captured and killed six alligators from the lagoon and stated that it was "very likely" that they caught the one that killed the boy, although it was impossible to be certain. Agency records revealed that Disney had caught and removed a total of 15 alligators from its property in just the five-month period prior to the attack from January to May 2016, and state records further indicated that Walt Disney Company had captured and euthanized more than 240 "nuisance" alligators from its property over the previous ten years.

Thus, it soon became clear that the resort's executive management knew very well that there were (and still are) some rather formidable, downright dangerous reptiles living in the lakes and lagoons on the resort grounds. They simply could not bring themselves to inform their guests of this reality-impinging fact. Evil, it seems, lurks even in the ultimate family paradise.

Apparently, if you're a Disney public relations executive, you think: We can't have big red, white, and black "WARNING—DANGER" signs posted in the Happiest Place on Earth! That's an absurd contradiction in terms; an illogic that can't exist! Besides, any "alligator" that might slink out of the Seven Seas Lagoon at Disney World would simply have to be a big, friendly, bright-green cartoon alligator with big eyes and a broad, happy grin; and it wouldn't "slink" out of the murky lagoon, all teeth and terror—oh no—it would have to dance out of sparkling waters wearing a top hat and spats and singing to all the children; probably it would be named Alvin or something. And it would probably sound a lot like Barney the Dinosaur while it delighted the children with festive song and dance. Now that would be a Disney World alligator!

I do not mean to make light of this horribly tragic death of a two-year-old boy in a place that he should have been as safe as one could possibly be on this otherwise dangerous planet. But the hard truth and undeniable fact is that a large measure of the reason why Disney officials failed to warn about the hidden hazard of real, live, dangerous alligators living in the lagoons and waterways of their world famous entertainment resort is simply because they could not bring themselves to post anything negative within the halcyon, manicured grounds and glittering attractions of the "Happiest Place on Earth." Harsh as it may sound, Disney's executive management were guilty of drinking their own Kool-Aid. And don't kid yourself: they also feared that such ominously scary signage, and the images of carnage it would necessarily evoke, would adversely affect reservations by protective and fearful (and presumably disillusioned?) families and, in turn, hurt their $17 billion worldwide theme park business. Really now; does that make any sense to anyone?

But that is not all, because once again in this case, the signage alone is not enough, in my opinion. I have advised Disney executives that guests arriving at their Florida resort hotels should be directly informed and advised verbally of the hidden alligator hazard right as they check in. Specifically, hotel front-desk representatives should be charged with the responsibility to orally warn guests as an integral part of the check-in routine as they're taking credit-card payment information and handing over the room keys. Face-to-face. That would really be the most effective way to communicate this crucially important message, and to make sure the message is received and understood by the consumers who are directly at risk in this instance.

It is not likely they will ever take this step, although the resort has since cordoned off the shore of the Seven Seas Lagoon with a rope-and-wood-post barrier that now bears at intervals along its length warning signs that state: "Danger," "Alligators and snakes in area," "Stay away from the water," and "Do not feed the wildlife" (*See Figure 5.2*).

FIGURE 5.2

Courtesy of Natalie Williams.

I began this book by stating that the world is an inherently dangerous place. Try as they might have, the tragic death of two-year-old Lane
Graves perhaps shows that the architects of Disney World could not
engineer a completely risk-free environment, and it proved that even the
Magic Kingdom cannot keep the wolves outside the door. Next, we move
from what should have been one of the safest places in the world to what
is inarguably one of its most hostile.

DEATH ON MOUNT EVEREST

In May 2017, Nepali Sherpas, ironically on the ascent of Everest to retrieve
the body of a Slovakian climber who had died only yards from reaching
the 29,035-foot summit, unexpectedly stumbled upon the bodies of four
other climbers at what is known as Camp 4. At 26,000 feet, Camp 4 sits at
the entry to what climbers call the Death Zone, the altitude at which the
human body stops trying to acclimatize and climbers are literally, slowly
dying until they can descend. But the four men whose bodies were discovered by the Sherpas did not freeze to death, nor had they suffered a terrible
fall. Instead, they apparently died from carbon monoxide (CO) poisoning
caused by using their propane stoves to keep warm inside their tents without proper ventilation.

In the U.S., the Centers for Disease Control and Prevention (CDC)
estimates that there are on average about 162 deaths per year due to carbon
monoxide (CO) poisoning. Most of these, about 78 percent, occur inside
the home or adjacent buildings like garages and barns. Approximately
12 percent (about 19 deaths per year) occur inside tents, camper-trailers,
ice-fishing huts, and other temporary structures, and another 6 percent
(about nine deaths per year) inside motor vehicles, including boats. But
let's look at the specific devices that are principally responsible for these
carbon monoxide deaths.

Using a survey period from 2008 to 2010, the CPSC found that the vast
majority of deaths (71 percent) were caused by faulty home heating systems
or by engine-driven CO-producing tools such as gas-powered generators

emitting CO. Interestingly, the same study found no CO-related deaths due to propane-fired camp stoves or portable lanterns. This remarkable statistic may be due in large part to the very clearly worded and explicitly designed safety warning labels that now appear prominently on all of the relevant products made by one of the world's largest suppliers of camping equipment, Coleman Company, Inc. This is the story of another company and industry leader that eventually did the right thing in embracing principled disclosure, although they had to undergo a serious learning curve in order to get there.

After experiencing a number of hefty lawsuits in the 1980s and 90s over fatalities allegedly caused by carbon monoxide poisoning due to its products, Coleman retained me to review and assess their warning labels, which did not seem to be doing the trick of successfully indemnifying the company against liability in the courts. I immediately found their warning labels could be significantly improved, not only in terms of the language and design that was used, but also with respect to their placement on the products themselves, which could stand to be made more prominent. As well, most of their on-product labeling simply referred consumers to the warnings and user instructions printed in the owner's manual, which of course some people never bother to read. Finally, while the labels on Coleman stoves and lanterns did warn against running these devices inside a closed pitched tent or small enclosure, like an ice-fishing hut, for example, they also needed to indicate precisely why it was so dangerous to do so.

That is, they needed to improve the precision and strengthen the language identifying the hidden hazard itself. This, of course, is the fact that devices that burn propane (or kerosene before propane became popular) inevitably produce a hidden amount of carbon monoxide, which can rapidly build up to deadly concentrations, especially in confined and closed spaces. Coleman's executives believed at the time that carbon monoxide is an open and obvious hazard that most consumers were very familiar with.

I began by assuring them that it is not; in fact, carbon monoxide might easily be described as the poster child representing the very concept of the term "hidden hazard." You can't see it and you can't smell it. You can't tell it's there until you've either passed out or passed on from breathing it. Even if most people know that burning propane or kerosene (or any type of fuel) inevitably and unavoidably produces a certain amount of unwanted CO, even the savviest of campers and "rugged outdoors-people" are also likely to believe that stoves and lanterns burn so efficiently that they produce only negligible and thus presumably harmless amounts of the deadly gas. One has to imagine that the four experienced climbers on Everest may have fallen victim to this false belief.

The thing is this: There simply is no "harmless" or "safe" amount of carbon monoxide gas. Even if today's camping appliances are vastly more efficient than they were years ago, some CO generation as a byproduct of burning is a hidden hazard that cannot be completely eliminated, and in an enclosed space even that minute, continuous emission of the gas eventually builds to deadly proportions. Not only that, but most modern camping tents are more airtight than they were a generation ago.

Coleman earnestly wanted to be proactive in addressing the problem. In fact, they had amassed a wealth of analytical data for me to work with, which they had compiled through extensive analyses in three important areas. These included a competitive analysis, a regulatory analysis, and perhaps most importantly, a market analysis to learn precisely how consumers were using their products and how they were typically being injured or killed by them. From there, the process of improving and upgrading Coleman's warning labels and safety instructions proceeded in much the same fashion as the one I described in connection with Daikin Industries in Chapter 4. Briefly, I created and designed four or five different warning label designs that we market tested extensively to determine which version was most easily understood by the majority of consumers, especially those who were most likely to use Coleman products.

However, ensuring the safe handling and use of flammable gases like propane packed in pressurized containers is quite a bit more complicated than simply warning about the risks of potential electrical shock or rotating fan blades that were the primary hazard flashpoints with Daikin's air conditioning units. So even as Coleman now features a short, cogent version of their warning labels placed prominently on their stoves and lanterns, the company also provides a much longer and detailed set of cautions and user instructions through its product distributors and in the printed owner's manuals that come packaged with the product. (For the full version of the Coleman Company's warning text and directions for use, see: https://manualsbrain.com/en/manuals/1075213/pdf/ 7ed282644d7cbc05105b0621f945495edf6a1a8652f6ca722dee1a70 fe1c9da1/coleman-propane-stoves-user-manual.pdf)

CHAPTER 6

TRAVELING: FOLLOW THE DEADLY BRICK ROAD

We're in a Lexus … we're going north 125 and our accelerator is stuck!
We're going 120 [mph]—We're in trouble; we can't—There's no brakes!
End freeway half mile! We're approaching the intersection! Hold on!
Hold on and pray … pray! Oh! OH!

—the last words of Christopher Lastrella, seconds before
he, his sister Cleofe, her husband, California Highway
Patrolman Mark Saylor (who was driving), and
their 13-year-old daughter Mahala all died
in a fiery crash as a result of Toyota's faulty
"sticky" foot-petal accelerator.[67]

If Americans like to play hard, it's certainly true that they love to travel, whether the purpose is pleasure or business. According to the U.S. Travel Association, domestic person-trips for both leisure and business purposes totaled 2.1 billion in 2014, an increase of over 50 million, or 2.4 percent, over the previous year.[68] Leisure trips accounted for 72 percent of all domestic travel, with personal business, general business, and conference, convention, and seminar attendance accounting for another 20 percent.

---

[67] Wert, "Toyota."
[68] U.S. Travel Association, "Travel."

At the same time, 139 million Americans commute to work daily and, according to the U.S. Census, in 2014 the average commute time was 26 minutes, although some 600,000 people dubbed "mega" commuters travel 90 minutes and 50 miles or more one way to work. The American Public Transportation Association reports that in the year 2016 alone, Americans took nearly 11 billion trips via passenger railroad systems (including heavy and light rail, as well as inner-city commuter and trolleybus lines) and public bus transportation systems.

With respect to air travel, recent figures from the U.S. Department of Transportation's Bureau of Transportation Statistics (BTS) show that U.S. airlines and foreign airlines serving the United States carried an all-time high of 895.5 million domestic and international (inclusive) scheduled service passengers in 2015, 5.0 percent more than the previous record high of 853.1 million reached in 2014. The combined increase was the result of a fairly equal rise of 5 percent in the number of passengers on domestic flights (696.2 million in 2015) and 4.7 percent growth in passengers on U.S. and foreign airlines' flights to and from the U.S. (199.4 million in 2015).[69] Clearly, we are a nation of people on the move.

We begin this chapter with a discussion of commercial airline travel because it involves a unique set of challenges to the whole issue of safety warnings, although it is one that is shared to some extent by passenger rail and bus service providers, as we will also see later in this chapter. In particular, the challenge centers largely around the specific population that must be warned about hidden hazards in order for transportation service-provider companies (or government-run authorities) to protect their customers from potentially serious injuries or worse. (Hint: It is NOT their base of customer-consumers or the public at large.) Our examples will demonstrate once again that, like alligators in Disney World's Seven Seas lagoon, hidden hazards do not always originate directly from the product or the nature of the service itself.

---

[69] U.S. Department of Transportation Statistics.

PUBLIC TRANSPORTATION: WHEN IT IS COMPANY EMPLOYEES WHO MUST BE WARNED

Travel and transportation experts are often keen to point out that flying on commercial airlines is by far the safest mode of travel for consumers. And indeed, modern commercial aircraft are incredibly safe, equipped with redundant computerized mechanical systems designed to kick in should any of the primary systems fail, which also rarely ever happens. Still, a 2015 survey conducted by *Forbes Magazine* listed airline pilots and flight engineers (combined) as America's third deadliest occupation, right after the much more obviously perilous occupations of commercial fishing first and logging second. The fact is that most airline crashes are caused by pilot error, and weather conditions are a far more prevalent factor in such incidents than any sort of equipment failure.

Actually, squaring these two seemingly contradictory facts is more logically intuitive than it might appear on the surface, and the answer points neatly to the challenge that commercial airline companies face in providing principled disclosure and in targeting and effectively reaching the right audience when they are obliged to warn about hidden hazards. This is a case where the audience to be warned is not the customer-consumer. Rather, the audience that must be warned consists of their employees, from pilots and flight engineers, to check-in personnel, baggage handlers, flight attendants, and all other staff involved in the safe conduct of commercial passenger flight. It may even be the case that the "audience" that most crucially must be warned is the company itself, as we will see in this section. And if consumers may be so often faulted for failing to heed safety warnings, companies and their executive management can be just as guilty for the same thing.

It would do no good, for example, to warn passengers about severe and dangerous weather disturbances like wind shear across an airport runway at take-off or landing or extreme turbulence at 30,000 feet. These are hidden hazards that must be communicated to pilots and onboard technicians responsible for flying the plane, and the warnings regarding these conditions obviously do not come from the airline company, nor are these hazards intrinsic features of the aircraft that could not be "designed out." Rather, the warnings come from a variety of other competent and authoritative sources, such as the U.S. and local weather forecasting services, or from instrument readings taken by air traffic control authorities working the towers at individual airports.

As well, increasingly today, the warnings come from technologically sophisticated, computerized onboard weather detection systems that alert pilots when the aircraft is about to encounter severe weather conditions. Loud buzzers, flashing red warning lights, and even pre-recorded auditory messages are used to warn pilots about all sorts of potentially catastrophic conditions from ground-level wind shear to storm turbulence, and even to flight situations like insufficient altitude while flying over mountainous regions. But it is also important to note that these onboard computer-generated warnings tend to be critically urgent emergency messages when the encounter with dangerous flying conditions is imminent.

However, the point for our purposes is that, regardless of the source, the audience for these warnings is the pilot and the flight engineers, not the consumer-customers sitting comfortably back in the passenger compartments. When you think about it, no other industry beyond transportation requires consumers so routinely and in such enormous numbers, to put their physical lives—not to mention their complete trust—into the hands of a very few, hopefully highly competent and diligent people. That goes for both public and private transportation from taxi cabs to busses to trains to ocean liners to cruise ships to commercial air travel; the last being perhaps the quintessential model of unequivocally handing control of your very existence over to someone else (outside of your surgeon, of course). And this exquisitely existential circumstance further leads us to the unique challenge that transportation providers face with respect to identifying hidden hazards within their respective industry segments and developing adequate warning messages against them in a manner that meets the criteria of principled disclosure for all parties concerned.

For the airline industry in particular, two recent and highly sensational incidents bring this dilemma into sharp focus. One is the crash of Germanwings Flight 9525 in the French Alps on March 24, 2015, which has fairly conclusively been determined to be a horrific case of suicide by pilot (co-pilot, in this particular incident). The other is the disappearance of Malaysian Airlines Flight 370 over the Indian Ocean and many miles off course on March 8, 2014, which remains a mystery to this day, and one whose actual cause will in all probability never be known definitively. However, since we do know, to a reasonable degree, that this was the case with the Germanwings tragedy, we will focus on that incident, and particularly on the several complex warnings questions that it raises.

THE HAZARD FROM WITHIN?

The hidden hazard here was that the copilot was apparently suffering from severe depression that rendered him unfit to work; meaning that if he worked in his present mental state, he could cause severe injury or death to passengers and other flight crew members. Later investigations into the sad, short life of the copilot, Andreas Lubitz, age 27 at the time of the crash, would reveal a history of manic-depressive episodes dating back over seven years. The first of these occurred in September 2008 and delayed, but did not prevent Lubitz from completing his course of study at the Lufthansa Flight Training Pilot School in Bremen, Germany, where students spend a full year studying aviation theory before putting it into practice at a Lufthansa-owned and operated flight-training school in Arizona.

Dropping out of the program after only two months, Lubitz sought help from a psychiatrist in his hometown of Montabaur, who diagnosed the young man as suffering from a "deep depressive episode," with thoughts of suicide, and treated him with intense psychotherapy. The psychiatrist (whose name is protected by German privacy law—more on that later) also prescribed not one, but two powerful antidepressants, Cipralex and mirtazapine. His symptoms included tinnitus, a near-constant ringing in the ears often associated with mental depression. In any case, the doctor attributed the collapse in part to the trauma or separation anxiety Lubitz apparently felt due to the move to Bremen, which had taken him away from his family and younger brother for the first time in his life. His parents would later tell crash investigators that their son, during the short time he was away, had developed an irrational and "unfounded" fear of failure.

After six months of intensive treatment and with the regular regimen of his medications, Lubitz's psychiatrist declared that "a considerable remission [has] been obtained." His satisfaction with his patient's recovery was enough to enable the doctor to write a letter to German aviation officials recommending that Lubitz be permitted to resume his training in Bremen, stating conclusively: "Patient alert and mentally fully oriented, with no retentivity or memory disorders. Mr. Lubitz completely recovered, there is not any residuum remained. The treatment has been finished." In spite of this essentially "all clear" message, however, the doctor continued to treat Lubitz—and to prescribe powerful mood-altering drugs— for another three months after having assured officials of his patient's full recovery.

Accordingly, however, when German aviation officials subsequently moved to restore Lubitz's student pilot's license and his fit-to-fly medical certificate, they rightly amended the documents with a crucial designation for "Specific Regular Examination" (SIC). This notation would stay on Lubitz's permanent record, and it would also mean that he would be required to report periodically to Lufthansa's Aero Medical Center to undergo regular psychiatric examination for signs of depression. Should his malady return, any further psychiatric treatment, and in particular, should he require any more medications, this would result in his automatic grounding, probably for life.

To this point, for the most part, all appears well and good. However, the fact that Lubitz's doctor continued to treat him with antidepressant drugs after declaring him fully recovered to aviation authorities remains problematic (and, admittedly in hindsight, quite disturbing). Lubitz seems to have recognized that he has some significant psychological issues, he has voluntarily and proactively sought out help from a medical professional, a psychiatrist, and undergoes appropriate intensive treatment leading to apparent recovery, or at least put him on the road to recovery. All of this is duly reported by the doctor to German aviation officials and Lufthansa, and the pilot to be is designated to receive regular medical/psychiatric examinations to detect any reemergence of his depression and to ensure his continued fit-for-flying status for the good of his passengers, the airline, and the pilot himself.

Finally, the planned regular examinations by Lufthansa's medical team as a function of his permanent SIC status are really in Lubitz's best personal interests as a human being, because among the one in six men statistically who are affected by major depressive disorder, 50 percent of those who recover will experience one or more relapses in their lifetimes. Yet, here is where the story begins to go sour, and it does so (somewhat exasperatingly) when the U.S. Federal Aviation Administration (FAA) first gets involved.

In order to participate in the four-month training program at Lufthansa's Arizona flight school, the FAA requires foreign (and U.S.) trainees to fill out a student-pilot application. Among the questions the document asks, predictably, is whether the applicant has ever been diagnosed with "mental disorders of any sort, depression, anxiety, etc.," Lubitz lied on the form, ticking off "no," and leaving blank the space below, in which he was required to detail any medical treatment he had received over the previous three years. However, the serious omission was caught four days later by a German aviation doctor who was responsible for vetting documents for the FAA, and who reported it to authorities. Anyone caught lying on an FAA application form risks receiving a jail sentence for perjury, or perhaps worse, being permanently barred from flying. Yet, once again, the detection of Lubitz's lie merely served to delay the obtainment of his student-pilot license and subsequent acceptance into the flight training program in Arizona.

Because inexplicably, the FAA responded to Lubitz's clearly and egregiously falsified application by saying lightly, "We are unable to establish your eligibility to hold an airman medical certificate at this time." It then, in effect, offered him a second chance to fill out the form properly and honestly, instructing, "Due to your history of reactive depression, please submit a current detailed status report from your prescribing physician." Thus, upon resubmitting his application, Lubitz came clean, explaining in detail his history of depression and treatment, as well as providing the status report from his doctor as demanded. And that was all it took, apparently, to satisfy both German aviation officials and the FAA. Lubitz successfully completed the Arizona training program, received further pilot training in his native Germany flying larger and increasingly more sophisticated jets, and in the fall of 2013, he joined Germanwings, where he quickly advanced to First Officer, qualifying him to copilot commercial flights across Germany and Western Europe.

Lubitz appears to have begun to relapse just before Christmas of 2014. Increasingly convinced that he was going blind, he began visiting numerous ophthalmologists and neurologists at the rate of three or four appointments a week. He complained incessantly that he was seeing stars, halos, flashes of light, streaks, and flying insects, as well as suffering from light sensitivity and double vision; certainly not good symptoms for a pilot, and, of course, this is when Lubitz began fearing, with neurotic intensity, that he would lose his job due to these troubling developments. Yet, doctors examining his eyes and brain using a variety of state-of-the-art diagnostic equipment could find nothing wrong, their universal conclusion being that they were, in fact, psychosomatic in nature. One ophthalmologist observed that Lubitz was "full of fear" and a neurologist diagnosed him as suffering from hypochondria, or acute anxiety disorder. So certain was Lubitz that the symptoms affecting his vision were real—according to one doctor's records, he would describe them with "remarkable frequency and detail"— that he refused, or perhaps was simply unable to accept, the very possibility of alternative diagnoses suggesting psychological rather than physical or neurological causes.

Ultimately, his own family doctor diagnosed an "emergent psychosis" and urged him to check himself into a psychiatric clinic. Lubitz chose to ignore her, and instead, abruptly broke off all treatment. That is, until returning to the same Montabaur psychiatrist who had treated him for nine months nearly six years earlier, back in 2008 to 2009. The deeply troubled copilot thus began a renewed program of intensive psychotherapy and—even while continuing his normal work and flight schedule—once again began taking powerful antidepressants including mirtazapine and lorazepam. Court records would later show that the psychiatrist knew full well that Lubitz's crushing depression and panophobia had returned big-time, yet he made no attempt at all to alert Lufthansa officials on his patient's relapse. The result of this doctor's decision would be unimaginably catastrophic.[70]

Over the final weeks and days of Lubitz's life, testimony from his friends, associates, and family after the tragedy paint a portrait of a tortured young man descending rapidly into mental illness and spiraling out of emotional self-control, a man who several people described as "living on the edge." Only two weeks before deliberately crashing the jetliner into an Alpine ravine, he learned that his long-term girlfriend was pregnant. The two had intended to be married; however, she had just broken off their seven-year relationship because his increasingly erratic and bizarre behavior left her fearing for her safety. According to reports in the German Newspaper *Bild*, one friend of the disturbed copilot said that Lubitz had begun to bully his fiancé, ordering her with regard to "what clothing she could wear, what men she could speak to, even the length of her skirts," adding, "He was a control freak of the highest order." Another friend said he was having problems with severe mood swings.[71]

Worsening matters, Lubitz was involved in an affair with a German-wings flight attendant over the five months leading up to the crash. Identified only as "Maria," she described Lubitz as increasingly "tormented

[70] Hammer, "Flight 9525."
[71] Ibid.

and erratic" and revealed that he would wake up from horrible nightmares screaming, "We're going down! We're going down!" German police who raided Lubitz's flat after the incident reportedly found "a small mountain of pills" and preliminary information from a report on the disaster by the European Aviation Safety Agency revealed that Lubitz had apparently rehearsed the maneuver by which he eventually would bring the plane down. Analysis of his seized computer indicated that he had recently searched the internet for various means of committing suicide, googling phrases like: "producing carbon monoxide," "drinking gasoline," and "which poison kills without pain?" And on March 20, less than four days before he would plunge Germanwings Flight 9525 into the French Alps killing himself and 148 other passengers and crew members, Lubitz googled the internet for information about the locking mechanism on an Airbus A320 cockpit door.

A CASE OF MULTIPLE FAILURES TO WARN—FROM ALL THREE LEGS OF THE SAFETY TRIAD

What lessons might we learn from the Germanwings tragedy? First, we might begin by wondering why the FAA wasn't more strident in reacting to Lubitz's blatant lie on his initial student-pilot application in 2009, rather than, apparently, simply giving him what amounted to a do-over. However, we're likely to never know the answer to that question. In point of fact, it might not have mattered in the larger scheme of things. Given a clean bill of health by his doctors at that time, we may reasonably conjecture that had he answered the mental disorders question honestly the first time around, he would likely have been granted his license to fly, and conceivably nothing would have turned out any different. Clearly, no one could have predicted the horrific actions he would take seven years later.

Nor does it appear that the FAA was alone in its lax attitude in this case. While the permanent SIC designation in Lubitz's medical records required Lufthansa's Aero Medical Center to examine him regularly for depression, to this day it remains unclear how often he was expected to report to Lufthansa doctors, and how thoroughgoing his examinations were. A disturbing report issued by a United Nations regulatory group in 2012—three years before the Germanwings crash—strongly criticized the airline industry for its lack of effective screening for mental illness, particularly with respect to younger pilots, as if they are somehow more immune to the development of significant psychological problems. The report essentially declared that the "traditional medical examination" currently in use is antiquated and wholly inadequate to facilitating accurate detection of potentially serious psychological disorders like those suffered by Lubitz. And according to an attorney (and licensed pilot) involved in pursuing a class-action suit on behalf of families of the Germanwings victims, such exams are notoriously lax. "There is a flaw in the system, allowing 'self-reporting' and concealment," he states, adding further, "You fill out this bullshit questionnaire, you lie, and you are off to the races."

Second, we need to take a hard look at how the airline industry (as well as other entities in the transportation sector) balances the personal privacy of critical employees like pilots and flight engineers with the need to ensure the safety and welfare of the flying public. We might phrase the question in savagely unambiguous language by asking: When and where does the airline pilot's right to privacy end and my (the passenger's) right to live begin?

Germany's data protection privacy laws are among the strictest in the world. That's because when first enacted in 1971, they embodied a strong sociopolitical reaction to the indelible memory of relentless Nazi surveillance and the Third Reich's pervasive invasion of personal privacy (especially of the Jews). These privacy laws were then even further tightened in 1990 after the fall of the Berlin wall and reunification, this time in direct response to the very similar policies and behaviors of the former German Democratic Republic (a.k.a. East Germany) secret police known as the Stasi. Nevertheless, even these most restrictive of national privacy laws do allow German psychiatrists and other medical professionals to alert (or warn) relevant parties—including employers—if they have professionally grounded reason to believe that a patient in their care could present a danger to the lives of others. This duty comes under a provision under German privacy law known as the "Interests of Public Safety Exception," which allows doctors to alert appropriate authorities without the knowledge or consent of the patient in question.

Despite this legally protected ability, however, the sacrosanct bar of personal privacy may have nonetheless precluded Lubitz's doctors from warning his employer over the extended weeks and months of his final depressive psychological breakdown, and unfortunately the one that led to his suicide and the deaths of so many others. From these facts, it is clear that current German law as well as the common culture gives far more weight to personal privacy than it does to the interests of public safety.

The U.S. has similar privacy laws—and similar exceptions for reporting by medical professionals—under the Health Information Portability and Accountability Act of 1996 (HIPAA), signed into law by President Bill Clinton, which has been amended several times since its original enactment. The HIPAA laws also allow certain exceptions for the release of personal medical data other than by the patient, including via court order or administrative non-judge request (only for relevant, very specific information regarding fugitives, material witnesses, and missing persons). One very interesting exception in U.S. privacy law applies to law enforcement officials who may use such personal information to prevent an imminent threat to the safety of the individual or the general public.

Appropriately, the Germanwings crash and the disappearance of Malaysian Air Flight 370, which may or may not have been a case of pilot suicide, prompted U.S. officials to initiate new regulatory scrutiny of pilot medical and psychological screening procedures. In May 2015, barely two months after the Germanwings tragedy, a panel of U.S. and international experts selected from government and industry began a comprehensive review of the methods and practices used by the FAA to evaluate and monitor the mental and emotional health of pilots as well as—quite critically—the barriers that might exist to reporting any issues.

Current U.S. regulations require pilots operating regularly scheduled flights to undergo a robust physical examination annually and every six months for captains and individuals over the age of 40. These physicals are administered by certified aviation medical examiners who are also responsible for inquiring into the psychological and emotional condition of pilots, and who are empowered to "defer any examination when … additional psychological testing may be indicated," according to the FAA. As we have already seen, pilots must also complete a yearly FAA medical application form that inquires about mental disorders, and pilots face fines of up to $250,000 if they are found to have falsified or failed to disclose pertinent information. Yet, as we have also seen in the unfortunate case of Andreas Lubitz, the self-report component of this still-current screening process may indeed be suspect. What is most important, however, is that medical professionals must be empowered, supported, and protected by proper and practical personal data disclosure provisions under privacy laws to allow them to be the issuers of warnings to airline companies and aviation authorities whenever a given individual poses a potential risk due to serious emotional distress or a diagnosed psychological disorder.

Finally, we need to look at the third leg of the Proactive Safety Triad, the consumer/general public itself, whose safety is ultimately at stake. Whatever obstacles the present German privacy laws (and U.S. laws as well) may represent to medical professionals in duly reporting patients at risk, the fact remains that other individuals and groups are not bound by the provisions of this law. Thus for example, Lubitz's friends, his fiancé (or the flight attendant he was seeing), his fellow pilots and coworkers—even his own family members—having clearly observed his disturbing eccentric behaviors, having experienced first-hand the torments and psychological stress he was under, could have attempted to intervene, either by confronting Lubitz directly or, if necessary, by way of warning his employer of his apparent state of mind and consequent potential danger to the lives of others. All of these individuals as private citizens (and thus not subject to privacy laws governing the disclosure of privileged confidential information) could have done so without fear of legal repercussions. None did.

In a palpable sense, we can all empathize: No one wants to "rat out" their friends or, god forbid, one's own family members to their employers or authorities, particularly when such action may lead to job suspension or firing, or even potential detainment or arrest by law enforcement officials for cause. Yet, the horrific consequence of the failure of friends, lovers, family, and associates to alert Lufthansa speaks for itself. Certainly, it would have been a much better outcome if Andreas Lubitz had gotten—even at minimum for his own sake—the help he needed, even if that meant he would never fly a commercial jetliner again. It would seem that the distinctly 21st-century proviso of the modern post-9/11 world—"if you see something, say something"—ought to apply to much broader circumstances than simply an errant backpack or briefcase left unattended in an airplane terminal or train station.

OUR NATION'S COMMUTER AND FREIGHT RAIL SYSTEMS ARE NO BETTER

To a meaningful extent, the same intimate level of direct responsibility for the lives of passengers is entrusted to the drivers of the nation's commuter trains. In fact, while the average commercial domestic flight might carry between 100 and 200 passengers, many commuter trains routinely carry more than double that number, day in and day out, to and from their places of employment.

Unlike air travel, however, as a strictly land-based means of conveyance running on permanent tracks, rail systems easily lend themselves to the application of automatic safety control mechanisms that can not only alert motormen and station-based managers to impending danger, but can also be designed to override or "fail-safe" train operators to avoid specific hazards—even to the point of automatically averting situations that might otherwise result in certain catastrophic disaster. In principle, the safety systems are hardly different from the ones used by control dispatchers to keep track of the locations and speeds of individual trains in order to make sure the overall transportation network is running on schedule, and which presumably allows for manual adjustments to be made—either slowing or accelerating specific trains—to keep everything on that proscribed schedule.

Regardless, the conspicuous question for American rail carriers is why such computerized hazard-avoidance systems—which have been available for decades and are currently used routinely throughout Europe and parts of Asia (particularly in Japan)—have not been more widely installed and implemented in the U.S. I am speaking, of course, about Positive Train Control (PTC). PTC utilizes a system of sensors and interactive Global Positioning System (GPS) technology that can alert a train and its engineers to all manner of track conditions, from sharp curves that require a routine reduction in speed at specific locations, to unexpected obstacles on the tracks that could present a collision danger and might require the train and its drivers to take emergency action to reduce speed or even come to a complete stop.

Just in recent years, horrific derailment crashes on the Metro North lines in Spuyten Duyvil, New York, in 2013 and in Philadelphia in 2015, along with a third crash of a New Jersey Transit train into the bumper block at the end of the line inside NJT's Hoboken terminal took a total of 13 lives and collectively injured 375 other people. The Metro North train derailed as it entered—at an estimated 82 mph—a dangerous curve through which the speed limit is 30 mph. The Amtrak *Northeast Regional* train running from Washington, D.C., to New York was traveling at 102 mph through a curved section of track with a speed limit of 50 mph just past Philadelphia. The NJ Transit train was only going 10 mph over the inside-terminal speed limit of 10 mph, but even that was enough for the train to plunge through the protective bumper block at the end of the rail line, careen across the end of the platform, and smash into the stone façade of the historic 1907 Hoboken Terminal building, killing a woman who had been standing on the platform. All three of these terrible disasters easily would have been avoided if the trains and the specific sections of the tracks where the incidents occurred were equipped with PTC, which would have warned the trains' engineers that they were going too fast. Nor is the benefit of PTC limited to the movement of trains themselves.

On February 3, 2015, Ellen Brody drove her 2011 Mercedes SL 350 onto a railroad crossing just before an approach to the Taconic State Parkway in Westchester County, New York, stopping in the middle of the tracks to check her car for damage after the crossing gate had come down and hit it. Brody may have been unfamiliar with this particular crossing. Investigators believe she may have been there because an earlier automobile accident near a more commonly used crossing less than a mile south had slowed traffic on the Parkway and pushed detouring cars onto side roads, including the one over which Brody had attempted to cross the tracks.

In any case, Brody hurriedly climbed back into her Mercedes but was unable to drive off the tracks before a Metro North train carrying 650 passengers rammed into her car, which immediately burst into flames as it was pushed 400 feet down the tracks. Brody was immediately killed, as were five passengers riding in the first car, horrifically, when the electrified third rail alongside the tracks was pulled up by the force of the collision and speared through both Brody's SUV and the full length of the first car of the train. There are about 130,000 public and 85,000 private railroad grade crossings across the U.S., and every year approximately 2,000 cars or trucks are hit by trains at these crossings, killing more than 250 people annually and seriously injuring hundreds more. If PTC were installed at every railroad grade crossing across the country, virtually all of these accidents, injuries, and fatalities could have been avoided, including the death of Brody and the five Metro North riders in 2015. So why has PTC not been more widely implemented? Money, of course; profit over safety.

By way of a brief history, the National Transportation Safety Board (NTSB) has been calling for the implementation of PTC for over four decades, prompted by the 1969 collision of two Penn Central commuter trains in Darien, Connecticut, in which four people were killed and 43 were seriously injured. For most of that time, little attention on Capitol Hill was paid to the NTSB's recommendations until a coincidental succession of rail accidents involving freight trains carrying deadly poisons occurred in the early 2000s. Of course, in the wake of these incidents, the renewed efforts by Congress to require the system-wide installation of PTC were fiercely resisted by the railroad industry.

However, the accident that finally spurred Congress to take substantive action was the spectacular head-on crash in 2008 between a Metrolink commuter train and a Union Pacific Freight train in Chatsworth, California that killed 25 people and injured 102. Congress finally responded by enacting the Rail Safety Improvement Act of 2008, which instructed the nation's railroads to install PTC on all 60,000 miles of tracks by the end of 2015. However, as the recent spate of derailment crashes amply serves to illustrate, the 2015 deadline came and went. As late as May 2015, the industry trade group known as the Association of American Railroads (AAR) acknowledged to Congress that the rail industry had thus far installed PTC on only about 8,200 miles of tracks, or less than 14 percent across all rail lines where it was federally mandated by the 2008 Improvement Act, citing the high cost among a number of reasons for the delay. In response, Congress passed the Surface Transportation Extension Act of 2015, which provides a three-year extension to the year 2018 for the installation of PTC nationwide.

According to its website, the AAR now claims that, as of February 2017, freight railroads:[72]

- Have spent more than $7.9 billion on PTC development and deployment
- Are spending $100 million a month on continuous development, testing, and installation
- Retained more than 2,400 signal system personnel to implement PTC
- Geomapped 96,000 miles of railroad and 486,000 assets

The AAR further reports that at the end of 2016:[73]

- 38% of 60,153 route miles have PTC
- 63% of 18,500 freight rail locomotives are equipped with PTC
- 51% of the 125,000 employees requiring training are PTC-qualified
- 87% of the 32,654 track-side signal systems are PTC ready
- 77% of the 3,968 base station radios are installed

---

[72] Association of American Railroads, "Positive Train Control."
[73] Ibid.

While the AAR's claims are somewhat encouraging, we now know that the industry did not meet the new deadline of 2018, and it may, in fact, take many more years to fully implement PTC on all 60,000 mandated miles nationwide. However, some hope for correcting this unacceptable situation comes from newer digital technology that has emerged in the 21ˢᵗ century.

Spurred by a 9 percent increase in railroad grade crossing accidents in 2014, the following year the Federal Railroad Administration (FRA) announced the formation of a partnership with Google to provide the locations of all U.S. railroad grade crossings in the company's Google Maps application. Google will be enabled to tap into the FRA's enormous data base in order to plug each location into its mapping program, and also plans to program audio and visual alerts into the application when drivers use the turn-by-turn navigation feature. At the time of the announcement of the partnership with Google, the FRA also indicated that it was reaching out to four other digital technology map makers—Apple, MapQuest, Garmin, and TomTom—in hopes of including similar grade crossing warnings in their mapping applications.

While such efforts may be promising for the future, the benefits of grade crossing warnings embedded in automotive computerized mapping applications remain questionable in the short-term. According to figures compiled in July 2015 by the marketing analytics firm IHS Automotive in conjunction with the U.S. Department of Transportation, the average age of cars and light trucks on America's roads and highways is 11.5 years and the average length of ownership for a new vehicle is 6.5 years. That means that it could conceivably take somewhere between six and 12 years for every car in America to be equipped with one or more of the newly available digital mapping technologies and the warning systems built into them. It also needs to be mentioned that in-vehicle warning technologies of this kind are secondary systems; they are not capable of automatically preventing serious accidents at grade crossings the way that PTC is capable of doing so. And, of course, there is always the issue of whether people will actually use or pay attention to them. A seemingly paradigmatic question might be: Does one really need to have their vehicle's GPS navigation turned on during their daily commute back and forth to work? Or will they prefer to listen to uninterrupted music or an audiobook?

Before we turn to cars, we examine at least one other warnings issue that will continue to confront the nation's railroads for at least as long as it will take them to finally implement PTC on a nationwide basis. Earlier, we saw how the depressive mental state of copilot Andreas Lubitz played such a tragic and central role in the Germanwings catastrophe. And while the commercial airline industry overall does a reasonably good job of requiring annual physical examinations that include psychological screenings for its cockpit-certified personnel, the U.S. railroad industry is comparatively and exceedingly lax in this regard, another fact that has come to light as a result of the spate of recent fatal rail accidents detailed earlier.

For example, the cause of the 2013 Metro North New York derailment crash at Spuyten Duyvil has been determined to be the condition of obstructive sleep apnea suffered by the train operator, and the same condition is suspected to be the cause of the NJT crash, at least preliminarily. Neither of these commuter rail lines has ever bothered to routinely test their operators for this condition prior to these fatal accidents. Further, in its final report on the New York crash, the National Transportation Safety Board (NTSB) faulted Metro North for not routinely screening for sleep disorders in employees in positions defined by federal regulations as safety-sensitive, however it also cited the Federal Railroad Administration for not requiring railroads to do so.

Finally, in perhaps the irony of all ironies, in December 2016, William Rockefeller, the sleep apnea suffering engineer in the middle of the Metro North crash, filed a $10 million lawsuit against the railroad claiming that Metro North should have either installed PTC on the dangerous curve in Spuyten Duyvil or alternatively, equipped the cab with "an alerter system of audible signals" that would serve to warn Rockefeller and other operators when their trains were exceeding posted speed limits. As if to make the circumstances even more befuddling, such an "alerter" system was, in fact, in place in the rear cab of the Hudson Line train, which becomes the front cab for southbound runs into Manhattan, but not in the front cab for the northbound run into Westchester County and where Rockefeller was stationed.[74]

Superficially, and to the casual observer—and to New York taxpayers who will ultimately pay the legal bills and pony up the inevitable settlement monies—Rockefeller's lawsuit may seem ludicrous: *The motorman is suing the railroad authority because* **HE** *fell asleep at the "wheel."* How is that any better or worse than absentmindedly spilling hot coffee on yourself and getting scalded like Stella Liebeck?

However, Rockefeller's lawsuit has serious merit. One of OSHA's fundamental requirements is that employers must provide a safe workplace or environment for their employees, or otherwise, adequately warn employees of hazardous conditions that may exist and that cannot be eliminated. By failing *both* to regularly screen its locomotive operators for potentially dangerous conditions like sleep apnea *and* to provide adequate warnings like the cab-based audible alerter mechanism (or positive train control as an even better alternative), Metro North categorically did neither. As a result, the railroad finds itself in the unenviable position (and one that must be politically excruciating for executive management) of being sued by *both* the class of injured passengers and families of those deceased in the accident *and* by its own employee for failure to provide a safe work environment as well as failure to warn. And once again, the question I have for Metro North as well as the rest of the railroad authorities across the country is: Was it really worth it, and does it really continue to be worth putting off the installation of PTC system-wide, and for that matter, nationwide?

---

[74] Zambito and Fitz-Gibbon, "Engineer."

ONE MORE LOOK AT THE AUTOMOBILE INDUSTRY

No chapter dealing with Americans on the move would be complete without talking about our love affair with cars and the open road. And while earlier we briefly touched on some classic cases of the automobile industry's failure to warn about hidden hazards and defects in their vehicles, few modern-day incidents tragically resemble a Hollywood script more than the opening epigraph to this chapter: the real-time 911 recording of the last words of Christopher Lastrella literally seconds before he and three other members of his family were killed in a fiery car crash caused by a sticky Toyota Lexus gas pedal. Released only days after the fatal crash on August 28, 2009, the recording seized the national media spotlight and served to highlight a defect that Toyota had known about for years but had done nothing to correct the problem, nor to warn consumers about the hazard it presented.

Toyota would ultimately agree to a $1.2 billion fine to avoid prosecution for covering up severe safety problems with what it called "unintended acceleration," according to court documents, and for continuing to make cars with parts the FBI said the car manufacturer "knew were deadly." FBI Assistant Director George Venizelos stated bluntly that Toyota, "put sales over safety and profit over principle," adding:

> *The disregard Toyota had for the safety of the public is outrageous. Not only did Toyota fail to recall cars with problem parts, they continued to manufacture new cars with the same parts they already knew were deadly. When media reports arose of Toyota hiding defects, they emphatically denied what they knew was true, assuring consumers that their cars were safe and reliable.*[75]

---

[75] FBI, "Toyota."

That's a much different story than the car maker told when it reached an out of court settlement with the Saylor family for an undisclosed amount (believed to be about $10 million) and did so, according to a report aired September 17, 2010, on ABC News 10 out of San Diego, "only under the one condition that [Toyota] wouldn't be held liable, and [upon agreement that] there's nothing wrong with its cars." In fact, according to the ABC News report, just two days before the announcement of the Saylor family settlement, and continuing to deny any wrongdoing, Toyota, "asked a California federal judge to dismiss hundreds of lawsuits claiming sudden acceleration, saying the suits were not based on fact."[76]

Unfortunately, the litany of such cases among car makers goes on and on, and they involve virtually all of the largest and most popular brand manufacturers. In 2015, across the automobile industry, there were 123 government-initiated recalls resulting in the recall of over 20 million cars over safety issues. An additional 83 safety recalls were initiated by the industry itself, without government intervention—a staggering and unprecedented number. These additional, voluntary industry recalls resulted in the recall of another over 40 million cars bringing the total number of cars recalled in 2015 to a mind-boggling 64 million and making 2015 the all-time leading year for total automotive recalls.

Previously, in February 2014, General Motors issued a relatively modest recall of 800,000 cars to repair faulty ignition switches that could inadvertently shut off the engine while driving, thus both directly causing crashes and preventing the airbags from deploying, in turn resulting in more grievous injuries to the helpless driver and passengers. Over the following months, the recall ballooned to nearly 30 million cars worldwide, and GM would eventually pay an undisclosed amount of compensatory damages for 124 deaths linked to the ignition key failure.

---

[76] SDNews, "Toyota."

GM had actually first discovered the defect with the ignition key in 2004, a full ten years before they issued the first recall. Accused of delaying the first recall for far too long after the company received field reports that revealed the problem, GM North American President Alan Batey responded glibly in a statement that, "The chronology shows that the process employed to examine this phenomenon was not as robust as it should have been." That's about as colossal an understatement as one can imagine! Even worse, amid the conga-line of wrongful death court cases that ensued, GM argued that the ignition key defect should be linked only to fatalities resulting from head-on crashes in which the air bag failed to inflate. In other words, for example, GM insisted that fatalities to back seat passengers didn't count, because those deaths were not caused by the failure of the airbag to deploy!

In one infamous case, GM had the temerity to argue that the ignition switch failure was not responsible for the death of Brooke Melton, a Georgia woman whose car subsequently "spun out, hydroplaned, hit an oncoming vehicle and rolled off the road, dropping 15 feet into a creek."[77] In addition to disabling the airbags, it should be noted that ignition switch failure also disabled the car's power steering and antilock brakes.

Furthermore, documents provided by GM to the U.S. Congress indicated that the fix needed to correct the defect ignition switch cost 57 cents. Yet, in late March 2014, GM CEO Mary Barra testified before a House subcommittee that the 57 cents represented only the cost of the parts needed to fix the problem and that a recall would have cost the company over $100 million had it been undertaken in 2007, and "substantially more," had it been undertaken in 2014 at the time of the hearings.[78]

What are we missing here? Ultimately, GM recalls 30 million cars worldwide and tells Congress that it's going to take "substantially more" than $100 million to correct the 57-cent ignition switch defect? So … that

---

[77] Wallace et al., "GM."
[78] AP, "Cost."

comes out to over $3.3 million per car? Maybe they should have simply given everybody a new car (with a nondefective ignition switch) and saved a few bucks!

In September 2015, the U.S. Environmental Protection Agency (EPA) issued a notice of violation of the Clean Air Act to Volkswagen Group after it was found that the German automaker had intentionally programmed the turbocharged direct injection (TDI) diesel engines of 11 million cars worldwide and 500,000 in the U.S. alone so that the emissions controls were activated only during laboratory testing. The programming caused the vehicles' nitric oxide and nitrogen dioxide output (collectively known as NOx level) to meet U.S. standards during regulatory testing, but allowing the engines to emit up to 40 times more NOx in real-world driving.

Let me state that more plainly: Volkswagen deliberately conspired to deceive the EPA and get around stringent U.S. environmental law, and they had deployed this programming in those 11million cars over a lengthy six-year period from 2009 through 2015. This was a decision that had to come from the very top echelon of VWs executive suite.

For more than a year before the scandal finally broke, Volkswagen executives insisted to the EPA that emissions test discrepancies the agency had found were merely the result of "technical glitches" and categorically refused to acknowledge that they had deliberately rigged the vehicle emission tests right up until the moment they were confronted with the smoking-gun evidence of the "defeat device." Even then, Volkswagen CEO Martin Winterkorn, while apologizing for having "broken the trust of our customers and the public," in his September 23rd resignation speech, *still refused* to admit culpability for the deception, insisting that the admitted wrongdoing was attributable to "the terrible mistakes of a few people." This, despite the fact that at right about the same time, the CEO of VW's America Group, Michael Horn, was finally taking full responsibility for the intentionally orchestrated deception, stating publicly, "Let's be clear about this. Our company was dishonest with the EPA and the California air resources board and with all of you, and, in my German words, we have totally screwed up."[79]

At long last, an admission of guilt.

Finally, the sheer enormity of the Takata fiasco demands a more in-depth exploration of the heinous actions of the company's executive management that ultimately led to the demise of the once third-largest auto parts manufacturer in the world, and the world's largest manufacturer of air-bag mechanisms.

We begin on November 4, 2008, when Honda Motors recalled 4,000 of its 2001 Accord and Civic models globally, citing concerns that the driver and passenger airbag inflators might produce excessive internal pressure causing them to rupture and spray jagged metal fragments into the car—and directly into the faces, necks, and upper torsos of the driver and front seat passenger.

Just over six months later, in May 2009, an Oklahoma teenager by the name of Ashley Parnam was killed when the airbag in her 2001 Honda exploded, shooting metal fragments into her neck. She became the first of at least 16 fatalities[80] (as of this writing) that have been directly attributed to exploding Takata airbags. Yet, both Honda and Takata denied fault, and settled with the deceased's family for an undisclosed sum.

However, in a similar incident that same year, which took the life of Gurjit Rathore of Virginia, Honda and Takata would eventually settle with her grieving family for $3 million, after nearly two years in litigation. On May 10, 2013, the same year as the Rathore settlement, Takata posted a record $212.5 million annual net loss. But that was just the tip of the iceberg for Takata, as the fatalities—and the lawsuits—mounted, and

---

[79] Sorokanich, "Volkswagen."
[80] Reynolds, "Takata."

the recalls by auto manufacturers mushroomed to almost inconceivable proportions.

The Takata defective airbag story is still being written: As David Kiley recently observed, it now represents a "full-blown" crisis that continues to spiral out of control.[81] The total number of vehicle recalls by many of the world's major automobile manufacturers is now topping 70 million in the U.S. alone—the largest automobile recall in American history—and over 100 million worldwide in the space of nine years. It has cost Takata and the auto industry billions of dollars, not to mention the loss of at least 16 lives. In fact, this crisis appears so out of control that it is nearly impossible to imagine when or how it will ever end.

Yet, the real outrage of the story is not only the sheer magnitude of the recalls or the colossal worldwide turmoil they have caused (and continue to cause). Rather, and as reported in the *New York Times*, it is the fact that Takata knew about the airbag inflator defect all along and chose to go ahead with manufacturing and distributing millions upon millions of the dangerous devices, in spite of the serious life-threatening danger they posed. Internal documents obtained through court proceedings and a series of hearings by the U.S. Senate revealed that Takata's own engineers had conducted a study that provided conclusive proof that the airbag mechanisms could explode, creating a deadly spray of jagged shards from the metal rims of the airbag container.[82]

In fact, according to the *New York Times* article, the engineers had presented the damaging report to Takata management in 2004, at least five years before the first fatality with the death of Ashley Parnam! Yet, Takata management instructed its engineers to bury the report and proceed with manufacturing, thereby brazenly putting corporate profits above the safety of millions of drivers around the world. As one former employee

---

[81] Kiley, "Takata."
[82] Tabuchi, "Takata."

put it, they were instructed to, "Pack [the study] all up, shut the whole thing down."[83]

It goes without saying that the company's decision to bury the engineers' glaring report was morally and ethically reprehensible—some might go so far as to say that it was morally depraved in its inexcusable indifference to public safety, even to the point of utter contempt for human life itself. Yet, not to diminish the colossal scale of that disregard and the loss of life it has caused, this fateful decision is hard to fathom, even on a much more fundamental, principled level of sound business practice. Takata had achieved the vaunted position of becoming the world's largest supplier of airbags to a dozen of the world's largest and most highly regarded automobile manufacturers, no doubt after decades of hard work and technological research, experimentation, and innovation, not to mention exceptional service in supplying its customer-automakers.

Regardless of that prestige and position and power—perhaps in part because of it—the management of Takata in their arrogance chose, bluntly stated, to screw over each and every one of the auto manufacturers to whom they had become the principal and trusted supplier of automobile airbags. In other words, they directly screwed over their entire essential, primary customer base in one fell swoop. If you are an auto industry executive in charge of contracting to buy millions of dollars' worth of parts for your company's line of 2018-model (and beyond) cars and trucks, would you be inclined to buy them from Takata? Thus, this catastrophic decision simply makes no sense on any practical level of Business 101, and there is only one motive that explains it: Greed.

Moreover, with that context in mind, one might conceivably have some empathy for car company executives loathe to issue staggeringly costly recalls of millions upon millions of their vehicles that might be equipped with defective Takata airbags. After all, Toyota, GM, Honda, Ford, and all the others are really not directly responsible for the deadly devices, and

---

[83] Ibid.

one could very reasonably argue that all of these car companies bought the units from Takata in good faith with the (equally reasonable) expectation that the units would perform as they were supposed to—that they weren't going to kill and gruesomely maim drivers and passengers.

WILL THE ROBOT CARS SAVE US ALL?

A lot of buzz in today's automotive world surrounds the "autonomous vehicle," or the emerging smart technology of self-driving cars and trucks. Some analysts estimate that by the year 2030, autonomous vehicles could account for as much as 60 percent of U.S. auto sales, and several auto makers have already introduced new, sophisticated models equipped with a number of autonomous features such as self-parallel-parking, lane departure warnings for highway driving, and automatic emergency braking. In fact, perhaps predictably (and exasperatingly), car companies like Hyundai are already airing commercials showing drivers literally taking their hands off the steering wheel to "test" or demonstrate the lane departure "safety" feature and aggressively stepping on the gas because, hey, with automatic emergency braking, you can go whatever speed you want without ever having to worry about hitting anything or anyone!

Still, setting such typically ludicrous advertising hype aside, most experts agree that ultimately, autonomous vehicles will be much safer than cars piloted by humans, and in evidence they point primarily to the National Highway Traffic Safety Administration's (NHTSA) estimate that human error accounts for over 90 percent of all U.S. traffic accidents, which includes some 35,000 fatalities every year. In an April 2017 LinkedIn article, Shelly Palmer, CEO of The Palmer Group, a strategic advisory and technology solutions firm, claims, "Remove human error from driving, and you will not only save a significant number of lives, you will also dramatically reduce the number of serious injuries … [of which] there were over 4.4 million in the U.S. in 2015 alone."[84]

---

[84] Palmer, "Self-Driving Cars."

Palmer suggests that consumer resistance to the fully autonomous car is largely emotional, having to do, in part, with that feeling of giving up control. If you have ever taken a son or daughter out in the family car to teach them to drive for the first time, you know the feeling. Palmer uses the analogy of people who are afraid of flying even when confronted with the fact that commercial airline flight is "the safest form of travel by several orders of magnitude," and insists that "by the numbers," statistics will show that "semi-autonomous vehicles crash significantly less often than vehicles piloted by humans."

Nevertheless, a survey published in March 2017 by the American Automobile Association (AAA) found that over half of Americans (54 percent) feel less safe sharing the road with autonomous vehicles, with only 10 percent indicating that they felt safer. Interestingly, while we might expect AAA's finding that 85 percent of baby boomers said that they would be afraid to ride in a fully self-driving vehicle, a surprising 73 percent of millennial and 75 percent of Generation X respondents also indicated that they would be fearful of riding in one. Overall, more than three-quarters of all Americans (78 percent) are afraid to ride in a fully self-driving vehicle. Yet, despite all of that expressed fear, 59 percent of the survey's respondents said they wanted to have autonomous features in their next vehicle. "This marked contrast," the study's authors conclude, "suggests that American drivers are ready to embrace autonomous technology, but they are not yet ready to give up full control."[85]

NHTSA clearly agrees that at least some, and perhaps many, autonomous features will vastly improve vehicle and driver safety. For example, the agency cites an agreement with 99 percent of U.S. automakers to include Automatic Emergency Braking (AEB) in all new cars by the year 2025. NHTSA believes adding that feature alone will prevent 28,000 crashes and 12,000 injuries annually when fully implemented. Further, support for the idea that the autonomous vehicle inevitably will be an integral part of our future comes from a seemingly unlikely source—that is,

---

[85] AAA, "Unsafe."

until you think about it. That's because it turns out the automotive insurance industry is already bracing for a significant drop in consumer policy sales, having also apparently concluded that more autonomous cars on the road will mean fewer accidents—and a diminishing need for collision and liability insurance.

A report issued in 2016 by the consulting firm KPMG indicates that, "over the next 20 to 25 years, the number of accidents will fall by 80 percent," according to Jerry Albright, principal of actuarial and insurance risk practice at the company. That's a startling forecast that, if achieved, will turn the automotive insurance industry upside-down. The report estimates that the $200 billion in annual premiums that insurers collect from policyholders could shrink by as much as 60 percent by 2040, as safer, autonomous vehicles reduce accident damage and personal injury—and revenues from premiums fall as a result. No less a corporate guru than Warren Buffett, whose Berkshire Hathaway conglomerate owns Geico, has said that autonomous automobile technology poses a "real threat" to the insurance industry.

And while not particularly germane to our concerns in this book, the potential woes that safer cars pose to the financial fortunes of the automotive insurance industry (how deliciously ironic is that thought to anyone who has seen their car insurance rate skyrocket after being involved in a fender-bender?) do serve to point us to the inescapable, $64,000 question. We are looking at what may well be the most intensive and sophisticated application of digital computer technology ever installed into an already complex consumer product: What could possibly go wrong?

WHAT ARE THE RISKS?

In May 2016, 40-year-old Joshua Brown became the first person to die "behind the wheel" of an autonomous car when his Tesla Model S, cruising on Autopilot, crashed into an oncoming tractor trailer that was making a left turn, the car going right under the trailer section and hitting a fence and a power pole before coming to rest. The Rand Corporation estimated that, up until the crash, "Tesla car owners had logged 130 million miles in Autopilot mode" without a single fatality.

In all fairness, it should be noted that Brown, a former Navy man who was responsible for dismantling bombs during the Iraq War, was something of a risk taker. Among experts and the people who knew him, it is widely acknowledged that Brown was knowingly pushing the limits of the still nascent autonomous vehicle technology much like a test pilot in a new experimental jet, going so far as to post self-narrated videos of his escapades—including demonstrations of situations in which the Autopilot did *not* perform well—indicating that he knew very well the risks of what he was doing.

In the ensuing investigation into the cause of the crash, Tesla acknowledged that its onboard camera failed to recognize the white broadside of the trailer against a bright sky, and therefore the Model S consequently failed to brake to a stop to avoid the collision. However, in a final report in which NHTSA looked at several other Tesla Autopilot incidents involving injuries in addition to the fatal Brown crash, the agency concluded that it "did not identify any [safety-related] defects in the design or performance" of Autopilot, or "any incidents in which the systems did not perform as designed." To be perfectly clear, NHTSA's investigation focused solely on whether there was a defect in the Autopilot system and concluded that, although Autopilot did not prevent the accident, it performed as it was designed and intended, and therefore did not have a defect, and did not warrant a product recall by Tesla. As Palmer states, apparently beaming with techie-aficionado pride, "the car didn't cause the crash."

Huh?

Quite contrary to Palmer's gleeful proclamation, however, NHTSA essentially acknowledged that what its investigation truly reveals is that even the most innovative car makers are not there yet with respect to inventing the fully autonomous car that can drive itself without any human oversight whatsoever. Upon release of the report, agency spokesman Bryan Thomas said, "Not all systems can do all things. There are driving scenarios that automatic emergency braking systems are not designed to address," as well as problematic situations such as crossing traffic that, he continued, "are beyond the performance capabilities of the system."[86] If that is indeed the case, would it be fair to say that the *limitations* of the system caused Joshua Brown's fatal crash?

In a statement that seems to run diametrically counter to the whole idea of the fully autonomous vehicle, Thomas insisted that "Autopilot requires full driver engagement at all times." In fact, regulatory agencies like NHTSA and the National Transportation Safety Board (NTSB) have strongly cautioned automakers about naming and marketing semiautonomous driving systems in ways that lead consumers to believe that they can mindlessly let the car drive itself while they sit back reading the paper or texting on smartphones while trying to drink superheated coffee without scalding themselves. Because you can't do that. And it may be decades before you will be able to do that, if it ever happens at all.

Accordingly, some critics have called on Tesla to rename Autopilot, arguing that the current name suggests drivers may cede most over-the-road tasks to the car's computers, cameras, and sensors. Also in 2016, Mercedes Benz pulled an ad for its own semi-autonomous system, pressured by complaints that it deceptively and dangerously overstated the technology's capabilities. When we think about the likely and potential limitations of autonomous vehicles themselves, it may be crucially important to keep in mind that some of the very systems that might need to go into those vehicles—you know, to make them "autonomous"—have their own inherently peculiar limitations to begin with.

For example, Tesla has the remarkable ability to wirelessly beam software updates to its cars. In September 2016, after the Brown crash, the company released a major update to Autopilot that enables the system to rely more on radar technology, rather than cameras alone, to identify other vehicles and obstacles and to automatically apply the brakes or take evasive action. Yet, while Tesla CEO Elon Musk has speculated that the new version might have prevented the Brown crash, as highly accurate as radar

---

[86] Boudette, "Tesla."

is in measuring distance to an object, it is far less precise in detecting the size and shape of objects or obstacles. In other words, there really is no way of knowing how radar would have affected the autonomous reactive—or nonreactive—"behavior" (if I may call it that) of Brown's Tesla that fateful day. (For more on the technological complexities involved in creating the fully autonomous vehicle—and most importantly, making them safe—see **"Autonomous Car Designers and Technologists Face Monumental Challenges in Making Them Safe for Consumers."**)

In the end, finding no defect or fault with the Tesla Autopilot or the vehicle itself, however obliquely, NHTSA in effect seems to lay the bulk of the blame for the deadly crash on Brown himself. Much like the black box recorders in commercial airplanes, investigators were able to determine from the Autopilot computer that Brown set his car's cruise control at 74 mph about two minutes before the crash, that he likely took his hands off the wheel (as he had also characteristically done in his posted videos), and that he should have had at least seven seconds to react to the truck crossing the road before crashing into it. From the fact that Brown did not apply the brakes, effectively overriding the Autopilot, NHTSA reasonably concluded that Brown was not paying attention to the road in front of him. In other words, it is not an exaggeration to say that he placed his life and personal safety completely under the control of his car's as yet imperfect Autopilot system, and paid the price for his overzealous faith in the technology. As noted earlier, Joshua Brown knew the risk he was taking. But what about the average consumer-car buyer who purchases a semi-autonomous vehicle based on the promise or the advertising by the manufacturer that it will be safer for his or her family?

JUST HOW SAFE ARE AUTONOMOUS VEHICLES?

It seems that the fundamental difficulty in trying to answer this crucial question is that presently we are essentially chasing after a moving target. Right now, there is no such thing as a fully autonomous car or truck that can exclusively drive itself safely. In the words of Michelle Krebs, a senior analyst at Autotrader.com, "No car buyer should think there are fully auto-mated vehicles on the market." What *are* increasingly on the market today are vehicles with specific autonomous features primarily for specific, lim-ited driving operations like parallel parking, highway lane maintenance, and emergency braking. More and more autonomous features will be rolled out over time. For just one example, both General Motors and Audi are presently working on systems that will monitor the driver's eyes to determine if he or she is paying attention to the road.

Proponents of the autonomous vehicle acknowledge that it is going to take many years of technological innovation and development before the first fully autonomous cars roll out onto America's highways, byways, and metropolises. Yet, most see that development as inevitable. Shelly Palmer of the Palmer Group even envisions a day when we "are going to need a special permit to manually drive a car and [we] will not be allowed to man-ually drive on certain streets and highway lanes because [it] will pose too great of a threat to the caravans of autonomous vehicles on those roads."

However, until that happens, it would appear that American consum-ers will face a protracted period of time during which the line of demarca-tion simply will not be sharply defined between the areas of responsibility that self-driving cars can safely handle by themselves versus those that the human driver must still operate manually. Not only that, but those responsibilities are likely to vary from one brand to another and may even vary among different models produced by the same car maker. And that is bound to lead to a lot of confusion among consumers, especially those who own cars built by different manufacturers.

And no one is denying that drivers will continue to be obliged to closely monitor *all* of the vehicle's functions, both those still manually operated *and* those ostensibly under the control of autonomous systems that are not yet fully realized or precisely differentiated. To reiterate the warning from NHTSA spokesman Bryan Thomas: "Autopilot requires full driver engagement at all times."

A major component of my concerns as a warnings consultant assessing risk for organizations and individuals is potential liability: failure to warn leads to costly negligence lawsuits and often even costlier out-of-court settlements, or perhaps jury awards, should a particular case actually go to court, as it did for Stella Liebeck, for example.

As tragic as Joshua Brown's fatal crash was, he was fortunate that he did not kill or seriously injure anyone else. But let's suppose for a moment that he had; that in colliding with another vehicle, he severely injured the other vehicle's driver, turning him into a quadriplegic we'll call Luckless Dan. Facing enormous medical bills for lifesaving emergency treatment and a lifetime of costly round-the-clock nursing care, we would fully expect Luckless Dan to hire a sharp attorney to sue Brown (or his estate) bigtime for damages. There are just so many questions that would come into play, but here, for example, are just a few of them:

Would Brown's defense be to blame Tesla for the accident, and turn around to sue the car company? We have already seen that NHTSA ruled that, not only was the car and its computerized Autopilot system not defective, the agency acknowledged that everything performed precisely as it was "designed and intended to."

Would Brown be held liable for not properly monitoring the Autopilot system while it was controlling the vehicle? That determination might hinge on whatever warnings, if any, Tesla may have provided about hidden hazards in the system, such as performance limitations or driving functions the company knew the system did not handle well.

But with that idea in mind, might Luckless Dan succeed in court by suing Tesla for failure to warn Brown about the limitations of Autopilot? In fact, would Brown's estate succeed in blaming Brown's death on Tesla for failure to warn?

Even in the absence of providing any warnings, would Tesla claim that Brown should have known that he needed to be actively monitoring the Autopilot at all times? In Brown's case, given his well-documented intimate knowledge of the autonomous system and its significant limitations, as well as his professed test-pilot mentality, such a claim might hold up in court. But what about the average car buyer who assumes—not unreasonably, especially if not informed otherwise—that when the Autopilot is on, it will stop the car rather than kill him by crashing into such an obvious obstacle as a huge tractor trailer crossing the road ahead?

AUTONOMOUS CAR DESIGNERS AND TECHNOLOGISTS FACE MONUMENTAL CHALLENGES IN MAKING THEM SAFE FOR CONSUMERS

We have already seen hand-held GPS mapping programs send unwitting motorists onto active railroad tracks that the systems apparently identified as roads, or onto nonexistent bridges over *very existent* waterways resulting in cars ending up in the drink, both scenarios to the immediate peril of their occupants. In the future, when GPS mapping is programmed into the vehicles themselves, will such systems be able to keep up-to-the-minute with respect to road closures or detours as a result of road construction and repair—especially spur of the moment, emergency repairs?

The media attention paid to Brown's fatal crash served to highlight the fact that current semi-autonomous vehicles employ a mix of old and new technologies, which, in turn, raises concerns about how compatible they may be. Incredible as it may seem, presently Tesla's Autopilot stays within highway lanes by tracking the dashed white lines painted on interstates and other multilane roads. Does that sound just a little too simplistic and vulnerable to you? What happens when it snows? What happens when, inevitably, heavy traffic causes the dashed white lines to become so worn off the road surface you can hardly see them—a common phenomenon on the East Coast that is only exacerbated by bad winter weather, heavy snow plows, and salt spreaders sometimes equipped with tire chains?

While the logical and admittedly obvious response to these questions might be that when you see the flakes start to fly or find yourself on a badly worn and potholed stretch of macadam, it's time to turn off the auto-control and take back the manual operation of the car. However, such weather and road condition-based variables further serve to highlight the substantially blurry line at the nexus of questionably reliable autonomous driving functions versus traditional, human-enacted manual ones.

They also indicate that fully autonomous tech is going to need to become much, much more sophisticated than being guided by lines painted manually on the highway! But the need for human, or human-like judgment doesn't end there, because in the typical driving environment, there are multiple situations or cues the average driver must attend to, and that a truly autonomous car will need to be able to react to safely as well.

WHITHER PRINCIPLED DISCLOSURE?

Earlier in Chapter 3 on playing, and specifically in connection with swimming pools owned and maintained by consumer-homeowners, I made the point that the boundary lines of responsibility for communicating warnings about hidden hazards often become blurred at the interface among the three legs of the Safety Triad. In no instance is that truer than with the autonomous vehicle. Certainly, for the foreseeable future, manufacturers of autonomous cars will need to be extremely careful about accurately and proactively informing consumers (and regulatory agencies as well) about precisely what each new generation of the technology is capable of doing and what it is not.

They may need, for example, to warn about unobvious system limitations that may represent hidden hazards. Joshua Brown's Tesla Model S was quite capable of cruising down the highway at a 74-mph clip, but perhaps the hidden hazard in this case was that the car was not capable of "seeing" a huge white truck against a bright sky. Unfortunately, from CEO Elon Musk's own words, it appears that even Tesla engineers did not know or expect this significant and disturbing limitation. (What else can't Autopilot "see" or detect?) At the same time, car manufacturers will need to define very clearly the responsibilities that will still fall to the driver. Based on my experience working with large corporations of every industry stripe, this may very well involve a level of transparency of disclosure that is unprecedented in American business.

For their part, consumers will need to be more responsible and personally accountable for informing themselves in terms of understanding what autonomous functions their cars can handle completely unaided, as well as what driving-related operations still require their hands-on human involvement, judgment, and expertise. Here again, and complicating matters, these system-specific characteristics may vary from brand to brand and model to model within the same brand. With that in mind, it may well be advisable, at some point, for new car buyers (and including all family members who might actually drive the car) to be required by law to undergo a hands-on training tutorial administered by an expert (provided by the dealer or manufacturer) so that they fully understand the performance parameters of the vehicle they are buying even before they take possession of it. Moreover, consumers will also have to harbor no illusions about the fact that even the most sophisticated autonomous systems to-date must be actively monitored at all times by the driver, and part of that expert instruction would involve clearly and thoroughly explicating all driver responsibilities.

Finally, government regulators are almost certainly going to need to step up efforts to make sure car companies accurately represent what their products are able to do safely in their advertising, promotion, product warrantees, and instruction manuals—and that they adequately warn consumers about any hidden hazards that might exist in their autonomous or semi-autonomous vehicles. Regulators may also have to consider the creation of explicit, industry-wide performance standards for autonomous vehicles, perhaps even a multitiered structure as each new generation of these vehicles achieves a greater level of sophistication in their capability to self-drive unaided by the human driver or occupants. Will future high-end brands necessarily entail a greater number of integrated autonomous features? One can easily imagine that this could be a matter of serious concern. How is the consumer to choose in comparing available autonomous functions versus out-of-pocket cost for the vehicle model?

While acknowledging that "previous studies of automatic emergency braking, adaptive cruise control, self-parking, and lane-keeping systems have shown strong promise," the 2017 AAA study also warns that semi-autonomous systems have demonstrated "great variation in performance." Further revealing that such substantial variation is vexing and problematic to most consumers, the AAA survey found that "81 percent of Americans feel that all automated vehicle systems should work similarly and consistently, *regardless of vehicle manufacturer*" (emphasis mine). While this notion makes perfect sense, clearly, NHTSA and other regulatory agencies have their work cut out for themselves! The same goes for the national and international car companies who would have to closely cooperate in adopting equivalent performance standards for their different classes of vehicles. In posing rhetorically the question as to whether competing car manufacturers (as well as the software design firms working with them) will openly share new technological data and innovation, Shelly Palmer confidently says he believes they will "absolutely."

But I'm not so sure of that.

For example, what happens when a deer bolts into the road ahead as you're traveling at, say, 50 mph: does the autonomous car automatically brake hard to stop the vehicle? Okay, but what happens when a deer bolts into the road ahead as you're travelling 50 mph and there happens to be a tailgating 80,000-lb tractor trailer bearing down on your rear bumper? Now what?

WHAT ABOUT COMPUTER HACKING?

There isn't a reputable computer or software technology expert in the world who doesn't freely and openly acknowledge the undeniable fact that *every* computer system is hackable. How far will car manufacturers be willing—or be required by regulators if it comes to that—to go in hack-proofing their vehicles as much as humanly and/or technologically possible? More practically, given that preventing hacking entirely is impossible, what sorts of explicit warnings should manufacturers provide to consumers about the potential that their vehicles may be susceptible to the hidden hazard of hacking? Or will hacking be regarded by the courts as criminal activity for which the car manufacturers cannot be held liable? And would such judgment by the courts demotivate manufacturers' efforts to prevent criminal hacking?

WHAT ABOUT COMPUTER HACKING, NOT BY CRIMINALS, BUT BY THE CAR MANUFACTURERS THEMSELVES?

Does that sound like a far-fetched, even ridiculous idea? Don't forget that Volkswagen conspired right from the executive suite to defraud EPA emissions tests. Now suppose that, all of a sudden, a popular, top-selling autonomous vehicle model becomes the focus of a spate of consumer lawsuits alleging a faulty self-driving feature, as yet unidentified, but nevertheless suspected of being responsible for a series of crashes resulting in serious injuries? Knowing that manufacturers are able to wirelessly make program changes without car owners knowing anything about it, what's to stop programmers from remotely going in secretly and fixing that self-driving glitch so that their team of defense attorneys can stand up in court and say that the glitch never existed at all, and demand that plaintiffs, "show us the proof"?

If you don't think that this hypothetical scenario—as distressing as the thought may be—is a distinct and very real possibility, then you haven't been paying attention!

CHAPTER 7

HEALING: PATIENT, HEAL THYSELF!

Lone Starr: *Listen! We're not just doing this for money.*
Barf: *We're not?*
Lone Starr: *No! We're doing it for a SHIT LOAD of money!*
—Spaceballs[87]

The pharmaceuticals industry in the United States is a $457 billion enterprise that now spends $6.4 billion on annual advertising, a figure that has jumped more than 60 percent over just the past four years. In fact, nine out of ten of the biggest drug companies spend more money on advertising than they invest in research and development. And Big Pharma spends another $24 billion marketing its products to doctors across the country. The median salary of $14.5 million among pharmaceutical company CEOs in 2015 was by far the highest of any industry, and that doesn't include performance bonuses and stock options.

These staggering numbers are clearly indicative of a highly lucrative industry, despite the hand-wringing lamentations of corporate executives and especially the industry trade group, the Pharmaceutical Research and Manufacturers of America (PhRMA), who complain about the high cost of bringing a new drug through required clinical trials and "excessive" regulatory scrutiny to market. And where there is a staggering amount of money at stake, you can bet that a great deal of effort is being made to

---

[87] Brooks, *Spaceballs.*

make even more of it. And by far, the most disturbing development in Big Pharma's effort to increase profits involves the unbridled astronomical growth of direct-to-consumer (DTC) advertising through slick television, magazine, and social media ads targeting the general public. Industry spending on DTC advertising over the past four years has dramatically increased by nearly a billion dollars a year, a breathtaking pace that shows no indications of slowing down (*See Figure 7.1*, which notably includes the preponderant television and magazine advertising, but *does not* include internet advertising).

FIGURE 7.1

SPENDING ON PRESCRIPTION DRUG ADVERTISING BY SOURCE. DIGITAL OUTLETS NOT INCLUDED

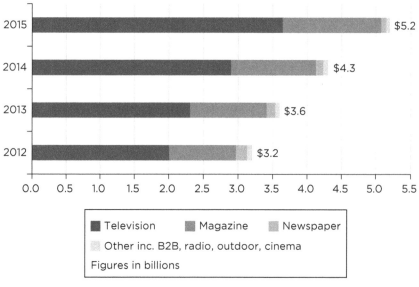

Source: Nielsen/STAT.

According to the website statnews.com, "Nine prescription drugs are on pace to break $100 million worth of television ad time this year."[88]

---

[88] Robbins, "Drug makers."

The graph in Figure 7.2 reveals the staggering amount of advertising dollars that Big Pharma is currently spending on their most popular drugs.

FIGURE 7.2

THE 20 MOST-ADVERTISED RX DRUGS IN 2015, BY SPENDING

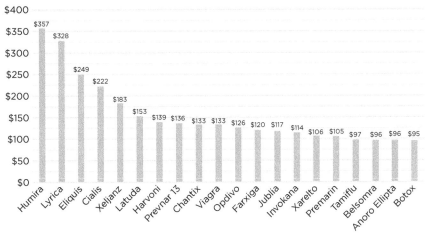

Source: Kantar Media. Figures in millions.

THE EROSION OF THE LEARNED INTERMEDIARY DOCTRINE: WHAT YOU THINK YOU KNOW CAN HURT YOU!

To understand the reasons—and there are many—why DTC advertising of prescription pharmaceuticals is so deeply troubling, particularly as it relates to principled disclosure through the appropriate and effective communication of safety warnings, it is first necessary to understand what is known in the law as the Learned Intermediary Doctrine. Simply put, this doctrine makes a crucial exception for prescription drug manufacturers to the general rule that manufacturers have a duty to directly and explicitly warn end-users about the potential risks of using their products. The theory underlying the doctrine is simple and, historically at least, foundationally sound. Since patients may obtain prescription drugs only from their doctors, the learned intermediary rule shields drug manufacturers from product liability as long as they have provided adequate warnings to prescribing physicians. Meaning they do not have to warn the patients directly or, for that matter, consumers at large.

The assumption that doctors are in the best position to assess the risks versus benefits of specific prescription medications for their patients based on intimate knowledge of their medical histories was perhaps best summed up by the Fifth Circuit Court in a decision in 1974:

> *As a medical expert, the prescribing physician can take into account the propensities of the drug, as well as the suscepti-bilities of his patient. His is the task of weighing the benefits of any medication against its potential dangers. The choice he makes is an informed one, an individual medical judgment bottomed on a knowledge of both patient and palliative.*[89]

So far, so good. One would think, intuitively, that most reasonable people would want their physicians to take full responsibility for their safety in choosing both the type and dosage of prescription medications that, as patients, they may be required to take to treat their various ailments.

University of Pittsburgh Professor Julie Donohue notes that, prior to the earliest beginnings of federal regulation of the pharmaceuticals industry in the Progressive Era of the early 1900s, American consumers were largely left to self-medicate, having to choose their remedies from among potions ranging from legitimate, medically proven preparations to the long list of "miracle cures" peddled by snake oil salesmen.[90] The former included standard drugs like digitalis, morphine, quinine, and aspirin that were universally recognized by the American Medical Association and listed in the United States Pharmacopoeia (USP). The USP is a compendium of standard drugs first established by 11 leading American physicians who met in Washington, D.C., in 1820. The latter included what generally

---

[89] Reyes *v.* Wyeth Labs.
[90] Donohue, "Drug Advertising."

were called "patent" medicines with carnival side-show names like Lydia Pinkham's Vegetable Compound, Hamlin's Wizard Oil, Warner's Safe Cure for Diabetes—and my personal favorite—Kick-a-poo Indian Sagwa. According to Donohue, "the main ingredient of many of these tonics, salves, and bitters was water, plus ... addictive substances such as alcohol or opium." But the truth of the matter, as far as consumers were concerned, was that nobody really knew what the hell was in these products.

As for the advertising by the drug manufacturers of the day, Donohue writes that while many of their advertising messages "invoked positive images of doctors and the promise of new medical science, most pharmaceutical advertising still emphasized self-treatment." In fact, the author points out that the objective of the 1906 Pure Food and Drug Act, one of the earliest pieces of legislation to advance federal drug regulation, was "not to discourage self-medication, as organized medicine wished to do (specifically, the American Medical Association (AMA), founded in 1847 but newly incorporated in 1897), but to give consumers more information so that they could identify effective medicines."

Interestingly, the 1906 Act specifically prohibited false or misleading statements *only* about the *ingredients* or the identity of a drug: It did not in any way prohibit false or wildly exaggerated advertising or on-the-label claims about the therapeutic effectiveness—or the safety—of those drugs. Paul Wax, a medical toxicologist at the University of Texas Southwestern Medical Center, observes that the 1906 legislation was weak at best: "There had to be some truth to what [drug companies] were selling ... but in terms of safety, let alone efficacy, that wasn't part of the equation."

That all changed in the fall of 1937 after more than 100 people, including 34 children, died after taking a concoction called Elixir Sulfanilamide to treat an eye-blinking panorama of ailments ranging from gonorrhea to sore throat. The product was manufactured and distributed by S.E. Massengill Company of Bristol, Tennessee, and was the first—and presumably last—liquid formulation of sulfanilamide drugs that had previously been manufactured by several pharmaceutical companies including Merck, Squibb, and Eli Lilly.

Under the 1906 Act, however, Massengill hadn't done anything terribly wrong. Toxicology analyses of the first six patients in Tulsa, Oklahoma, who died of renal failure after taking the Elixir revealed the ingredients in the bottles to be exactly what the company said they were right on the label. There was one minor infraction: Massengill had actually broken the law only in calling their drug an "elixir," which, at the time, was a designation reserved for preparations containing ethanol. While not empowered to reprimand Massengill for this impending catastrophe, the fledgling FDA (launched in 1906 as the Bureau of Chemistry) was able to take advantage of this minor technicality to aggressively track down and seize bottles of Elixir Sulfanilamide across the country, a bold move that some experts credit for saving as many as 4,000 lives.

In any event, Donohue explains that writing was already on the wall for self-medication by American consumers. "By the 1930s," she writes, "federal drug regulators had abandoned the belief that consumers, armed solely with information about a drug's ingredients, could safely self-medicate. Throughout the decade, FDA officials, supported by New Deal activists including newly founded consumer groups (e.g., the National Consumers League), tried to expand federal authority over drugs."[91] However, it was the intense public outcry over the Elixir Sulfanilamide scandal that pushed this reformist effort over the top, forcing Congress the very next year to pass the 1938 Food, Drug, and Cosmetic Act (FDCA). Passage of this Act marked the first time in U.S. history that drugs had to be proven safe and to receive the FDA's approval before they could be marketed.

Also an expert in the Elixir Sulfanilamide tragedy, toxicologist Paul Wax laments, "Unfortunately, it took a disaster … to get the senators to vote and empower the FDA like it should have been empowered to begin with." Yet, remarkably, it would take Congress another 25 years—and another infamous drug-related disaster—to get around to requiring pharmaceutical companies to provide clinical *scientific evidence of the efficacy of their drugs*—in addition to product safety—in order to gain FDA

---

[91] Ibid.

approval to market and distribute them to American consumers. This time, the disaster was the outbreak of morose deformities among thalidomide babies throughout Europe, which hastened the calamity-driven response in Congress resulting in the swift passage of the Kefauver Harris Drug Amendments in October 1962.

The history of federal legislation and FDA regulation over the pharmaceuticals industry becomes rather complicated over the latter half of the 20th century, but initially, in the decades after World War II, the model of pharmacological treatment under the direction and guidance of physicians took precedence over self-medication. Yet, the ways that the FDA would regulate drugs would, in turn, directly affect how those drugs were advertised by the manufacturers, as well as to whom they were marketed. In 1951, for example, Congress passed the Durham-Humphrey Amendments to the FDCA, which created a statutory definition of prescription drugs to include those that "because of [their] toxicity or other potentiality for harmful effect, or the method of [their] use, or the collateral measures necessary to [their] use, [they are] not safe for use except under the supervision of a practitioner licensed by law to administer such drug[s]."[92]

Before the Durham-Humphrey Amendments, it was left up to the manufacturers to decide whether a drug should be categorized as prescription only or could be sold over the counter. However, Donohue explains that FDA officials came to view some drugs "as potentially so dangerous that no amount of information provided to consumers would make self-medication safe." Indicating how thoroughly the physician-prescribed model took hold, by 1969 prescription drugs made up 83 percent of spending on pharmaceuticals by American consumers.[93]

Of course, like any savvy for-profit industry, Big Pharma understood the necessity to follow the money. Once it became clear that only doctors could write prescriptions, the pharmaceutical companies virtually ceased trying to directly target consumers and instead focused all of their

---

[92] 65 Stat. 648

[93] Donohue, "Drug Advertising."

advertising and marketing efforts on doctors and other health care professionals. Accordingly, throughout the 1960s, more that 90 percent of Big Pharma's spending on marketing was aimed at doctors (with the rest targeting pharmacists and hospitals), completely reversing the pattern that existed only 30 years earlier. In other words, the Learned Intermediary Doctrine was in full force, and business for Big Pharma was very good and rapidly getting enormously better and bigger. In fact, from 1939 after the passage of the FDCA to 1959, drug sales rose from $300 million to $2.3 billion, with prescription drugs accounting for over 98 percent of the increase!

So how did we get from there to where we are today?

In 1969, the FDA promulgated its final, ostensibly definitive advertising regulations, which required advertisements to present a "true statement of information in brief summary relating to side effects, contraindications, and effectiveness."[94] The new regulations also stipulated that pharmaceutical advertising must present a "fair balance" between information about the drug's side effects and contraindications as well as information about its effectiveness. The FDA also endeavored to define precisely how an advertisement could be considered false, unbalanced, or otherwise misleading.

Born out of an era in which increasing control of medical practice—as well as sole authority over the prescription of drugs on behalf of patients—was aggressively being turned over to physicians, the FDA's 1969 regulations did not directly tackle the issue of prescription drug advertisements to the general public. However, they contained two controversial provisions that would unwittingly set the table for profound and sweeping regulatory changes to allow DTC pharmaceutical advertising nearly three decades later, as we will shortly discuss.

The first provision stated that drug ads broadcast over television and radio media:

> *shall include information relating to the major side effects and contraindications of the advertised drugs in the audio or audio*

---

[94] Ibid.

and visual parts of the presentation, and unless **adequate provision** *is made for dissemination of the approved or permitted package labeling in connection with the broadcast presentation, shall contain a brief summary of all necessary information related to side effects and contraindications.*[95]
(emphasis mine)

The problem with the wording of this guideline is obvious, if only in hindsight: What exactly is the meaning of "adequate provision" in this context, and exactly what specific means of "dissemination" of required package labeling information would meet FDA requirements for full disclosure? The definition of this terminology would remain unclear, and the answers to those questions a matter of intense debate and controversy, until 1997 when the FDA at last clarified the ways that pharmaceutical advertisements could meet regulatory requirements, and, in the process, effectively opened the floodgates to broadcast DTC.

The other questionable provision was that some specific types of drug advertisements were exempted from the regulatory requirements. This exemption was primarily aimed at what were called "reminder advertisements" intended by Big Pharma to run in professional medical journals, and which contained only the name of the drug, but making "no [stated] claims for the therapeutic safety or effectiveness of the drug."[96] I probably don't need to tell you that these were called "reminder advertisements" because the drug companies were simply trying to "remind" your doctor to be sure to prescribe their products to you as a patient. Yet, the FDA went even further by exempting *any* advertisements from the regulations, including broadcast DTC, as long as the proprietary name of the drug itself was not directly stated or given.

By the early 1990s, the pharmaceutical manufacturers would seize, in wholesale fashion, the opportunity to capitalize on this gaping loophole

[95] Ibid.
[96] Ibid.

to run both reminder and help-seeking advertisements that mentioned, alternatively, either a specific disease or ailment or the name of the prescription drug designed to treat it, but never both in the same ad, thus skirting the FDA restrictions. (See **The Birth of DTC Prescription Pharmaceutical Advertising** for an intriguing tale of what many industry observers regard as possibly the birth of modern broadcast DTC pharmaceutical advertising.)

THE BIRTH OF DTC PRESCRIPTION PHARMACEUTICAL ADVERTISING

Incredibly, the DTC advertising technique that would become the overwhelmingly successful model utilized by Big Parma to take advantage of this loophole, thus circumventing informed disclosure requirements, was not developed by executives in the corporate boardroom or devoted pharmacological chemistry scientists in the lab. Nor was it the brainchild of some gifted creative advertising industry genius in a tower office on Madison Avenue. Rather, the ultimately lucrative scheme was hatched by a package goods salesman by the name of Joe Davis. Interviewed some years later, Davis reflected on the underlying social context of the mid-1980s, which had enabled his pioneering (if somewhat dubious) marketing breakthrough: "Nobody had ever thought that these drugs should be or could be advertised to the patients. It was just outside of people's brain [...] They thought that only doctors could understand the products. They're technical products. They're scientific products. But that's not what I thought."

Davis enlisted the help of William Castagnoli, then an executive at the medical advertising agency Medicus. With Castagnoli's help, Davis devised a way to recommend drugs in both print and broadcast advertising that exclusively extoled the positive effects of a hypothetical drug with the exact attributes of a specific pharmaceutical, but without naming the drug specifically. Omitting the name was the key to sliding the ads through the FDA loophole, and Davis' and Castagnoli's commercials all ended with instructions for interested consumers to see their doctors for more information.

The very first unnamed drug marketed in this fashion was Seldane, which the commercials described as an "antihistamine that did not cause drowsiness." As if all went according to Davis' plan, when patients asked their doctors for the exact type of drug described in the ads, sure enough, they were prescribed Seldane. The results were phenomenal. Seldane sales skyrocketed from $34 million in 1985 to $800 million annually only a few years later.

An ironic postscript to the groundbreaking story of Seldane is that the drug was eventually removed from the U.S. market when it was found that it could cause serious heart arrhythmias. That happened in 1997, the same year that the FDA's current regulations essentially released the hounds of Direct-To-Consumer broadcast pharmaceuticals advertising that we see ad nauseam today.

All of this was only the beginning, however, and a number of profound social, economic, and political forces through the 1970s to the 1990s would reshape the ways that prescription drugs were advertised and sold to patients and consumers. One such major factor was the consumer advocacy movement of the 1970s that, when it expanded into the arena of health care, demanded that drug manufacturers provide more information to consumers as a matter of patients' rights. Advocacy groups argued that patients were entitled to assume a greater role in their own health care and decision-making regarding treatment options. Historically, while patients previously had been seen as *buyers* of health care services, in the legal sense, they had not actually been viewed as *consumers*. Heretofore for instance, the "consumer" function of health care might have been limited to selecting one's health insurance plan. In essence, even as the Learned Intermediary Doctrine persisted (as it should), the notion that doctors acted as (knowledgeable) consumers on behalf of their (uninformed) patients was beginning to erode in significant ways.

In addition, the skyrocketing cost of health care and the rise of managed health care plans such as Health Management Organizations (HMOs) respectively raised the financial stakes of treatment decisions and involved other people or organizations in those decisions, namely the for-profit entities that would be paying the bill. The fact that these organizations increasingly came to be seen by the general public as making life-and-death decisions for their members solely on the basis of cost, without consideration of what would be best for the patient, only served to heighten the advocacy efforts of the patients' rights movement.

Finally, the conservative movement in Congress in the 1990s placed significant counter-regulatory pressures on the FDA on a number of fronts, including DTC advertising of pharmaceuticals. In 1994, Republican House Speaker Newt Gingrich called the FDA the "number 1 job killer in America," charging that its protracted drug approval process discouraged innovation and seriously delayed or even prevented profitable products from coming to market. Ironically, conservatives' criticism was echoed by a new breed of disease-specific consumer advocacy organizations, for example, a group that, at the time, was urging the FDA to accelerate significantly its approval process for drugs specifically designed to fight the raging HIV/AIDS epidemic. By the year 2000, there were more than 3,100 politically active, disease-specific advocacy groups putting pressure on both Congress and the FDA to force greater transparency on the pharmaceutical and health care industries, while at the same time championing patients' autonomy in medical decision-making.

The preceding presents only a brief overview of the forces that led the FDA to throw the doors open to DTC pharmaceutical advertising in August 1997, effectively clarifying, for better or worse, the meaning of the phrase "… *adequate provision* … for dissemination of the approved or permitted package labeling …" which had initiated such confusion in 1969. The agency's release of its "Draft Guidelines for Industry: Consumer-Directed Broadcast Advertisements," specifically enumerated the ways that pharmaceutical manufacturers could meet the brief summary requirement in broadcast ads by referring consumers to other sources such as:

- a toll-free telephone number,
- print ads (with more complete and definitive fine print),
- a website, and/or
- their pharmacists or physicians, from whom they could obtain complete information about the product's risks and benefits.

For a much more detailed and extremely fascinating account of the history of drug advertising, I recommend reading Julie Donohue's "A History of Drug Advertising: The Evolving Roles of Consumers and Consumer Protection" from *The Milbank Quarterly*.[97]

As we will see, particularly in the case of its massive and unrelenting television and internet media advertising assault, it is the last of these four general options that Big Pharma beats like a rented mule to exploit, or circumvent in my opinion, the Learned Intermediary Doctrine.

As a final historical note, today it remains a matter of debate whether these new guidelines were deliberately intended to loosen the 1969 (and subsequent) restrictions or simply to clarify existing rules; however, the undisputable consequence of this policy change was that it made DTC advertising—and particularly broadcast DTC—all the easier for Big Pharma. Within a year, television advertising by the pharmaceuticals industry more than doubled from $310 million to $664 million, and overall spending on DTC advertising rose from $1.3 billion in 1998 to $3.3 billion in 2005. As we saw earlier in Figure 7.1, Big Pharma spending on DTC continues to grow at a mind-boggling $1 billion a year.

BIG PHARMA CASHES IN

The bottom line is that, by all indications, Big Pharma's grand marketing and promotional scheme over the past several years has paid off enormously, providing the top companies with scandalous operating profit margins— led by Amgen at a whopping 42.6 percent—that far and away exceed the average of 10.4 percent for S&P 500 companies (*See Figure 7.3*). In fact, Big Pharma's margins literally dwarf those of huge and highly profitable multinational companies in other business sectors, for example General Motors (5.7%) and Exxon (3.7%).

---

[97] Ibid.

FIGURE 7.3

HOW PHARMACEUTICAL EARNINGS COMPARE

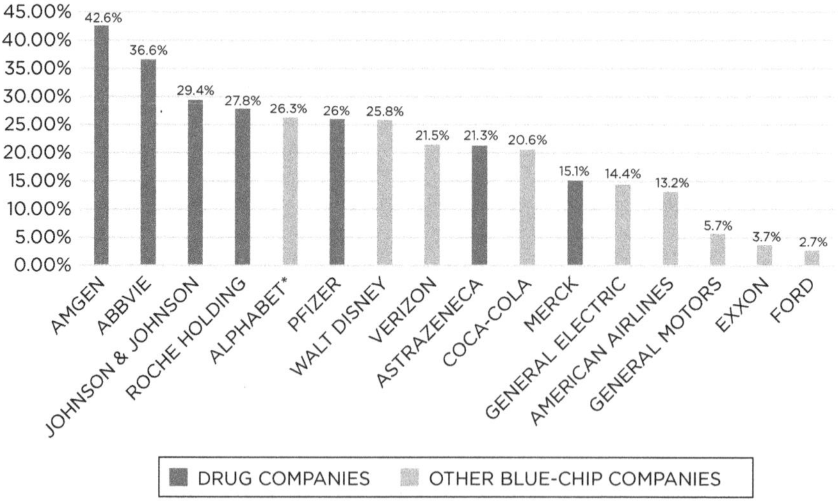

| DRUG COMPANIES | OTHER BLUE-CHIP COMPANIES |

This chart compares some prominent drug manufacturers' operating profit margins to other successful American companies. The average margin for S&P 500 companies that same year (2016) was 10.4 percent.
*PARENT COMPANY OF GOOGLE
SOURCE: MORNINGSTAR

Source: AARP, Inc., 2017.

It should come as no surprise that DTC advertising has proven to be enormously profitable for Big Pharma. It is estimated that every dollar spent on drug ads returns $4 in retail sales. If you do the math, that means the $6.4 billion the industry spent in 2016 brought in $25.6 billion in sales, not a bad ROI, especially if you consider that that figure represents only a scant dozen or so of the latest and most popular medications among a whopping total of 18,130 FDA-approved prescriptions (and counting!) available in the U.S. today. Industry critics have accused the industry of indiscriminately raising prices on their most popular drugs to the point of price gouging, in part to pay for their aggressive DTC marketing, but ultimately to increase profits exponentially out of sheer heartless greed.

AARP, Inc. estimates that drug prices in the U.S. rose a staggering 208 percent from 2008 to 2016 and underscores that the increases are by no means limited to the newest or most technologically advanced drugs that have come onto the market over recent years. The organization points for examples to two critical lifesaving medications, noting that between 2003 and 2013, the cost of insulin tripled "despite no notable changes in the formulation or manufacturing process," and that the four-decade-old EpiPen has seen a price hike of 500 percent since 2007.[98] According to CBS News Moneywatch, U.S. drug manufacturers raised prices across the board in January 2016, "boosting some list prices by as much as 42.3 percent."[99]

Predictably, the pharmaceuticals industry blames excessively high prices for drugs and the recent need for substantial increases on the high cost of research and development that accompanies the arduous gauntlet of the FDA's approval process in bringing a new drug to market. The industry cites a 2016 study published in the *Journal of Health Economics* claiming that it can take as long as ten years and as much as $2.3 billion to bring a single new drug to market.[100] However, many industry experts and consumer watchdog organizations dispute those numbers, arguing that they wildly overstate the actual costs. By the way, the *Journal* article in question was based on research conducted at the Tufts Center for the Study of Drug Development. The Tufts Center for the Study of Drug Development gets a significant portion of its operating funds from the pharmaceutical industry.

Where have we heard this before?

Of course, if you still want to believe Big Pharma's claims about the formidable costs of R&D, I suggest you take another look at those operating profit margins in Figure 7.3. One imagines, at the very least, that major shareholders don't find them terribly excessive. What's not to love? And remember that earlier in this chapter, I noted that nine of the top ten Big Pharma companies spend more money on marketing and promotion than they do on R&D. Let me add that at last count, and

---

[98] AARP, "Drugs."
[99] Picchi, "Drug ads."
[100] Wilson, "New technologies."

according to the Center for Responsive Politics, in 2019, the number of paid professional pharmaceutical industry lobbyists working the halls of Congress in Washington, D.C., was 1,265, up from a total of 804 only two years earlier in 2016![101] That's nearly three lobbyists for every member of Congress.

Certainly, all of this represents an alarming cause for concern for consumers and especially for the ability of average Americans simply and basically to afford the prescription drugs they need to stay in good health. While clearly the economic impact of these outrageously escalating costs for essential medications has become a national crisis all of its own, my central focus remains on the issue of whether drug manufacturers are providing adequate warnings about the hazards that may be hidden in their vast array of products. However, in the case of strictly physician-prescribed pharmaceuticals, the issue becomes a lot trickier because of the Learned Intermediary Doctrine, and the traditional notion that doctors are principally responsible for warning their patients about the hidden hazards of certain drug formulations or medical remedies. However, with DTC advertising designed specifically to influence consumer-patients who are, by no means, medical professionals, where does the warnings responsibility of drug manufacturers' end, and the responsibility of attending physicians kick in?

BURYING THE WARNINGS MESSAGE, PLACATING THE LEARNED INTERMEDIARY DOCTRINE

In the case of prescription medications, such hidden hazards might generally take the form of unintended side effects that could have significantly detrimental or dangerous health consequences, and can even cause death. Perhaps the most serious hazard of all is the insidious and highly addictive nature of some very powerful drugs like painkillers and psychotropic medications, as the current festering opioid epidemic across

---

[101] OpenSecrets.org, "Profile."

our country today clearly and tragically demonstrates. And let me be clear: the addictive properties of opioids qualify, in no uncertain terms, as hidden hazards. While consumers might be vaguely aware of the basic fact that opioids tend to be addictive, they generally do not know which specific prescription drugs are so, nor do they know how incredibly powerful the addictive properties might be for specific medications they might be considering, or that their doctors may prescribe for them. In fact, a rational argument can be made that many doctors do not fully understand the sheer addictive power of these drugs, which some critics have referred to as legalized heroin.

So the two-fold question becomes first, how well do Big Pharma's *Direct-to-Consumer* broadcast drug commercials warn consumer-patients about the hidden hazards in their products, and second, do those drug commercials acknowledge (and perhaps more crucially, do they *affirm*) the fundamental propriety of the Learned Intermediary Doctrine—especially in an electronic-age environment in which consumers are increasingly able to direct their own care as well as obtain potent medications through means other than their attending physicians, such as the internet and less formal managed health care organizations?

Anyone who has looked at their television monitor or smartphone screen in the last 15 minutes knows intimately, indelibly, and excruciatingly how the paradigm drug commercial goes. You can't miss them: Kantar Media recently reported that in 2016, the last full year for which data is available, 771,368 drug commercials were broadcast on television; that's an average of 88 commercials every hour of every day.[102] But have you ever thought about the deliberate underlying formula that they use to hook consumers? Let's begin our analysis by examining Figure 7.4. Essentially, the drug manufacturers employ a two-pronged strategy that is designed to deflate, deflect, or counteract both of the questions I raised earlier.

---

[102] Kaufman, "Drug Ads."

FIGURE 7.4

HOW DRUG ADS WORK

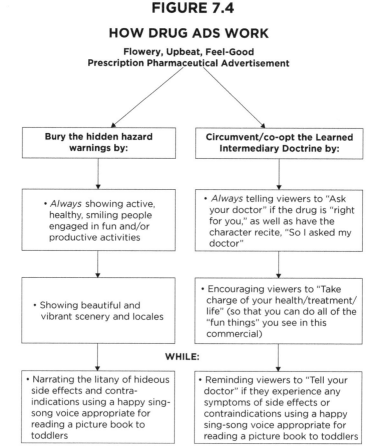

**Flowery, Upbeat, Feel-Good
Prescription Pharmaceutical Advertisement**

Bury the hidden hazard warnings by:	Circumvent/co-opt the Learned Intermediary Doctrine by:
• *Always* showing active, healthy, smiling people engaged in fun and/or productive activities	• *Always* telling viewers to "Ask your doctor" if the drug is "right for you," as well as have the character recite, "So I asked my doctor"
• Showing beautiful and vibrant scenery and locales	• Encouraging viewers to "Take charge of your health/treatment/ life" (so that you can do all of the "fun things" you see in this commercial)

WHILE:

• Narrating the litany of hideous side effects and contra-indications using a happy sing-song voice appropriate for reading a picture book to toddlers	• Reminding viewers to "Tell your doctor" if they experience any symptoms of side effects or contraindications using a happy sing-song voice appropriate for reading a picture book to toddlers

Created by Art Lizza

Visually, the commercials show smiling, happy, and attractive people doing fairly strenuous things like hiking through the woods, swimming in (or diving into—yikes!) an Olympic-sized swimming pool, or biking (properly helmeted of course) down winding country roads or urban streets. They show people restoring old houses, playing violins at a concert, or fishing from a boat floating serenely on a pristine lake. They show people relaxing at the beach, picnicking at the lake, tossing the Frisbee with their kids, walking multiple dogs at the park, or barbequing in the back yard—that's a really popular one. Some of them even show people engaged in relatively dangerous activities like zip-lining, rock-climbing, or downhill skiing.

These, presumably, are all people enthusiastically living utterly happy, abundantly healthy, and prosperous lives thanks to taking the remarkable, life-enhancing drug being promoted in the particular broadcast ad.

Against these sometimes breathtaking, sometimes spiritually halcyon visuals, however, the narrator recites a seemingly endless horror show of eye-blinking, downright terrifying unintended side effects and contrain-dications that *may occur* in someone taking the drug, potentially leading to serious and life-threatening complications and even death. Before we go any further, it is important to note that the carefully (and deliberately) chosen wording is quite crucial here. The announcer specifically states that such complications among users of the drug, "have happened," or "have occurred," but never, never states the obvious: that those complications may have been, or indeed were, "caused" by the drug. That's a little like saying some fatalities "have happened" to people who lingered on railroad tracks too long as the train was coming.

But the broader idea here is to bury this litany of very real, very sober-ing warnings about the often very significant hidden hazards of these sophisticated drugs against a picture-postcard panorama of otherwise afflicted men and women abundantly living life to the fullest without the slightest care or worry about their various chronic illnesses or physiological conditions. It goes without saying that we are a very visually oriented soci-ety, and researchers who study communication science generally agree that pictures speak louder than words. The hope of the drug advertisers is that consumers will, in effect, barely hear the warnings while being enthralled and mesmerized by the very humanly and environmentally attractive visual images on their screens.

But observe what happens when some viewers of these commercials inevitably *do* hear the cautionary warning words. A typical reaction even from the viewer who might be shocked by these warnings revelations is to laugh nervously and then say in effect, "Boy, with all of those crazy side effects, I'd never take that drug in the first place!" Pretty soon everyone in the room is laughing about it; the warnings come to be seen as so outrageous that they become something of a running joke. Like: "You can't be serious." And that's just what the drug manufacturers want. They want you not to take the warnings seriously. The goal is to bury in plain sight the very significant, red-flag warnings that should give pause to anyone who is seriously thinking of taking these powerful medications. And as direct consequence, American consumers are seeking out these medications in droves, despite the risks.

INTO MR. PEABODY'S WAY-BACK MACHINE: IS SELF-MEDICATION MAKING A COMEBACK?

The available data bears out this phenomenon. In recent years, DTC drug advertising has raised the prescription rate for the advertised drugs by 30 percent, an ominous indication of how aggressively consumers are seeking them. A May 2011 study found that DTC advertised drugs are now prescribed nine times more than similar counterpart medications that are not intensively advertised directly to consumers.[103] Meanwhile, doctors across the country complain that patients are increasingly insisting on getting the brand name prescription medications they've seen on television even when other drugs or generics might be more effective, with fewer potential side effects, *AND* less expensive. In some cases, the desired medication may be completely unnecessary, but consumers become convinced they need, or would benefit from it, expressly because they saw it on television.

However, critics of the system charge that if doctors want to hang on to their patient-clients, and if giving a prescription for a drug that patients ask for (or more likely badger them for) keeps them happy, they're probably going to write that prescription. Peripherally, while consumer advocacy, informed consent, and the general idea that patients have a right to participate in their own course of medical care and treatment are all good things

---

[103] Lo, "Ethics."

within reasonable limits, there are significant aspects of these sophisticated drugs that nonmedically trained consumer-patients simply do not know or understand. Yet, doctors may feel significant pressure to yield power just to keep their patients happy, despite the potential risks.

That brings us to the second prong of Big Pharma's DTC advertising strategy, which is nothing short of hijacking the venerable Learned Intermediary Doctrine and effectively co-opting it to support, not the health and welfare of you as the patient, but instead, the industry goal of getting you to buy their celebrated prescription drugs from your doctor. Here again, it is critical to understand the precise wording that, in reality, is intended to shield Big Pharma legally from liability while seductively playing into that whole feel-goody, advocacy-driven "patient empowerment" perception that all self-respecting 21st-century consumers seem to feel they want so badly. And they do this by using a formula that takes full advantage of the largely impotent guidelines for broadcast DTC advertising issued by the FDA in 1997 that we examined earlier. It's a formula that ought to resonate immediately with anyone who has viewed even a mere handful of these commercials.

If you observe closely, you'll notice that the basic script of every single DTC drug commercial consists of a consistent, deliberate pattern of repeatedly encouraging, suggesting, or instructing viewer-consumers to "ask your doctor" about "whether [INSERT MIRACLE DRUG NAME HERE] is right for you." Often, the people in the commercials look at the camera pointedly and say something like, "At the hospital, they prescribed Brand X, but I asked my doctor if I could do better, and my doctor prescribed ..." BINGO! The drug being advertised! In some commercials, the person in the ad might say alternatively, "I needed to do something more to control my type 2 diabetes," or "My blood sugar numbers weren't where they should be," followed immediately by, "So I asked my doctor ..." As ought to be obvious, this technique serves very nicely to advance the consumer advocate's theme of patient as empowered director of their own health care treatment while still invoking appeal to the learned intermediary. Most importantly for the drug manufacturers, however, it expressly is not Big

Pharma telling you to take these drugs, but rather, it is you, ostensibly along with the sound advice of your attending physician, willfully and independently making the informed choice to take them.

One of the more curious phrases—and a telltale one in my view—is the admonition to "Be sure to tell your doctor about other medications you are taking." Even the casual viewer hearing this puzzling remark might be inclined to ask, "Shouldn't my doctor already know about the 'other' drugs I'm taking?"

Of course, he or she should, but that's not the point.

The point is that, once again, the commercial adeptly "positions" you to be taking charge of your care by appealing to your particular learned intermediary for advice; the language theoretically absolves the drug manufacturer if, for example, you happen to take incompatible drugs in combination or have a bad reaction to their drug—either with or without the advice of your physician—that leads to a catastrophic result. You've been duly informed and warned; now the onus is on you. The only positive thing we might be able to conclude about the multiply repeated proviso to "ask your doctor" is that it is probably more effective than the other options provided by the FDA's 1997 pronouncement.

That is to say, intuitively, it is probably more likely that consumer-patients will, in fact, consult their doctors versus calling an 800 number plastered on the screen or actually going out and buying the print literature containing a particular drug's full safety warnings text ("See our ad in the October issue of *Nirvana Thru Drugs Digest*"). And while drug websites certainly provide a medium in which large amounts of information and clinical data may be compiled and displayed, let's be perfectly clear: people are not going to be any better at reading "the fine print" disclaimers concerning prescription pharmaceutical warnings than they are at reading the service agreement contract terms that some website services require for membership.

Nevertheless, the dilution of the warnings messages—that whole sense of "you can't be serious" that I illuminated earlier—makes it all the more likely that patients will similarly minimize or even dismiss their own learned intermediaries. That is to say, consumer-patients who have already become de-sensitized to the severity of the otherwise hidden hazards of these drugs, essentially by commercials that effectively make a mockery of them, may be less inclined to take the advice of their own doctors when provided.

Meaning that, in reality, patients risk following somewhat subconsciously the not-so-subtle advice of DTC advertisements to take particular drugs even over the advice of their physicians either not to do so, or their professional recommendations to take something else that might be cheaper and more effective with fewer adverse potential side effects. To reinforce this subliminal message, all of the people in these commercials appear to be very self-confident and very strongly self-assured; they know what they want to do, and by gum, they are doing it, even if it's hang-gliding or bungee-jumping or taking a highly potent and powerful prescription drug.

The bottom line appears to be that we are hurtling back regressively to a time when consumer-patients were allowed to "choose their own poison." And this despite the fact that today's drugs are more sophisticated and complex, are more powerful than ever before, and also carry an ever-expanding landscape of serious side or interaction effects ranging from addiction to debilitating complications to … death!

Finally, as disturbing as this continuing backward trend certainly is, there are indications that it may get intolerably worse before it gets better. That's because in the last year or so, there have been subtle rumblings that Big Pharma is presently but quietly seeking FDA approval to expand its DTC advertising efforts to promote off-label uses of its premier drugs. "Off-label" refers to uses for which a drug wasn't originally intended, but may have tentatively been shown to have some (*unscientific*) positive effect, even though it may never have been fully tested for those alternative uses. (The drug Sildenafil, sold most famously as the brand name Viagra, as well as others, was originally designed to treat a variety of cardiovascular disorders; its other widely celebrated "potency" was only discovered when appreciative men started showing up at their doctors' offices eagerly asking for more.)

But DTC drug advertising for off-label uses would be nothing short of a colossal disaster. A joint study conducted by U.S. and Canadian researchers in 2014 found that patients using off-label drugs without strong scientific evidence of effectiveness were 54 percent more likely to suffer adverse side effects ranging from simple allergic reactions to much more serious gastrointestinal, cardiac, and respiratory complications.

Bob Ehrlich, the Chairman and CEO of DTC Perspectives, a direct-to-consumer industry services group, has vehemently denied that anyone in the pharmaceuticals industry or at the FDA "is seriously thinking of allowing drug companies to advertise off-label use to the public through DTC." Yet, in the same post published on his organization's website, Ehrlich openly contends that "courts have ruled drug companies can use commercial-free speech to discuss studies reflecting off-label uses," and insisted that "drug companies want the [First Amendment free speech] to tell the medical world about legitimate off-label studies." However, he stops short of indicating whether he believes Big Pharma has the equal First Amendment right to tell the general consumer-public about successful off-label studies. Some industry insiders have obliquely alluded to the notion that drug websites represent a promising vehicle for compiling large amounts of clinical trial results and other research data to "inform" consumer patients about the properties of specific drugs—both on- and off-label uses.[104]

My question for Mr. Ehrlich is: In reality, wasn't "loosening the regulations for discussions with doctors" with respect to drug on-label uses just one step in the sinister progressive march toward "loosening the discussion" about them with consumers through DTC drug advertising? It seems quite clear to me that occurred when loophole-seeking drug advertisers found a way to leverage "reminder ads" to directly target consumers and bypass the learned intermediary.

So, what has the FDA been doing or saying about all of this over the 20 years since releasing its guidelines for DTC broadcast ads in 1997? You

---

[104] Ehrlich, "Media."

might be surprised to learn that, despite the deceptive tactics I have illuminated here, the FDA must formally approve all DTC drug advertisements. In fact, Ehrlich loudly bemoans what he regards as unfair and excessive FDA interference in broadcast drug advertising, whining, for example, that the agency "goes nuts when the background music is too loud on DTC ads."[105] But the FDA's inaction is tied to a much more systemic problem that we explore next.

THE REVOLVING DOOR AT THE FDA

The historically incestuous relationship between the FDA and Big Pharma is so endemic that it is difficult to decide where to begin in talking about it. But we begin with one of the agency's typically flagrant heinous appointments, that of naming Scott Gottlieb as a deputy commissioner for medical and scientific affairs in 2005. At the time, Gottlieb's only qualification consisted of being a 33-year-old Wall Street insider with a reputation for recommending hot medical and pharmaceutical stocks. He found himself in hot water almost immediately. No sooner after arriving at his new position, Gottlieb was instrumental in rushing to the market Pfizer's new stop-smoking drug varenicline, marketed as Chantix. Chantix was linked to a series of suicides through 2006, and may have played a significant role in the violent and tragic death of Dallas musician Carter Albrecht.

By all accounts from his friends and associates, Albrecht was a gentle and peaceful man who, according to his girlfriend, had almost immediately begun to suffer severe hallucinations after taking Chantix for less than a week. On the night of September 3rd, 2007, the talented keyboardist for the band Edie Brickell and the New Bohemians flew into an uncharacteristic rage that his doctors and the medical examiner would later theorize may have been caused by a bad reaction to a combination of alcohol and Chantix. Albrecht first assaulted his girlfriend and when she locked him

---

[105] Ibid.

out of her house, he ran to a neighbor's home and began wildly kicking the front door and banging on it with his fists.

Fearing a burglar or worse, after yelling repeatedly for the man to leave, the neighbor fired a single shot through the front door. He deliberately fired high, hoping that a warning shot would be sufficient to scare off the would-be intruder. But Albrecht stood 6'5". The bullet struck him in the head, killing him instantly.

Next, when a series of clinical trials of a new multiple sclerosis drug had to be abruptly halted because three people suffered serious loss of blood platelets and one died, Gottlieb called the stoppage "an overreaction,"[106] further speculating that the disease, not the drug, might be to blame. Gottlieb's strong ties to Big Pharma were so blatantly obvious and well-known that he was forced to recuse himself in numerous instances. One of those instances concerned agency preparations for a possible bird flu epidemic, in which Gottlieb had to step aside because of his financial involvement with pharma companies Roche and Sanofi-Aventis. In other instances, Gottlieb had to bow out of important clinical research efforts related to Eli Lilly, Procter & Gamble, and five other drug companies. But one is only left to wonder with incredulity if Gottlieb was so regularly required to recuse himself from vitally important ongoing research studies during his tenure at the FDA—that his connections to the drug industry were the obvious elephant in the room during his confirmation hearings—why had the agency tapped an individual in the first place who would be precluded from performing critical aspects of the job?

However, this is nothing unusual. Clueless politicians charged with the profound and substantial responsibilities of nominating and confirming the best candidates to lead the federal government's key regulatory agencies— including Presidents Obama, Bush, and Clinton—have all sung the same logically flawed chorus, "Who better to oversee [INSERT INDUSTRY SECTOR HERE] than someone who intimately knows the industry from the inside?" The question might more accurately be rephrased as, "Who bet-

---

[106] Rosenberg, "Lilly."

ter to design toothless, smoke-and-mirror regulations that enable [INSERT INDUSTRY SECTOR HERE] to do whatever the hell they want than someone who already knows where all the loopholes are?"

And the beat goes on.

Enter Robert Califf, a cardiologist nominated to lead the FDA by President Obama in September 2015 and confirmed to the Commissioner's post by the full Senate less than six months later. Califf's credentials read like a Who's Who of Big Pharma and make Scott Gottlieb look like a contestant on the reality show *The Apprentice*. Califf's "vitae" at the time he assumed leadership at the FDA included:[107,108]

- 2009–2013: Paid consultant for Merck Sharp & Dohme, Johnson & Johnson, GlaxoSmithKline, AstraZeneca, and Eli Lilly. One such consulting payment alone, received in 2012 from Johnson & Johnson, amounted to $87,500 and included an unknown amount of funds for numerous individual trips and consulting engagements under $5,000;
- 2013–2014: Paid a total of $52,796, by a succession of Big Pharma companies including Merck Sharp & Dohme (which paid the highest amount at $6,450), Amgen, F. Hoffmann-La Roche AG, Janssen Pharmaceutica, Daiichi Sankyo, Sanofi-Aventis, Bristol-Myers Squibb, and AstraZeneca;
- Director of Portola Pharmaceuticals, Inc., from July 2012 to January 26, 2015;
- Advisor to Proventys, Inc.;
- Chairman of the medical advisory board of Regado Biosciences, Inc.;
- Member of the medical advisory board since June 2, 2009 and concurrently a member of the clinical advisory board of Corgentech Inc.;

---

[107] Rosenberg, "FDA."
[108] Tavernise, "Califf's Ties to Drug Makers."

- Significant financial interests, amounts undisclosed, in Gambro, Regeneron, Gilead, AstraZeneca, Roche, and others;
- Holder of equity positions in four medical companies;
- Served Genentech in a variety of capacities, from director, officer, partner, advisor, consultant, and trustee;
- Founding Director of the Clinical Research Institute at Duke University School of Medicine, an organization with an annual operating budget of $320 million, of which as much as 60 percent is funded by at least 23 drug industry companies.

Even more shockingly, Califf actually had the temerity to go on public record in *support of collaboration* between industry and regulators, once telling a National Public Radio interviewer, "Many of us consult with the pharmaceutical industry, which I think is a very good thing. They need ideas and then the decision about what they do is really up to the person who is funding the study."[109] Califf was also well known for defending Vioxx, used to treat arthritis and other conditions causing acute or chronic pain, but reportedly responsible for at least 50,000 heart attacks and strokes associated with long-term, high-dosage use. It is widely believed that Merck knew about Vioxx's dangerous cardio effects but marketed the drug anyway. The company's sales yearly revenue from Vioxx alone topped $2.5 billion in 2003. When Merck was forced to pull the drug off the market the following year, they reserved $970 million to pay for Vioxx-related legal expenses through 2007, and set aside $4.85 billion as a settlement slush fund in anticipation of a legion of legal claims from U.S. citizens.

It doesn't end there: while at Duke, Califf directed the clinical trials and later championed the blood thinner Xarelto before the FDA approval board despite strong warnings from medical experts who objected to its approval; he continued to promote Xarelto even after it was linked to 379 deaths. And at the time of Califf's appointment, Duke University was

---

[109] Rosenberg, "FDA."

still reeling from a major research fraud scandal that resulted in retracted papers, terminated grants, and a *60 Minutes* television special, prompting one industry observer to remark that Duke was at the time, "the least appropriate place from which to choose an FDA commissioner."

So excruciatingly white-hot glaring were Califf's ubiquitous and insidious conflicts of interest, not to mention his brazenly public anti-regulatory allegiance to Big Pharma, that he ultimately became an embarrassment to the politicians who had confirmed him to begin with. Although, only four senators had the courage to vote against it: Edward J. Markey (D., Massachusetts), Kelly Ayotte (R., New Hampshire), Richard Blumenthal (D., Connecticut), and Joe Manchin III (D., West Virginia)— the same Joe Manchin, by the way, who is fighting for better safety for coal miners under the Robert C. Byrd Mine Safety Protection Act back in his home state. Nevertheless, Califf wouldn't last a year as Commissioner of the FDA, resigning the post in January 2017. Subsequently, four months later, on May 11, 2017, a new man was sworn in as the 23rd Commissioner of the FDA.

His name is Scott Gottlieb.

CHAPTER 8

COMMUNICATING: CAN YOU FEAR ME NOW?

In the 1952 presidential election, soft-spoken Midwesterner and Democratic candidate Adlai E. Stevenson faced the unenviable task of going up against the immensely popular World War II hero and Republican standard-bearer, Dwight D. Eisenhower. Stevenson had been reluctant to run in the first place, despite being personally selected by incumbent Harry S. Truman. With his own popularity plummeting largely due to a stalemate in the increasingly unpopular Korean War, Truman had decided not to run, throwing the Democratic Party into disarray. In stark contrast on the Republican side, the analog television and radio airwaves of the day were ringing with the catchy "I like Ike" jingle—the tune written by Irving Berlin and paired with the famous animated television cartoon produced by none other than Disney Studios—still widely regarded as the most memorable and perhaps most effective political slogan of all time.

The story is told that, one day early in the campaign, Stevenson was awakened from a nap by a knock at the front door. The then-governor of Illinois threw on a bathrobe and answered the door to find a man with a briefcase in one hand standing on the stoop of the governor's residence.

"Can I help you?" he asked.

"I'm your television consultant, Mr. Stevenson," the man replied politely.

"Oh," Adlai Stevenson said. Still groggy from his interrupted siesta and thinking there must be something wrong with his television set, Stevenson led the man into the residence and, waving a hand toward one corner of the living room, said, "The set is over there."

Stevenson, in that moment at least and perhaps well beyond it, had seen the television only as the device itself, the physical set with the glowing screen attractively encased in furniture-grade, polished hardwood and standing in the corner. He did not see the profound power of the medium behind it, the instantaneous ethereal information channel that ran through its complex electronic circuits and vacuum tubes to display compelling images and persuasive, verbalized, opinion-forming content to millions of people in America and around the world. Perhaps, given the fact that the 1952 presidential campaign was the first in which television advertising was used to promote the major party candidates, history should forgive Stevenson for his colossal miscalculation. The voters of the day surely didn't: Eisenhower would go on to win the election in a landslide, taking 442 electoral college votes to Stevenson's 89 and winning the popular election by nearly seven million votes.

"BEAM ME UP, SCOTTY!"

On the basic nuts-and-bolts level, the telecommunications industry faces much of the same product safety challenges, difficulties, and constraints with respect to the ingenious devices and innovative equipment they manufacture and distribute, as do the makers of cars or massive commercial air conditioning units or residential water heaters, and so on. Which is to say, for example, that the hand-held devices and portable laptops or tablets are equally prone to the same sorts of unanticipated hidden hazards as any other consumer products: high-powered laptop computers have been known to catch fire; lithium ion batteries in cell phones have been known to explode. The most recent notorious case involves the recall by Samsung of every single one of its Galaxy Note 7 smartphones—some 2.5 million worldwide and one million in the U.S. alone—at an estimated cost of $17 billion in revenue from production through to completion of the recall. Even at those numbers, this was not the largest electronics recall in history. In August 2006, PC maker Dell recalled 4.1 million laptop computers because the lithium ion batteries that powered them could overheat and catch fire.

The fundamental similarity here is that these are largely hardware issues not unlike faulty automobile air bags or ignition key mechanisms, or the resident dangers posed by pilot lights and propane cook stoves that cannot always be designed out. We might even be inclined to give the R&D technicians and inventors working in the telecommunications industry a little leeway. Like the people who are trying to develop the autonomous car, telecom innovators are working at the cutting edge of technologies that have revolutionized the ways that we communicate; a revolution that is still continuing without a foreseeable conclusion. This is a marvelous thing, but one has to expect glitches to occur, though the hope, of course, is that no one should have to be injured or killed in order to discover them.

For example, the National Cancer Institute (NCI) has expressed concern over the potential of electromagnetic radiation from cell phones and other wireless devices to cause certain types of cancer and other health problems. Cell phones emit radiofrequency energy commonly called radio waves, which are a form of nonionizing radiation. Nonionizing radiation is a very low-frequency, low-power form of electromagnetic radiation, but cancer researchers are nonetheless concerned because tissues near these devices can absorb even these low levels of energy. We generally hold cell phones up to our ears—many of us do so constantly—so to be plain, we are talking about pretty important brain tissues here, for starters.

And while thus far there is (thankfully) no conclusive scientific evidence to suggest that cell phones cause brain or any other sorts of cancer, the NCI points out that cell phone use has increased exponentially in the 21st century. The organization estimates that, as of 2014, there were 327.5 million cell phone users in the U.S.; in the year 2000, there were only 110 million users. What the NCI is saying, of course, in at least sounding the alarm, is that our use of cell phones (and our dependence on them to stay connected and informed) has dramatically increased. We make more mobile phone calls than ever before (probably a *Zillion* more than we ever made using the phone that used to be plugged into the wall next to the refrigerator at home), we likely stay on those calls for longer amounts of time than ever before, and there are many, many more cell phone users out there to talk to, to say nothing of nonhuman wireless communications such as GPS and other data-sharing applications that keep our phones humming with flowing energy. Yet, even the invisible peril potentially posed by electromagnetic radiation, should it turn out to be real, will likely have to be solved by hardware modifications that reduce ambient radiation from the devices, perhaps through some sort of dampening mechanism or material. It's not like you can change the physics of radio waves. In fact, the NCI acknowledges that significant improvements in cell phone technology have already produced devices with lower power outputs.

With all of that said, if the safety and warnings issues that attend the ways we communicate were just about the now-myriad devices we use and depend on to do that, I could end this chapter here. I could say to the telecommunications industry, "Just make cell phones and wireless devices that don't heat up to the point of spontaneously catching fire that are powered by safe batteries that don't explode. And while you're at it, please make sure that while I'm talking on my smartphone I'm not getting so much electromagnetic radiation pulsing through my brain (or body) that I'm likely to develop cancer." I might add, "If you can't completely design out the potential risk of cancer, however minimal, caused by electromagnetic radiation due to 'excessive' cell phone use, please give me a call and we'll set up an appointment to design a warning label to go on your devices that will adequately warn consumers of this hidden hazard; a properly communicated label that will protect you against liability by providing consumers with informed consent." And we'd be done.

But the phone is no longer just a phone. In fact, we should stop calling it that. iPhones, tablets, and other handheld devices are powerful minicomputers capable of gathering and storing an almost infinite amount of our personal information, as well as information about just about everything else. Further, with the help of the internet, these devices become potential portals through which other individuals or entities might gain access to that information, whether we choose to share it or not. The GPS capability built into these devices, for one very basic and relatively mundane example, is able to track our location like no land line was ever able to do, and yet, by today's standards with the millions of applications already out there and growing by the hundreds every day, GPS capability is pretty small potatoes. Exercise monitors like Fitbit and others record your physical vital signs like blood pressure, heart rate, calories consumed, and calories burned and more; in fact, the company's website boasts that the wrist-worn device "tracks every part of your day" from "activity, exercise, food, weight, and sleep." Under Armour and other apparel companies are working on ways to incorporate similar tracking technology into the clothing we wear when exercising or playing sports. With apologies to Captain Kirk and the rest of the crew aboard the Starship Enterprise, calling these things "communicators" doesn't even seem to do justice the incredible things they are capable of doing, the information they can store and analyze right in the palm of your hand, and the tasks they can enable us to accomplish remotely, efficiently, and with only the tap of a tiny screen.

Another crucial phenomenon of the information age is that we willingly (if not always knowingly) share much more personal information than we realize. To cite another example, a theory that for a number of years has been gaining wide acceptance among experts in the field of product marketing and branding is that brand loyalty as a measure of product popularity is no longer measured by how often consumers buy certain products, but rather by how much personal information consumers are willing to share with the companies and organizations they regularly buy from or align themselves with. Just as our physical movements can be tracked, so too can our buying patterns be tracked. And our buying patterns reveal a great deal about our behaviors at work and play. Through social media, to some extent, even our political views and beliefs can be tracked.

For example, say you are an outdoors person who likes camping and hiking, river rafting and mountain climbing, or hunting and fishing, and so on. You can easily buy the equipment needed for these activities from any number of reputable companies that manufacture or sell a wide range of outdoor products. However, studies have shown that if one or more of those companies advertise their support for say, the national park system or through financial contributions to environmental advocacy groups like the Sierra Club, not only are outdoor-enthusiast consumers more likely to buy from those companies, but they are also much more likely to share their personal information with organizations they see as kindred spirits—whom they see as helping to protect the things they value.

HOW DOES ONE WARN ABOUT THE HIDDEN HAZARDS OF COMMUNICATION ITSELF?

All of this, in turn, has profound implications for our personal privacy, and the questions that are raised are many. Here are just three that come to mind immediately:

- How do/will companies and organizations use the personal data they acquire about individual consumers?
- How does the act of communicating in and of itself affect the conduct of our everyday lives?
- What happens when communication itself becomes "commoditized"?

The answers to these questions are quite complicated. To try to begin to understand them, you first have to understand the power of information itself—and by that, I mean *information that is effectively communicated*. Information in isolation, or in a vacuum, is essentially useless for all practical purposes. Consider three brief examples from the world of noteworthy political movements:

- Virtually every school kid across our country who is taught the history of the American Revolution knows about Thomas Paine and his influential pamphlet *Common Sense*. But few people know that there were dozens of pamphleteers operating in Colonial America in the mid-to-late 1700s, writing everything from regular news to political opinion. The way this worked, an activist might compose a political opinion or editorial and have someone like Ben Franklin set it in type and publish multiple, though limited, numbers of copies in print form—no internet in those days, of course. Every pamphlet had a number of blank pages at the back. Once the copies were distributed, people who read the editorial were encouraged to use the blank pages to add their own commentary and pass the pamphlet along to the next person to do the same.

Here's one for the Nothing New Under the Sun file. It is fiendishly intriguing—and impossible not to notice—how, despite all of its 21st-century cutting-edge digital technological wizardry, the means of communicating ideas and concepts via the World Wide Web so directly mirrors the "ancient" methodology of print, pass, and comment. The comments sections or strings that follow the billions upon billions of news and feature articles, editorials, blogs, and posts that populate today's internet have effectively taken the place, it would seem, of the blank pages provided for same by the colonial pamphleteers whom we might reflect were more visionary than they could have known!

Most American history books also fail to mention that, by some scholarly estimates, fewer than half of the colonists favored independence from Great Britain, and thus came to be called "Patriots," while a solid 20 to 25 percent remained loyal to the crown. In fact, some 30,000 Americans fought for the British during the Revolution, and 80,000 Loyalists eventually fled to Canada and England during and after the conclusion of the war. What really makes the efforts of Paine and other pamphleteers so crucially important in this world-shaking 18th-century struggle for American independence is not so much their political ideology itself, but more their ingenious ability to cogently and efficiently communicate their views to tens of thousands of the so-called "fence-sitters," which many scholars credit with ultimately turning the remaining 40 to 45 percent of American colonists into Patriots supporting independence. A reasonably convincing argument may be made and defended that, without this marshaling of grassroots support through the effective communicating of the common cause, the American Revolution might have failed.

• For most Americans old enough to remember, the most indelible images of the Islamic Revolution in Iran in 1979, in which the Pahlavi dynasty under Mohammad Reza Shah Pahlavi ("the Shah of Iran") was overthrown, will undoubtedly be the hostage crisis in which 52 U.S. diplomats were held captive for 444 days by Iranian revolutionaries. Following the revolution, with the Shah's departure and after 14 years in exile in Turkey, Iraq, and France, the Ayatollah Khomeini returned triumphantly to become the Islamic Republic's Supreme Leader under its new constitution, making him the highest ranking political and religious leader of the nation.

Much in keeping with all of the seemingly endless political histories that originate in or revolve around the Middle East, Iran's Islamic Revolution is a vastly complex story encompassing many decades of turmoil incited by a myriad of competing interests and implicating many political players—not to mention, as well, the world's largest and most internationally powerful oil companies. The seeds of the revolution itself arguably date back, at the very least, to the 1953 coup, orchestrated and executed by the CIA and Great Britain's intelligence wing MI6. That was the coup that ousted the democratically elected nationalist leader Mohammad Mossadegh, and that installed the Shah in power in the first place.

For our purposes, however, the most interesting backstory to the Iranian Revolution is revealed by the fact that many Middle

East historical scholars refer to it as the "Cassette Tape Revolution." While in exile, the Ayatollah had succeeded in remaining the spiritual leader of the people of Iran. He had done so by making a series of audio cassette tape recordings urging opposition and civil resistance against the Shah's brutal dictatorship, which were then smuggled into the country and secretly distributed.

By the mid-1970s, according to Stephen Zunes, a Professor of Politics and Chair of Mid-Eastern Studies at the University of San Francisco, the Shah had largely crushed "most of the leftist, liberal, nationalist, and other secular opposition leadership ... through murder, imprisonment or exile," and subsequently banning their organizations, as well as by successfully terrorizing the population over more than two decades of "widespread killings, torture and mass detentions." However, suppressing the predominant Islamist opposition wasn't nearly as easy, and that, according to Zunes, was why "it was out of mosques and among the mullahs that much of the organized leadership of the movement against the Shah's dictatorship emerged." And a key component to effectively undermining those repressive efforts was simply that the Shah's regime could not prevent the Ayatollah's clandestine audiotapes from infiltrating the country, nor from being secretly copied and passed among the people.

Escalating matters, in 1977, Khomeini began calling for open resistance through organized worker strikes, boycotts, tax refusal, and other forms of nonviolent noncooperation with the Shah's regime. Continuing through the end of the conflict, and even in face of a brutal retaliatory crackdown by the government, Zunes asserts that the unceasing stream of the Ayatollah's audiotapes fomenting dissent were instrumental in inspiring the continued mobilization of the revolutionary movement. Abolhassan Sadegh, an official with the Shah's Ministry of National Guidance (how's that for a scary totalitarian governmental title?) put it more poetically when he openly complained that "tape cassettes are stronger than fighter planes."

- When the Berlin Wall finally came down, many patriotic politicians hailed the triumph of democracy over totalitarianism; they hailed America's unwavering hardline, anti-Communist diplomatic rigor and staunch military vigilance in defense of freedom for all peoples, and they said that all of these unified efforts lead to the U.S. victory over the Soviet Union in the Cold War. As presidents do—regardless of historical accuracy—President Ronald Reagan and his tough-minded conservative administration garnered much of the credit, with flag-waving Americans recalling his famous speech on June 12, 1987 in front of the Brandenburg Gate in which he demanded with all the dramatic flair of the Hollywood actor he once was, "Mr. Gorbachev, tear down this wall!" All of those things did what they did, but it was a communications media genius and, ironically, perhaps the greatest television sports producer of all time who truly pinpointed the fundamental reason why the Berlin Wall fell, Roone Arledge, the creative powerhouse behind ABC Sports who launched Monday Night Football.

   An expert in media rather than political science, Arledge contended that it was communication that brought the wall down, noting that the East German regime could not keep the information out any longer. Arledge was spot-on correct: For all of the West's unyielding stance against Moscow, the Soviet bloc nations largely collapsed from within, because, in a word, their own people simply wouldn't take the propagandist line anymore. They knew better.

These are just a sampling of innumerable and remarkable stories that demonstrate the power of communicating information that, in turn, often leads to coordinated action in support of a cause leading to social change. However, what might be the most remarkable aspect of all of them, particularly as seen through the lens of our digitalized 21st-century culture, is that they all predate the creation and global launch of the World Wide Web, which did not "go live" until nearly two years after the Berlin Wall fell. Granted, the American Revolution, the Islamic Revolution in Iran, the collapse of the Soviet Bloc, and the Reunification of Germany all took years, even decades of increasing discontent and gathering opposition to reach their crescendos of revolt and wholesale regime change. But we have already seen how wireless cell phones—along with increasingly sophisticated built-in cameras capable of streaming live video in real time—aided monumentally by social media platforms like Facebook and Twitter, with literally billions of active on-line participants, can significantly accelerate this process.

The Arab Spring of 2011, for example, was touched off by a single incident in the town of Sidi Bouzid, Tunisia. That's where, in December 2010, a fruit and vegetable seller by the name of Mohamed Bouazizi took to the extraordinary measure of setting himself on fire to protest what he felt was harsh treatment by a policewoman in the street who tried to confiscate his cart because he did not have a permit. Bouazizi's extreme and desperate defiance resonated with the general discontent of the townspeople. Before the day was over, protests erupted everywhere throughout the village, captured by cell phone videos and shared around the world on the internet, sparking similar uprisings in nearly a dozen Middle East countries, at least.

The result?

- On January 14, 2011, the government of Tunisia was overthrown when President Zine el Abidine Ben Ali fled the country and went into exile; democratic elections for a constituent Assembly would later be held on October 23.
- On February 11, the U.S.-backed government of Egypt was overthrown. Attempting to simply step down, President Hosni Mubarak was subsequently arrested and imprisoned to face charges of murdering unarmed opposition protesters during his hard-fisted authoritarian tenure.

- On February 15, in Muammar Gadhafi's Libya, violent anti-government protests erupted, leading to full-scale civil war between opposition forces and Gadhafi loyalists. The government was overthrown when Tripoli fell to the opposition on August 23rd. Transition forces later doggedly tracked down and then killed Gadhafi on October 20, mutilating his body in a bizarre video that, of course, also went viral over the internet.

- Also, in early February, ongoing sporadic and isolated protest demonstrations in Yemen became dramatically more widespread, threatening to paralyze the national economy. Injured in a direct attack on June 4th, President Ali Abdullah Saleh was finally ousted less than six months later when he signed a power-transfer agreement on November 23rd, officially ending an incredible 33-year dictatorial reign.

- In March, pro-democracy protests erupted in the city of Deraa in southern Syria after the arrest and torture of some teenagers who had painted anti-government slogans on a school wall. When government security forces opened fire on the crowd, killing several demonstrators, cell phones with streaming video capability were there to record and broadcast it live, further enflaming the region. By July, hundreds of thousands of Syrians all across the country had taken to the streets to protest the totalitarian regime of President Bashar al-Assad and plunging the country into a horrifically bloody civil war that the UN estimates had taken 400,000 Syrian lives by April 2016[110] and still rages today.

- Finally, the Arab Spring movement brought cell phone-, video-, and social media-fueled civil protests and opposition uprisings in at least six other countries: Algeria, Iraq, Jordan, Kuwait, Morocco, and Oman.

---

[110] Wikipedia, "Casualties."

While it is certainly true that some measure of civil discontent either existed and/or had been building for years and even decades throughout all of these countries (name for me one nation in the entire world that is without any civil discontent!), I think it's fair to assert that never before in human history has a call to activist political protest spread so quickly across international borders while subsequently resulting so effectively in direct participatory action by so many peoples in so many nations, virtually all at once.

The phenomena of instantaneous electronic communication has clearly come to validate the predictions made over a half century ago by visionary media theorist Marshall McLuhan, who in the 1960s coined the term "global village" and theorized (even before it actually existed) that the electronic media of the internet would informationally make the world into a single unit in ways that are both potentially good and potentially very bad. According to McLuhan:

> *With this "continually sounding tribal drum" in place, "everybody gets the message all the time: a princess gets married in England, and 'boom, boom, boom' go the drums. We all hear about it. An earthquake in North Africa, a Hollywood star gets drunk, away go the drums again." The consequence? "We're re-tribalizing. Involuntarily, we're getting rid of individualism." … No longer concerned with "finding our own individual way," we instead obsess over "what the group knows, feeling as it does, acting 'with it,' not apart from it."* [111]

The instantaneous and virtually unstoppable communicative power of social media—as well as its propagandist power—are entirely like smuggled audio cassette tapes on steroids.

But I believe that's not all of the story. A lot of political scientists and politicians on both sides of the aisle are inclined to point to international

---

[111] Wikipedia, "McLuhan."

policy mistakes as the reason for the rise of more formidably organized and potent terrorist groups in the Middle East, Asia, and several other places around the world. I contend that international politics—whether diplomatic or military, whether flawed or soundly reasoned, whether deemed "successful" or failed—have nothing to do with this distinctly new phenomenon of the digital electronic era of the 21st century. The hard fact is that Al Qaeda and ISIS would not exist today without Facebook, Twitter, and some of the other global social networks that enable these terrorist groups to promote their cause, to recruit and deploy their "soldiers" worldwide, to coordinate with ample precision their subversive ground-game activities and operations, and of course, to engage in cyberterrorism via computer hacking and other means. When Osama Bin Laden was finally caught and killed, the first thing the SEAL team seized was his computer, believed to contain virtually all of the extant information about his operations and contact cells around the world. And here is where the technology comes full circle, in that the devices themselves can be used as terrorist tools. Handheld devices can be used as timing devices or detonators for bombs. It's a matter of pure speculation, but it's reasonable to conjecture that the close coordination required to pull off the 9/11 attacks might not have been possible without cell phones.

Now, would anyone want to say that we should hold Mark Zuckerberg and Jack Dorsey and his founding team at Twitter responsible for providing the means for the rise of terrorism in the world? Probably no more than we want to hold Philo Farnsworth responsible for all of those annoying direct-to-consumer drug ads now glutting the television he and others invented. But another controversial question concerns the role of government and the extent to which it should have "jurisdiction," whether directly or through appropriate agencies like the Federal Communications Commission (FCC).

In San Francisco in 2011 and for the first time in U.S. history, the Bay Area Rapid Transit (BART) shut down mobile-internet and cell phone service in an effort to head off a planned protest demonstration over the shooting death of a knife-wielding man by BART police a month earlier. Officials deliberately cut power to four underground service towers, fearing a crippling, system-wide protest fueled and propagated by social media. The move caused outrage and prompted comparisons to the same kinds of speech suppression exercised by tyrannies around the world to quell dissent—and any Political Science 101 student knows that the first thing totalitarian regimes do when they seize power is either shut down or take over the media. Some constitutional scholars likened the move to an unlawful suppression of First Amendment speech—a digital application of prior restraint. Should constitutional, democratically elected governments have the right to shut down internet communications on a grand scale? Or is this any different than shutting down newspapers, radio, and television broadcasts?

CREATING A COMMUNITY, OR FEEDING AN ADDICTION?

What all of this reveals is that wireless, ubiquitous, and instantaneous real-time electronic communication through social media possesses a tremendous power to build a palpable sense of community that few social or political scientists (outside of McLuhan, apparently) could have predicted, and the limits of which we probably have not yet seen. However, as we have already seen on a political plane, this can be a community devoted to promoting good, or one clearly dedicated to propagating evil. And it can also be a community tethered together through the same kinds of compulsive inducements and behaviors that characterize various forms of addiction.

Perhaps the easiest way to illustrate the curiously unanticipated community-building power of social media is to take a brief look at what might legitimately be described as revolutionary changes in the casino gaming industry, and conveniently, one that is no stranger to the issue of addictive behavior; that being compulsive gambling. Consider, in particular, the continuing saga of Atlantic City, New Jersey. Once the crown jewel of legalized gambling on the East Coast, Atlantic City casino operators fell on hard times only a few years ago, in part due to the intense competition from a rapid proliferation of new gambling venues across ten eastern states from Maine to Ohio to Florida. Beginning in 2014, five major casinos in the storied seaside resort town closed up in less than two years, including arguably the pinnacle of excess in architectural decadence, the $1.2 billion Trump Taj Mahal (which eventually wound up in the possession of Carl Icahn, purchased for $50 million, or $.04 cents on the dollar). That and other financial woes led to a controversial state takeover of the once-proud resort city at the end of 2016.

Coming to the rescue: As unlikely as it might seem on the surface, online internet gambling is turning out to become Atlantic City's casino operators' savior. Approved only recently by the New Jersey state legislature in November 2013, online gambling revenues surged more than 32 percent in 2016, according to a report published by gaming industry research group Eilers & Krejcik Gaming.

However, much to the shock of critics who argued that allowing casinos to offer online gaming would kill the patient (at least, the brick-and-mortar palaces of Atlantic City), it has instead resulted in a 9 percent revenue gain across all Atlantic City Casinos in 2017, bolstered by a staggering 40 percent increase in online gambling revenue. But rather than taking business away from the city itself, online gambling is, in fact, driving more consumers to visit the brick-and-mortar establishments. "Online gambling is becoming a highly effective tool for Atlantic City's casinos," the Eilers & Krejcik report states, further noting that "Increased integration between the online and live casino [experiences] appears to be driving additional play and visitation at land-based properties."

All of this may seem surprising, that is, until you understand that the ability of electronic social media to build community may be infinitely more powerful than face-to-face, in-person interaction. Yet, it may also foster more in-person community interaction. Rummy Pandit, executive director of the Lloyd D. Levenson Institute of Gaming, Hospitality & Tourism at Stockton

University, asserts that it's no surprise that online gaming may be leading to more brick-and-mortar business, as many gamblers getting a taste of the thrill online will then seek a first-hand, in-person "experience." Even players who enjoy wagering in their pajamas in the comfort of their own home, Pandit suggests, will likely crave the real casino atmosphere from time to time, interacting with others—whom they've probably "met" previously online. All the more reason to go visit the casino! And indeed, it's hard, if not impossible, to imagine a community-building device more powerful than one that provides instantaneous access to your "friends" at any second of any day 24/7.

One need only observe the way casinos now advertise to confirm the growing online trend in consumer gambling. That is, casinos used to advertise by showing large groups of diverse people, mainly very attractive, well-dressed young men and women inside their casinos gathered intimately around a roulette table, cutting to a shot of them at the bar or in the restaurant, or on the dance floor, or playing the slots together. Commercials for Atlantic City casinos also typically included gorgeous images of the group out on the boardwalk, often with dawn peering over the beach-side railing, presumably after an exciting night of unending partying and gambling. The message clearly was: Come on down to the casino, spend a few carefree days in our hotel, and have a fabulous time.

Today, however, the focus of broadcast casino-style gambling advertising is almost exclusively on online gambling. In the New York Metropolitan market, this applies not just to Atlantic City, but to many casinos in New York State, Connecticut, Pennsylvania, and beyond. The commercials' announcers tout "Real dealers" and flash images of attractive "live" female dealers in low-cut blouses sitting behind blackjack tables "ready to play with you!" A good thing, as we have seen, for the casino industry, but is online gambling and the attractive broadcast advertising that promotes it also contributing to a rise in compulsive gambling addiction?

Probably.

However, for the most part, the only warning message contained in advertisements for online gambling or for land-based gambling establishments is the very quickly voiced phrase, "Gambling problem?

Call 1-800-GAMBLER," which also shows on the video screen, but of course, in very tiny and hard to read disclaimer-sized type.

But let's take this a bit further. Compared to the community-building power of already like-minded consumers, such as outdoors-men and—women or combination online/land-based casino gamblers, the addictive draw of social media is arguably downright diabolical in power and scope. That may be because it draws on the peer pressure to be part of the group; or, as observed by McLuhan and cited earlier, social media causes us to obsess over "what the group knows, feeling as it does, acting 'with it,' not apart from it."

You know this feeling if you've ever had a dear friend who may have persisted in sending you invitations to play Candy Crush or Words with Friends or some other internet game (as I have from time to time!). Sometimes you're sitting in an airport waiting interminably for the call over the intercom to board your flight, and you might have some time to kill. But most other times, you're busy with something important and you are obliged to decline the offer. But if you're like me, you feel guilty for doing so; you've received an open invitation to the ball, but you've turned it down; you're the ultimate party-pooper.

Regardless, the real danger of the hidden hazard posed by the potentially and often highly addictive properties of social media can be much more serious than a little psychological guilt over reluctantly deciding to not play an online game with your friends and focusing on your work instead. It can even be deadly:

- Social media addiction may have contributed to the death of a nine-month-old infant in 2001, when Tony Lamont Bragg locked his son in a closet so that he could concentrate on playing his favorite internet video game. When he finally realized to check on the baby 24 hours later, his son was dead. Bragg is now serving a 15-year prison term after pleading guilty to manslaughter.[112]

---

[112] IGN, "EverQuest."

- On Thanksgiving morning in 2002, 21-year-old Shawn Woolley committed suicide while sitting in front of his computer, his favorite video game still up on the screen when he shot himself. Overweight and prone to epileptic seizures, Wooley routinely logged 12 hours a day playing *EverQuest*, an internet game so addictive in nature that regular players often refer to it as "Ever-Crack." Acknowledging that her son had psychiatric problems that may have contributed to his tragic act of self-destruction, Elizabeth Wooley nonetheless blamed the addictive game of exacerbating his mental illness and threatened to sue Sony Online Entertainment for failure to warn.[113]

- Today, Elizabeth Woolley oversees a website called "Online Gamers Anonymous," which lists, allegedly as a direct result of online social media and gaming addiction: at least six known infant and child deaths due to parental neglect (in addition to little Tony Bragg, Jr.), at least six known suicides (in addition to that of her own son), and seven known murders including that of two police officers. One of the deaths listed as a suicide occurred in 2004 when 13-year-old Zhang Xiaoyi jumped off a 24-story building in a rather misguided effort to re-enact a scene from the online game *World of Warcraft*.[114]

- Finally, in 2005, after sitting in a gaming café playing the online game *StarCraft* for 50 straight hours, breaking only to use the bathroom or take a quick nap, a 28-year-old South Korean man expired from heart failure.[115]

All of these cases point to a potentially very dangerous, yet largely hidden hazard of the addictive properties of social media and internet gaming interaction that threatens the safety of consumers. Yet, how best or how ade-

---

[113] Miller, "EverQuest."
[114] LevelSkip, "Addiction."
[115] Ibid.

quately the creators and purveyors of internet content should be required to warn consumers about this and other potential hazards resulting from participation in online social media offerings remains unclear. Had Elizabeth Woolley gone ahead to sue Sony Online Entertainment for failure to warn, would she have succeeded? Most legal experts say no.

For its part, Sony Online Entertainment CEO (and co-creator of *EverQuest*) John Smedley insisted categorically that the game did not cause Shawn Woolley's suicide, averring that, "it's really one of those terrible things that happens ... *EverQuest* is a game. And I don't see any connection between a form of entertainment and somebody's tragic suicide." Smedley fiercely rejects any notion that the game is addictive, calling that notion "nonsense," and adding "It's entertainment. Is a book dangerous? Is a television show dangerous? I think the answer is no. People need to take responsibility and say, 'Hey, you know, this is too much. Enough's enough.' It's a game!"

Similarly, Dr. J. Michael Faragher, dean of the School of Professional Studies at the Metropolitan State College of Denver and co-director of the Center for Addiction Studies, doesn't think there's much of a reasonable case to hold Sony Online Entertainment responsible for Shawn's untimely death. "If it wasn't this (*EverQuest*), it would have been something else," Faragher said. "I don't see a culpability as much as I see a lack of feelings of Sony's social responsibility. I don't think this kid would have played any less if Sony had posted a warning."

In the end, however, neither of these explanations seems even remotely to be an adequate or satisfactory response to the very serious and very troubling life-and-death hazard that may lie hidden within the power of social media and the addictive behaviors that it clearly supports, and may very likely encourage. Are we simply to throw up our hands, or should game creators and the media companies that promote and distribute them be required to issue prominently communicated warnings regarding the potentially addictive nature of internet games and other attractions?

CYBERBULLYING AND THE DESTRUCTIVE
POWER OF THE INTERNET

McLuhan's concept of "re-tribalization" and specifically this profoundly disquieting notion of "feeling as the group does" and consequently acting as the group does—often rather than as an independently thinking individual—further serves to explain the rise of the phenomenon of what's been termed cyberbullying. Indeed, the same power that instantaneous internet communication exhibits to rally politically motivated action on a grand scale, and that social media possesses to exert peer pressure to play games to the point of dangerously addictive behavior, is also quite capable of inciting dangerously irrational and aggressive group behavior as well. Cyberbullying is mob mentality gone viral, and the consequences are as tragic as they are well documented:

- On September 22, 2010, 18-year-old Rutgers University student Tyler Clementi committed suicide by jumping off the George Washington Bridge only two days after his sexual encounter with another man. The encounter was secretly viewed via webcam by Clementi's roommate, Dharun Ravi, with the help of a female student, hallmate Molly Wei, whose computer was used to view the webcam video feed. The case garnered national attention when Ravi and Wei were federally indicted in the webcam invasion of privacy incident, though neither was charged with having any role in Tyler's suicide itself. In March 2012, Ravi was convicted on 15 counts of invasion of privacy, bias intimidation, tampering with evidence, witness tampering, and hindering apprehension or prosecution. Wei escaped prosecution in exchange for turning state's witness against Ravi and 300 hours of community service. Ravi's convictions were later overturned on constitutional grounds, whereupon he pleaded guilty to one third-degree felony count of attempted invasion of privacy. He was sentenced to time served and fines paid, all other charges were dropped, and he was released.[116]

- More recently, in April 2017, 11-year-old Tysen Benz hanged himself in his room after reading text messages that led him to believe that his girlfriend had just committed suicide. Authorities later revealed that they had charged the 13-year-old girl, unidentified due to her age, with two counts of malicious use of telecommunication service and using a computer to commit a crime, both misdemeanors, but punishable by sentences in juvenile detention of up to six months and up to a year, respectively. It turned out that Tysen had been having a texting conversation on SnapChat with his girlfriend, who, unbeknownst to him, was using someone else's account and posing as that person when she told Tysen that his girlfriend had died. No one told Tysen that it was a prank.[117]

- In June 2017, 20-year-old Michelle Carter was convicted of involuntary manslaughter in the 2014 suicide-by-carbon-monoxide-poisoning of Conrad Roy, 18 years old at the time, whom Carter referred to as her boyfriend. Carter had sent an unrelenting barrage of hundreds of text messages urging and pressuring Roy to commit suicide, which he ultimately did by getting into his truck and using a gasoline-powered water pump in order to choke on the truck's fumes. At one point, when Roy exited the truck and texted to Carter that he was scared, she texted in reply, "Get back in." And when it was over, Carter texted to a friend that she was "talking on the phone with him when he killed himself ... I heard him die." Handing down the guilty verdict, Massachusetts Judge Lawrence Moniz called Carter's reprehensible actions "wanton and reckless conduct" and concluded that she had caused his death by instructing "Conrad Roy to get back in the truck."[118]

---

[116] Wikipedia, "Clementi."
[117] Phillips, "11-year-old boy."
[118] Shapiro and Lantz, "Carter."

Should social media providers or outlets like Facebook, Twitter, Snap-Chat, and all the others be required to warn users about the clearly potent force of cyberbullying as a "hidden hazard"? Or is cyberbullying an instance of the misuse of social media by individuals or groups for subversive purposes and even criminal behavior or activity for which the providers simply are not responsible? After all, criminal charges of wire and mail fraud over the more traditional communication channels of telephone and surface mail have always been generally brought against individuals, not against telephone service companies or the U.S. Post Office.

So, what can we do about the hidden hazards of communicating? Difficult as it might be for me, as a warnings expert, to concede, the fact is that information isn't always going to prevent the outcome. We might not be very comfortable with sentiments like those of Dr. Faragher when he speculated that consumer safety warnings most likely would not have resulted in Shawn Woolley curtailing his online game playing, perhaps even averting his suicide. And without meaning to be cruel or unfeeling, it must be acknowledged that even the federal prosecutors in the Tyler Clementi case were not inclined to directly charge Dharum Ravi—and in a way implicate social media as a factor by extension—for Clementi's suicide. Sometimes it just isn't about devising better warnings; sometimes there has to be a sociological solution. To sum it up, not all outcomes are predictable, and information alone is not always the solution.

In a profound way, this rather powerfully brings to mind a line from the movie *War Games*. The storyline of the movie according to its IMDb web page is:

> A young computer whiz kid accidentally connects into a top-secret super-computer which has complete control over the U.S. nuclear arsenal. It challenges him to a game between America and Russia, and he innocently starts the countdown to World War III. Can he convince the computer he wanted to play a game and not the real thing?[119]

---

[119] IMDb, *War Games*.

The outcome of the whiz kid's actions is never certain. But at the end of the film, having narrowly avoided actually starting a *real* WWIII, the computer tells the much-relieved whiz kid that nuclear war is "a strange game" in which "the only winning move is not to play." It may be the case, with regard to some of the more profoundly sinister aspects of the power and scope of modern instantaneous communication, that consumers will need to learn to not play the game.

PART II

THE SAFETY TRIAD

In the three chapters of Part II, we examine the major communication role of the three entities that make up the Principled Safety Disclosure Triad: companies, regulatory agencies, and the general public, as represented by millions of everyday consumers. Through their combined efforts, each will benefit, and ultimately, our society will be a safer place to work and live.

CHAPTER 9

COMPANIES: THINK BIG, WARN SMALL

WHY I'M NOT A GAMBLING MAN

I am sitting in a small jet-propelled airplane. It is not a commercial airplane, but one provided by the company to whose headquarters I've been invited for an important meeting. The company is a world-class maker of roofing, insulation, and composite materials for home and office builders, as well as do-it-yourself homeowners, and the leading supplier of spun-wool fiberglass insulation with well over a 60-percent market share at the time, and growing. I had been retained as an expert witness on behalf of the company to design warnings and safety communications to prevent health-related injuries to workers as a result of handling and installing fiberglass insulation made by the company. The one-hopper flight from Buffalo, New York, is so lightning fast and short that the flight attendant barely has time to get me a drink over the few seconds we are at flight's apogee before we immediately begin our descent, tray tables up, to the tarmac of an airfield in the upper Midwest. It is like riding inside a tactical missile with windows.

At the tiny airport I am greeted by corporate counsel, and together in a big black stretch limo we are whisked off to the company headquarters. My expectation is that we will sit down with all of the executives and most of the board members to engage in a discussion over the issue of exactly what sorts of warning labels should appear on rolls and batts of the company's fiberglass insulation to adequately protect people from health hazards resulting primarily from inhalation of fiberglass dust. I have a complete, definitive proposal in my briefcase. It is in the back of the limo that the attorney first informs me that the company's marketing director and a couple of key members of his team will also be there.

Uh-oh.

On the elevator up to the corporate offices, I make a tiny wager with the attorney. I say, "I bet you that I am not in that conference room for ten minutes presenting my proposal before someone, and by 'someone' I mean the marketing director, proclaims that putting warning labels on their products is going to adversely affect their profits."

The attorney smiles. He thinks I'm just joking.

So, I said, "Seriously. You need to go into that room first without me and tell them in no uncertain terms that no one is to say anything whatsoever about product warning labels hurting profits or adversely affecting sales or anything of that sort."

Now, the reason this is so critical is because, as an expert witness for the defense, I will be taking the stand to testify. Almost invariably in this situation, I will be asked under cross-examination by plaintiff's attorney if anyone at the company I am representing ever expressed any concern that the safety warning labels I proposed might have a detrimental effect on profits. Fundamentally speaking, under no circumstances will I perjure myself. I will be under oath, and if I heard it, I will have to say so.

Well, I lost the bet—although I would argue I lost it on a technicality. Because it was actually less than *five minutes* into the meeting that the marketing manager impatiently interrupted the proceedings, blurting, "Won't product warning labels hurt our pro—"

That's when the CEO—fortunately sitting right next to his marketing chief—kicked him in the shins under the table. The CEO was this close to putting a hand over the marketing guy's mouth.

"What Mr. Shmedlap [name changed to protect the clueless] means," the CEO interjected, "is that we want to do this the right way by providing sensible warnings that go far enough to protect our customers from injury,

Dr. Goldhaber. So please advise us on how we need to go about achieving that. We're listening."

TOO BIG TO CARE

The now infamous subprime mortgage crisis that led to the enactment of the Emergency Economic Stabilization Act of 2008, or more popularly (or unpopularly, depending on your perspective) known as the Big Bank Bailout also added a new phrase to the American lexicon. Specifically, presidents and politicians on both sides of the aisle, big-bank CEOs, and at least some otherwise reputable financial gurus declared and openly defended the notion that some of the largest banks in the world are simply "too big to fail," even as hundreds of thousands of average, hard-working Americans faced imminent foreclosure on their largest investment in life: their homes.

When it comes to warning consumers about hidden hazards in the products they manufacture and sell, we might turn that phrase to read that the biggest and most profitable corporations in America (and multinationally, in today's increasingly global marketplace) are simply "too big to care." Such was certainly the case with Coca-Cola and PepsiCo, as we saw earlier, when both companies abjectly refused to provide a warning to consumers about the defective plastic bottle caps that were prone to explode and cause serious eye injuries. Instead, they opted to raise prices across the board to increase revenue to, in turn, pay out settlements for (and elicit NDAs from) customers who inevitably sued these companies for compensation for their injuries. Coke and Pepsi could get away with this. They collectively owned as much as 90 percent of the soda pop market and had the power to snub their noses at government regulators—and at the general public, for that matter.

Yet, it doesn't have to be so. In spite of that nervous marketing manager at the meeting I attended so many years ago, that company, in fact, proved that it doesn't have to be so. While there are as many as 35 manufacturers of various kinds of fiberglass insulation around the world, the company that retained me as a consultant has for decades been the industry leader owning more than 50 percent of the market.

In fact, you have to go overseas to China and Europe to find the next largest manufacturers in the world, before you come to Johns Manville and CertainTeed as the second- and third-largest in the U.S. In that market-commanding position, my client could easily have done just like the two biggest soft drink companies and quietly dismissed the idea of putting safety warnings on their products. And they also could have raised prices incrementally to cover settlement costs from the inevitable lawsuits for injuries blamed on the company's failure to warn.

They chose instead to fully adopt my warnings proposals. But here is the most interesting phenomenon about their decision: In this case, when the industry leader unilaterally put safety warnings on its products, it forced all of the other manufacturers to follow suit, however grudgingly. Now, nobody forced these competitors to do that—there were no government regulations or advisories at the time. So, if we were to try to analyze these other companies' reasoning, we might conclude that they did not believe that consumers would think their fiberglass insulation was any safer than that manufactured by the industry leader simply by virtue of not bearing a warning label.

Their move to follow that lead was very likely motivated by the fear that consumers, quite conversely, would be suspicious of their failure to warn about the hidden hazard when the biggest player on the field was openly doing so. In other words, they feared losing more of the market share *because* of their failure to warn—a fact that turns on its head the tightly held myth that safety warnings on products hurt sales and profits. In fact, they can increase sales and profits *and* be a case of doing the right thing for consumers. Not all consumers are dummies. Sales of do-it-yourself home-improvement products at hardware stores, home centers, and lumberyards in the U.S. totaled an estimated $380 billion in 2017. And many DIY homeowners do want to know how to use tools and materials properly and safely.

There is no hard-statistical data I know of that indicates that putting appropriate and properly messaged warning labels on products that warrant them has ever resulted in a decrease of sales or a loss of profits. While it must be conceded that there may not be statistical data directly linking adequate product safety warnings to an increase in sales or profits, we do know that consumers do expect the products they buy to be safe to use. And for the most part, they do expect to be warned about hidden hazards. We know this because when they aren't warned about them and accidents ensue as a result, they sue. They sue big time. Not just for compensation for injuries, but often for enormous punitive damages as well. And even if 90 percent of liability cases never go to trial, plaintiffs often secure substantial amounts of money in settlement deals.

The CPSC estimates that over a trillion dollars is expended every year in liability litigation and settlement payments on behalf of American consumers injured or killed either by defective products or by products with hidden hazards that were not properly warned against. Wouldn't it be easier—and a lot less expensive—to warn consumers and avoid as much of that as possible? Moreover, lest we be too "humanitarian" about it, do you think casually that it might be nice for companies to endeavor to avoid or prevent at least some of the more than 135,000 fatalities and the nearly 40 million injuries that occur as the result of product-related accidents annually?

Unfortunately, what so often seems to happen to companies is that they become locked into what I call the Reactive Economic Model of product development. The flaw in this model may be that it is often too heavily driven by a myopic desire to appeal to market demand and a frantic race to beat the competition in meeting that market demand. This often results in rushing new products to market without due diligence attending to safety concerns. This is particularly true in the case of hidden hazards that are easily overlooked when "laboratory" product testing is less thorough than it should be, or isn't even performed in any responsible way at all.

More specifically for our purposes, I call this economic model "reactive" because the manufacturer typically warns about hazards after the fact, when either a regulatory body mandates it or litigation verdicts and/or settlement costs begin to exceed the expected cost to sales for providing safety information. It will be useful to take a closer look at the Reactive Economic Model, as well as the one with which I propose to replace it, which I call the Proactive Economic Model.

The Reactive Economic Model for companies wishing to bring new and innovative products to the marketplace goes something like this:

1. *Conduct (sometimes questionable) market research, which often asks the wrong questions (e.g., "Do our consumers want a 5-inch or 7-inch screen on their iPhones?" instead of, "How will the next-generation iPhone enable our customers to be more effective at work, home, leisure, etc.").*

This first step in the reactive model merits some explanation. Asking the wrong questions usually involves focusing on gimmicky and often fickle consumer desires at the expense of product utility and safety. For a particularly blatant example, consider the great deal of media hype that surrounded the release of a pink- or rose-colored iPhone just a few years ago, presumably to cater to the preferences of mostly young teenage girls—certainly a prime market for cell phones to begin with. One has to imagine that the pink phone sold very well, if only because pretty soon all of the major cell phone manufacturers were offering their own versions of the distinct color phones. That is all well and good, but it is hard to imagine a more superfluous and inconsequential "innovation"—though admittedly, it's a pretty harmless one without any detrimental drawbacks. By contrast, however, one has to wonder: Had Samsung conducted more rigorous laboratory testing of the *practical safety* of its new Galaxy Note 7 smartphone, the company might have discovered the problem of the exploding battery-phone interface *before* releasing the new version to the public. Perhaps it might have avoided the massive and costly recall of millions of Note 7 phones around the world. The next two steps are largely self-explanatory:

2. *Design products based almost solely upon market-driven considerations.*

3. *Manufacture products.*

That takes us to step 4:

4. *Market and sell products, collecting profits while awaiting reports of injuries and/or deaths supposedly linked to the products' hazards.*

If you think it seems presumptive to state that companies literally "await" reports of injuries or deaths linked to known but often hidden hazards in their products, you need to think again. In each of the consumer activities chapters in this book, we have seen examples of companies marketing products or creating environments while knowing of inherent defects or hidden hazards that pose dangers to consumer health and safety. These companies fully anticipate being sued by consumers for injuries or fatalities resulting from these hazards. Accordingly, they have teams of lawyers waiting in the wings and ready to serve as defense counsel when litigation arises.

5. *Defend and, ultimately (90 percent of the time), settle the inevitable lawsuits resulting from the accidental deaths and/or injuries, including as part of the settlement a nondisclosure agreement that prevents government regulators and the public at large from learning about the hazards lurking in the products or environments.*

Our examples of this regrettable practice run from Ford Motor Company's infamous Pinto memo, literally placing a monetary value on human life, to General Motors' decision that the alleged high cost of recalling 30 million vehicles worldwide to fix their faulty ignition switches outweighed the anticipated costs of personal injury litigation resulting from serious accidents linked to the switches. Oh, and the recall cost also apparently outweighed the loss of at least 124 lives. And there are thousands of other cases then and now.

As we have seen in one case after another, many companies literally calculate—in purely economic, bottom-line terms—the litigation and settlement costs they are willing to bear before going to the expense of retooling their manufacturing operations to correct defects. The same is true when they fail to engage in the kind of meaningful and meticulous market research and product development testing that seeks to eliminate potentially dangerous defects by engineering out hidden hazards in products before going to market with them in the first place; that is, by proactively redesigning products to eliminate such hazards. What that means, whether the corporate executives would admit it or not, is that they are willing to allow their companies to be responsible for countless numbers of serious injuries and—yes, even fatalities—as a result of the defects or hidden hazards in their products of which they are fully cognizant.

6. *Invest profits into growing the product line while continuing to design new, also potentially dangerous products for sale to an unwitting public.*

Basically, the strategy of the Reactive Economic Model enables the beat to go on. Sadly, it would appear that once you have gotten comfortable with the ideas that: (1) you are going to need to set aside $$$—billions of dollars as a litigation and settlement fund; (2) that X number of people will be injured or killed by the dangerous products that you or your organization are responsible for putting on the consumer market; and (3) you are further able to keep that hidden hazard information away from federal regulators and the general consumer-public, it's apparently easy to rationalize these factors and to simply continue on that course. Paying for litigation and hopefully out-of-court settlements simply becomes part of the cost of doing business. And if a few people die, well, it's like I said in the first sentence of this book: It's a dangerous world out there.

Fortunately, we have also seen examples of companies that have taken a different course. One such company that I discussed in detail is Daikin Industries, which stands out as an exemplar for its fundamental efforts to engage in principled disclosure, right from the very beginning, upon entering the new marketplace (for them) of North America for the first time in the company's history. As I noted, Daikin's actions were even more remarkable given the fact that their executives came from a culture in which lawsuits over personal injuries due to corporate negligence or failure to warn are largely unheard of. But you can't argue with the positive results because, to this day, Daikin has not been hit with a single lawsuit charging negligence for failure to warn.

Then there's Rheem Manufacturing Company. Their forthright response to the growing number of lawsuits in connection with accidental explosions and fires caused by the pilot lights or ignition modules in the company's line of water heaters was to hire expert consultants to devise effective warning labels to inform consumers of a hazard that could not be designed out of the units themselves. Thus, instead of denying responsibility, or trying to sweep the hazard under the rug, or blaming consumers who "should have known better," Rheem also chose the high road of principled disclosure by prominently placing their warning labels on product packaging and in high-visibility locations on the units themselves. Both Daikin and Rheem can be credited with holding up their respective industry's leg of the Proactive Safety Triad.

These examples, as well as many others, prove that manufacturers can have both profits and safety, provided they reverse the perverse Reactive Economic Model and replace it with what I call the Proactive Economic Model, which consists of the following steps:

1. *Conduct meaningful market research that produces product ideas based on what people **need** to become more effective in various aspects of their lives.*

2. *Design products based upon this research while, simultaneously, with the help of expert facilitators who aren't involved in the product's design, conduct a valid, reliable and thorough hazard analysis that strives to identify the most likely and severe hazards that could result from the product's use.*

   (Note: In some cases, it may be advisable that the expert facilitators are NOT employees of the company or members of the company's R&D team, but outside, independent individuals or firms with primary expertise in hazard identification and elimination, where possible. When elimination of a hidden hazard proves impossible, companies should also consider seeking expert facilitators of warnings communications that are clear and effective enough to preclude consumer lawsuits based on negligence or failure to warn.)

3. *If attempts to eliminate or guard against these hazards are not totally possible, then design and communicate effective warnings and safety communications (with the help of a warnings expert, if needed) so both workers and consumers have sufficient information to make necessary **informed choices** about whether or not to manufacture or buy the product and, if so, how to use it safely.*

4. *Manufacture products, while making sure to include all necessary warnings and safety communications.*

5. *Market and sell products and collect profits, knowing that if there still are a few lawsuits resulting from injured workers or consumers, they can now be strongly defended, at least on the central issue of failure to warn about hidden hazards.*

6. *Invest profits (and savings from significantly reduced litigation costs) in further growth and designing new and even safer products with a continued commitment to thorough hazard analyses, efforts to eliminate hidden hazards where feasible, and complete transparency about hazards that cannot be completely eliminated.*

THE TASK OF DEFINING HIDDEN HAZARDS

As a warnings expert for nearly 42 years, it is inescapably my task to look for the hidden hazards in manufactured products, foods, and medications lurking in the human work, home, travel, play, and communication environments we create and inhabit. As I have described in numerous places throughout this book, when I am advising corporate clients, nonprofit organizations, or government entities, the goal is most often a singularly pragmatic—and yes, a strictly financially driven one. The purpose, plain and simple, is to protect these clients from lawsuits brought by consumers or workers that lead to expensive, often drawn-out litigation and the paying out of substantial monetary settlements, or worse, massive judgments handed down by judges or sympathetic juries. In this sense, quite frankly from industry's perspective, it is, indeed, "all about the money."

Of course, I would point out to industries in general that being *all about the money* is what leads corporations into the murky and unforgiving legal swamps of negligence and product liability in the first place. Being all about the money is what leads otherwise rational, business-savvy corporate executives at the highest levels to willingly ignore dangerous product defects while denying responsibility for them. They sink even deeper into the morass, engaging in what has been legitimately classified by U.S. federal prosecutors as potentially felonious criminal behavior.

To try to counter this downward spiral, no doubt the questions that I must ask nervous CEOs and other company executives must seem pointedly and furtively negative-sounding—even self-incriminating. Questions like the following:

- What is (are) the hidden hazard(s) in your product or environment?
- How can people be hurt or killed by those hazards?
- What segment(s) of the population is(are) most at risk of injury or death from using your products without knowledge of the hidden hazards?

I need to know these things in minute detail—the worst-case scenarios of course—but also the less obvious dangers that may, nevertheless, result in consumer lawsuits for failure to warn, for example, and which, in turn, may result in judgments that go against my company clients, or more likely will involve significant monetary settlements to make the cases go away. This may seem cold and calculating and, frankly, from industry's standpoint at least, it certainly is. When all is said and done, business is ultimately about one thing: making money and maximizing profits—for the executives, the employees, and, let's not forget, the shareholders of public corporations.

As for my own standpoint, however, I would argue that it is not all so "clinical" or solely economically driven as it may sound.

I need to know these things in order to craft, design, and test warning labels when the hidden hazards pose dangers to consumer health and safety. I need to know the things that cannot be entirely or reliably designed out of the product or environment. In other words, my foremost and overriding goal is to design effectively communicated warnings that protect ordinary people from potentially serious harm. Do I believe that American industries should feel the same way about principled disclosure and the consumer's right to informed consent? Absolutely.

It is also important to assert strenuously that I am not an alarmist naysayer bent on discovering product flaws or dangerous negative impacts of environments. Nor am I a critic or in some way opposed to modern technological innovation and change. Quite the contrary, I am enthusiastically in favor of innovation that results in brilliantly conceived and designed products and user-friendly environments that make our daily tasks more efficient and our lives more enjoyable, while also making our world safer for everyone from children to families to workers and to consumers in general.

In fact, when I am working with a company that has been experiencing problems with lawsuits arising out of hidden hazards or legal accusations of failure to warn about those hazards, truly the best outcome I can achieve is when my efforts directly put an immediate end to that conga line of lawsuits. How do we achieve that? Through principled disclosure that provides informed consent for consumers and workers. To state it differently, the lawsuits invariably stop when manufacturers have given consumers all of the information and all of the warnings they need to use products safely while avoiding fully disclosed hidden hazards. In effect, it is only when principled disclosure is provided that a CEO or a judge or a jury can legitimately say that a consumer who nevertheless willfully ignores it "should have known better."

The ten key steps for principled disclosure are:

1. *Warn specifically for hidden hazards not likely to be known by users at the time of purchase or use.*
2. *Don't warn for open and obvious hazards that have high awareness among the public.*
3. *Follow all appropriate warning codes, standards, and regulations.*
4. *Communicate efficiently without sacrificing needed warnings and safety information.*
5. *Avoid information overload/obfuscation with clear, succinct, easily understood language.*
6. *Clearly communicate both the nature of the hazard and the consequences of exposure.*
7. *Provide appropriate instructional information to avoid the hazard and/or its consequences.*
8. *Design warnings conspicuously (appropriate size, color(s), signal words, location(s), etc.).*
9. *Use pictographs to enhance the comprehension of a warning's written language.*
10. *Use the best, most appropriate communication channel(s) to deliver the safety message.*

Let's review each of these ten points.

THE TEN KEY STEPS TO PRINCIPLED DISCLOSURE

1. *Warn specifically for hidden hazards not likely to be known by users at the time of purchase or use.*

To state it in positive terms, we might be inclined to say that it is a curious irony of innovative product design that, perhaps because we as consumers tend to focus on what tasks the product can do for us, we fail to see the product's shortcomings or the ways that it might harm us, particularly if we use it the wrong way, either accidentally or intentionally. That's, of course, why they are "hidden" hazards, as well as why the manufacturers must clearly warn about them. To use a very 21st-century example, it's why at least some of the well-meaning creators of various social media channels may not have imagined how some individuals and groups might deliberately exploit such channels for destructive or subversive purposes—such as bullying or inciting violence or to steal personal and/or credit card and financial information.

2. *Don't warn for open and obvious hazards that have high awareness among the public.*

This point recalls Supreme Court Justice Warren Burger's famous edict that when you "warn about everything, you warn about nothing." We had a glimpse of this phenomenon when we examined the 21 warnings in small print plastered on labels affixed to the common 8- or 10-foot folding ladders that practically every homeowner probably has in their garages or garden sheds. However, in the case of the household ladder, at least some of those warnings were reasonably meaningful and legitimately useful for avoiding accidents and potentially serious injury. But the fact is that sometimes companies can go too far.

In a short, admittedly entertaining book subtitled, *The 101 Stupidest, Silliest, and Wackiest Warning Labels Ever*, Bob Dorigo Jones leads off with Century company's Travelite SPORT collapsible baby stroller, which folds up for easy storage. The stroller's very first warning on the label is "Remove child before folding" (which Bob, shall we say, "appropriated" as the title of his bestselling book). While ludicrously funny on one level, the danger of such ridiculous warnings against the patently obvious is that people subsequently tend to ignore *all* warnings related to the product whatsoever—even valid ones that could save them from serious injury or worse.

As a result, when the consumer-homeowner sees an essentially brainless warning on a step ladder to "always use caution getting on or off a ladder," he or she is very likely to avoid other, more significant warnings on the label regarding objectively real hazards that do deserve attention and avoidance.

3. *Follow all appropriate warning codes, standards, and regulations.*

It goes without saying that companies should comply with all codes, standards, and regulations required or imposed by the government regulatory agencies responsible for overseeing their particular industry. We will discuss regulatory responsibilities in greater detail in the next chapter.

4. *Communicate efficiently without sacrificing needed warnings and safety information.*

Quite simply, use only as many words as are necessary to succinctly convey the nature of the hidden hazard. My diving hazard warning sign uses simple words like "DANGER," "SHALLOW WATER," and "NO DIVING." As Rudolf Flesch contended in his watershed book, *The Art of Readable Writing* and elsewhere, in order to be most effectively communicated, the message must consist of no more than five to seven words.

5. *Avoid information overload/obfuscation with clear, succinct, easily understood language.*

In addition to using as few words as are necessary, the terminology itself should be simple and direct, employing terms that are the most easily understood potentially by the most number of people, regardless of their education level.

6. *Clearly communicate both the nature of the hazard and the consequences of exposure.*

My studies have shown that it is not enough to identify the hazard and leave the warning at that. Call it a "fear factor" if you will, but an important and integral feature of any truly effective warning label is to directly communicate to product users, in no uncertain terms, the horrible things that can happen to them if they choose to ignore the warning. For example: "DIVING MAY CAUSE DEATH OR PERMANENT SPINAL INJURY."

7. *Provide appropriate instructional information to avoid the hazard and/or its consequences.*

My research and that of many other experts has universally found that the warnings communication that is truly the most effective not only identifies the hazard and the consequences of exposure to it, but also communicates helpful information on how to avoid the hazard altogether. Sometimes this is as simple as essentially saying, "Do not," as in "**DO NOT DIVE!**"

8. *Design warnings conspicuously (appropriate size, color(s), signal words, location(s), etc.).*

One of the abundant lessons I have learned from hundreds of field tests of product warning labels is that strategic placement is critical. It is not unusual for a matter of mere inches up or down, or to one side or the other, to mean the difference between whether the warnings are actually seen—and thus hopefully heeded—by consumers or workers or totally missed and consequently ignored.

9. *Use pictographs to enhance the comprehension of a warning's written language.*

Whether we like it or not, English language literacy across America varies tremendously, whether due to large populations of nonnative English speakers or to significant differences in educational level. Fortunately, internationally adopted pictographs have proved to be highly effective in conveying the danger of hidden hazards to one's personal self. These include the pictograph used by Daikin and others to pictorialize severe electric shock, the stick man on fire used in Rheem's pilot light fire hazard warning label, and the wheelchair logo I designed for diving hazard signs.

10. *Use the best, most appropriate communication channel(s) to deliver the safety message.*

Perhaps the easiest way to illustrate this final key to principled disclosure by industry is to cite the most flagrant example in which the best and most appropriate communication channels are most certainly *not* being used, but through a channel that is accordingly being seriously *abused*. That, in my opinion, is the way that Big Pharma "warns" of hidden hazards in its broadcast direct-to-consumer drug advertising through the channels of television, radio, and the internet. They do so by drowning out the message through the use of all sorts of beautiful visual and harmonious audio distractions.

One company in particular that really took the importance of optimal warnings placement to heart was Playtex. In July 2005, the FDA issued urgent new guidelines requiring feminine menstrual tampon product manufacturers to warn consumers about Toxic Shock Syndrome (TSS) associated with a new generation of superabsorbent tampons. According to the Mayo Clinic, TSS is a rare, life-threatening complication of certain types of bacterial infections, primarily resulting from toxins produced by *Staphylococcus aureus* (staph) bacteria or less frequently by toxins produced by group A *streptococcus* (strep) bacteria. The FDA order allowed manufacturers to place the required and rather extensively worded warning on either the outside or the inside of the product packages, but in an admirable abundance of caution, Playtex went above and beyond.

First, after retaining me to create, design, and field test for the most effective warning label design and wording, the company's executive board approved as a matter of course the final design I recommended. Next, they opted to put the label both on the outside *and* the inside of the packaging, although again, they were only required to do one or the other; not both. But they didn't stop there.

Because initially, Playtex planned to print the exterior version of the warning label on the top of the box. They assumed, logically enough, that the top was where the consumer would typically be expected to open the package, thus presumably seeing the crucial warning. That was until one of their engineers pointed out that it was just as easy for consumers to open the box from the bottom. In response, Playtex spent a small fortune on new package assembly equipment that enabled them to tightly seal the bottom of the box to make it nearly impossible to open the package from the bottom. Then they proceeded to print the warning on the top, sides, and bottom of the outside of the package, in bright red print, as well as prominently including the same warning inside the box. Bottom line: Playtex made it virtually impossible for anyone to be able to claim in court that they were never warned about the risks of toxic shock syndrome.

However, one more thing about the voluntary proactive safety labeling precautions taken by Playtex, which, by the way, were not adopted immediately by their competitors: One of the driving forces behind the company's bold and decisive action was their chief corporate counsel, Joel Coleman. Not once in any of my meetings with the Playtex board did I hear the word "profit" uttered by anyone. In fact, the company took the opposite approach in saying essentially, "Money be damned; let's reengineer the packaging, print the warning all over the box, and do the right thing right from day one [of the FDA order]."

In contrast to so many companies in so many industries that grudgingly adopt warnings messages solely because they are mandated by federal regulation or forced to do so by the leapfrogging cost of consumer lawsuits, Joel Coleman made an impassioned plea to the board to "spend the money to do this right, save lives, and make us the leading conscience of the industry. We don't want women contracting life-threatening conditions as a result of using our products."

National survey studies conducted after the FDA mandate went into effect would later reveal that a majority of respondents learned about the hidden hazard of TSS from the Playtex company packages more than from those of any other tampon-manufacturing company. And sales of Playtex's line of tampon products continued to rise accordingly.

In stark contrast, think of the enduring legacy faced by the principals of Takata Corporation, even after the company filed for bankruptcy on June 25, 2017. According to an *Insurance Journal* report, as of December 2018, some 16.7 million of the recalled air bag inflator mechanisms were still in use in vehicles traveling on U.S. roads alone.[120] That was one full year after the government-ordered deadline for replacing all of these defective and extremely dangerous devices. But it gets even worse, because in early 2019, the National Highway Traffic Safety Administration ordered the recall of an additional 19 to 24 million vehicles with defective Takata airbags, bringing the grand total to between 65 and 70 million.[121] It may be decades before the last exploding airbag is sent to the scrap heap of corporate folly.

THE (NECESSARY) FUTURE OF PRINCIPLED DISCLOSURE FOR INDUSTRY

I cannot conclude a chapter posited on the responsibilities of industry to actively embrace principled disclosure and fulfill its role as one of the three essential legs of the Proactive Safety Triad without saying a few prescriptive words—and issuing a stern warning of my own to today's companies—about the new reality of the rapidly evolving version of the information age in the 21st century. My warning is simply this: Do not fail to heed the words of Marshall McLuhan a half century ago when, as I noted in Chapter 8, he accurately predicted that instantaneous communication and

---

[120]Krisher, "Takata."
[121]NHTSA, "Takata."

worldwide interconnected media would bring about a global "retribaliza-tion" of people through the creation of an information environment in which "everybody gets the message [immediately] all the time."

Today, a consumer who has a problem with the headlights of his or her car can go online, google the make, model, and year of the vehicle, and find perhaps 15 other people who had the same problem, as well as what they did to fix it. That means that they are also able to discover if the problem is a chronic one that may indicate a manufacturing defect—whether it's one acknowledged by the car manufacturer or denied to exist at all. The point is that it's becoming a much more informationally transparent world out there and, going into the future—indeed even at the present moment—it is a lot more difficult for industry to keep their dirty little hidden hazards a secret from consumers and the general public than it used to be even a short decade ago. The cautionary proviso that "people talk" used to apply only to petty gossip. Now, thanks to the internet, it may easily apply to everyone and everything.

So, to all businesses and industry that wish to survive and prosper in the 21st century, I say simply this: Social media has its eyes on you. And while certainly not the noblest of motivations, the notion that the news of deliberate corporate failure to adequately warn consumers of known defects or hidden hazards in their products ought to be more than enough to convince any CEO in America to think twice about finally embracing principled disclosure and to participate in the cooperative dynamic of the Proactive Safety Triad.

CHAPTER 10

REGULATORS: HOW DO YOU CLOSE A REVOLVING DOOR?

"We have been legislated to death."
—James T. Hoyle, Secretary of the Manufacturers'
Association, spearheading the opposition to new
worker safety laws proposed in the wake of the
Triangle Shirtwaist Co. factory fire that killed
146 textile workers on March 25, 1911, a disaster
unsurpassed in New York City until the 9/11 attack
on the World Trade Center.[122]

There is only one singularly decisive thing that can and someday must be done in order to solve once and for all the systemic and long-standing problem that has plagued virtually all U.S. governmental regulatory agencies, authorities, and commissions historically right from their respective inceptions. It is a fundamental reform that is critically necessary if these regulatory bodies are individually ever going to be truly able to fulfill their industry-specific missions of protecting the general public as well as collectively acting to strenuously support the regulatory leg of the Proactive Safety Triad that I propose.

---

[122] Baram and Stone, "Triangle."

Actually, it's two things, and they are both major concerns. And they are both, quite unfortunately, highly unlikely to happen anytime soon.

END THE REVOLVING DOOR

The first is to end, once and for all, the "revolving door" that continues to spin freely as top executive industry insiders jump to the helm of agencies whose function is to regulate the very industry from whence they came, and then just as easily jump back into positions of power as CEOs and other top-ranking heads of companies within the very same industry. We saw this very clearly in Chapter 8 in the example of the abbreviated 11-month tenure of Robert Califf as head of the FDA. There, we profiled an individual so deeply plugged into the pharmaceutical industry that even Congress—with its long and storied history of installing Big Pharma puppets at the FDA—could no longer support his embarrassing continuance in the top post.

However, gross conflict of interest is by far the rule rather than the exception at virtually all U.S. regulatory agencies. In a nonscientific survey conducted by my own organization, we found that nearly 67 percent, or two-thirds, of all senior staffers in positions of authority with such agencies had come either directly or indirectly from careers in the very industries they were hired to oversee and regulate. Making matters worse, there is nothing in their federal contracts that prevents them from blithely switching back and forth. There's no clause to, in effect, prevent them from being enriched through the kinds of "regulations" they impose, or more likely, fail to impose as so-called regulators—when they inevitably return to senior positions in the same industry.

There is actually a very simple strategy that could effectively correct this intolerable yet nonetheless pervasive situation almost immediately. Moreover, it is a solution that is available right now if and when lawmakers ever summon the courage to invoke it. Of course, therein lies the rub.

Consumer advocates have long maintained that executives hired into certain key leadership positions among the most essential U.S. regulatory agencies must be required to agree to a clause in their contracts that restricts or prohibits them from working in or profiting from that industry for a specified period of time after they leave the government agency. This is by no means extreme, nor without legal precedent. Big business in the corporate sector routinely requires senior executives to sign employment contracts that contain a noncompete clause that legally prevents them, should they decide to leave the firm, from working for other companies or organizations engaged in the same industry.

Not only that, but such contracts also often prevent ex-executives from disclosing trade secrets and other sensitive internal information they may have been privy to while a standing member of the firm. So, think about it: Even if they leave the firm under amicable circumstances, like retirement, for example, executives bound by this contractual obligation are not even allowed to discuss their former employer's internal dealings from their retirement homes in the Hamptons or their yachts in Boston Harbor.

In order to effectively reform the regulatory process across all U.S. agencies, many outspoken consumer advocates have called for agency executives to be contractually prohibited from working in the regulated industry for a period of five years after leaving the agency. I believe that's not enough. I believe that the prohibition must be for a full ten years. And I also like the idea of including a restriction against disclosure of the agency's internal information.

After all, this could include sensitive information about ongoing investigations into questionable or dubious industry practices, or attempted cover-ups of known hidden hazards, product flaws, and so on. Why allow former executive regulators, even after they have left the agency, to tip off a company or industry practice under investigation that might, in turn, result in the company dodging responsibility for injury liability or negligence in court? But the broader and more critical question is this: If noncompete clauses are good enough for American and international business and industry, why should anyone object to their being equally applied to the important "business" of government regulatory oversight?

END INTRUSIVE LEGISLATIVE AND EXECUTIVE
MEDDLING IN REGULATORY AUTHORITY

The second requirement for effective reform is for the various regulatory agencies to be given real and unabridged power to initiate and enforce meaningful regulations on industry without interference or overbearing oversight by Congress as well as by the executive branch. In order to carry out its mandate, any regulatory agency or department charged with the responsibility of protecting the general public or consumers or workers and so on, must be empowered to both set the safety and hazard warnings rules and take aggressive, impactful action when they are not followed.

Yes, the safety rules, or the stipulated warnings requirements for hidden hazards in products or environments, must be based on solid scientific or empirical evidence of potential danger. That is to say, regulators must refrain from issuing nuisance rules and regulations that only serve to hamper business and industry and to confuse the general public. But when the dangers to public safety are real and demonstrable, regulators must be able to order companies to comply with full, principled disclosure of the hazards without having such orders—and the agency's autonomous authority—abridged by any other governmental authority, particularly one that is heavily influenced either directly or indirectly by the industry itself.

Examples include the EPA's decades-long effort to lower the standard for maximum allowable worker exposure to beryllium dust based on tested, scientific evidence only to be thwarted, time and again, by the U.S. Department of Defense and the Atomic Energy Commission working in direct collusion with the principal manufacturer of the metal. More recently, and very much in the news in the wake of several railroad fatalities over the past three years, in August 2017, the federal government under the Trump administration ordered two agencies within the Department of Transportation to drop plans for a regulation designed to combat obstructive sleep apnea among truck drivers and train engineers.

In a joint statement, their hands forced, the Federal Motor Carrier Administration and the Federal Railroad Administration announced that they "have determined not to issue a notice of proposed rulemaking," adding, in Caspar Milquetoast fashion, that they "believe that current safety programs" and other rules "addressing fatigue risk management are the appropriate avenues to address" the issue of sleep-related disorders.[123] What about the fatalities—nearly a dozen—in three railroad crashes that have been linked to sleep apnea in New York, New Jersey, and Pennsylvania alone? Never mind that the National Transportation Safety Board (NTSB) has been calling for better sleep apnea screening of truck drivers and railway motormen since 2009, to no avail.

At the same time, regulators must have the courage to step up to the plate when it comes to setting definitive guidelines rather than allowing specific industries to "police" themselves, as we have also seen so often throughout this book. Even more fundamentally, the prevailing culture within any regulatory agency must include unassailable and uncompromising autonomy. Recall EPA Deputy Director Jess Rowland's willingness, upon learning that the World Health Organization's International Agency for Research on Cancer (IARC) was about to classify glyphosate as a probable carcinogen, to try to quash the DHHS study for his executive friends at Roundup manufacturer Monsanto![124]

For regulators to be able to do even this, they need the full support and backing of the legislative and executive branches of government. A case in point that clearly illustrates all of these serious and troubling flaws plaguing the system is the ongoing story of a chemical called BMPEA and the Office of Dietary Supplement Programs (ODSP). ODSP is a tiny branch of the FDA with the formidable responsibility of overseeing the ever-burgeoning vitamin and dietary supplements industry.

WHEN INDUSTRY IS ALLOWED TO POLICE ITSELF: AMPHETAMINE AS A DIETARY SUPPLEMENT

According to the FDA, as of 2015, the dietary supplements industry had grown to over $35 billion in sales in the U.S. alone. The international

---

[123] Cullen, "Sleep Apnea."
[124] Rosenblatt et al., "EPA."

marketing analytics firm of Zion Market Research estimated that worldwide sales of dietary supplements topped $138 billion in 2016 and projects that they will surpass $220 billion by the year 2022.[125]

Yet, the ODSP is modestly staffed. An FDA spokeswoman indicated that as of 2016, the ODSP had only 23 full-time employees. Meanwhile, it is estimated that there are over 50,000 different dietary supplements available on the market today, with new products being added virtually every day.

BMPEA is a powerful chemical stimulant nearly identical to amphetamine that, according to a Canadian government public health alert, "can increase blood pressure, heart rate, and body temperature; lead to serious cardiovascular complications [including stroke and heart attack] at high doses, suppress sleep and appetite, and be addictive."[126] To its credit, in 2013, the U.S. FDA was the first agency to investigate the use of BMPEA as an ingredient in weight-loss and power-workout supplements, reporting its findings in *The Journal of Pharmacological and Biomedical Analysis*. It documented levels of BMPEA, in some products as high as 19 to 31 milligrams, in nine out of 21 dietary supplements.[127] Mostly in pill form, a number of these supplements boast names suggestive of street drug jargon like Black Widow, Yellow Scorpion, and Hardcore.

At this point, it is important to note that none of these products specifically lists BMPEA on their labels as an ingredient. Instead, they all list a little-known plant called *Acacia rigidula*, a shrub native to Mexico and southern Texas from which BMPEA can be synthesized. This deception is deliberate and calculated. One independent scientist who investigated the presence of the chemical in supplements was Dr. Pieter Cohen, an assistant professor at Harvard Medical School. Cohen indicated that it is a common practice for companies to spike workout-exercise and weight-loss dietary supplements with high stimulant, amphetamine-like chemicals

[125] Zion Market Research, "Dietary Supplements."
[126] O'Connor, "Dangers."
[127] Advisory Board, "Diet supplements."

and then hide those ingredients on the product labels under the names of obscure plants to give the impression they are natural botanical extracts. Calling the label listing of *Acacia rigidula* as an ingredient in so many supplement products a red flag, Cohen and academic scientists at some other universities conducted their own analyses. Quite disturbingly, Cohen and his group initiated their study only after the FDA refused to tell them which supplements contained BMPEA. Undaunted, Cohen and his colleagues found the stimulant in 11 of 21 products, including many of those previously tested by the FDA. These findings were subsequently published in the journal *Drug Testing and Analysis*.[128]

However, unfortunately, the FDA's due diligence with respect to "disclosure" ended with the quiet publication of its findings in a scholarly journal with limited (primarily professional) readership. The agency correspondingly failed (through the ODSP branch) to issue an alert that these products contained a dangerous and potentially addictive chemical. Further, it also did not make public the names of the products containing BMPEA or the companies that manufactured them. In fact, when Canadian health authorities determined that the chemical posed "a serious health risk" and ordered supplements containing BMPEA to be pulled from that country's store shelves, the FDA/ODSP responded with a statement saying that its review of these products "does not identify a specific safety concern at this time."[129] How do we reconcile such a disparate, conflictive, and unsatisfactory response?

Public health experts critical of the FDA's failure to act in the case of BMPEA blame a long-standing pattern of conflicts of interest resulting from the agency's proclivity for hiring top agency regulators from among the executive ranks of the food and supplements industry itself—the revolving door in full swing once again. During the years that BMPEA came under close scrutiny by the FDA and other public health officials, the head of the ODSP was none other than Daniel Fabricant (from 2011

---

[128] Cohen et al., "Amphetamine Isomer."
[129] O'Connor, "Dangers."

to 2014). Prior to taking the post as head of ODSP, Fabricant had been a senior executive with the Natural Products Association (another name you have to love for its sublimely self-contained, subterranean deception).

As the largest and most powerful dietary supplements industry lobbying and trade group, the NPA spends millions of dollars every year lobbying to block new laws that would require supplement-makers to meet stricter standards for product ingredient disclosure and consumer safety. And when Daniel Fabricant later resigned his post as head of ODSP at the FDA, just where do you suppose he went? He became the Executive Director and CEO of … you guessed it … the Natural Products Association. (Meanwhile, upon Fabricant's departure, the FDA installed as the temporary, interim head at ODSP, Cara Welch, another alumnus of the NPA. Is the needle stuck on this record or something?)

Even after leaving the FDA, Fabricant unflinchingly maintained that having former industry officials in charge of the FDA's dietary supplements division was "an incredible benefit to the agency," and reviving the tired and logically flawed line about the "efficiency" of having people who know the "ins-and-outs" of the industry. Michael Jacobson, executive director of the Center for Science in the Public Interest, has an ominous and decidedly different point of view, stating that having "former officials in the supplement industry become the chief regulators of that industry at the FDA is like having the fox guarding the henhouse."[130]

Meanwhile, the NPA's lobbying efforts against government efforts to increase regulatory scrutiny and power of control over dietary supplements of any kind has been ferocious. According to the nonpartisan Center for Responsive Politics, the NPA spent $1.5 million in 2013 and 2014 lobbying the FDA, key members of the House and Senate, and the Federal Trade Commission. The NPA was instrumental in clearing the way for passage of the 1994 Dietary Supplement Health and Education Act, which specifically exempted dietary supplements from the kind of rigorous oversight and strict disclosure requirements applied to prescription pharmaceuticals

---

[130] Ibid.

and medical devices, and, for all intents and purposes, allowed the supplements industry to police itself.

That piece of legislation, by the way, was sponsored by Senator Orrin Hatch of Utah, in whose state many of the largest supplement companies happen to be not-so-coincidently headquartered. To make things even more cozy, the senator's son, Scott Hatch, is a founding partner of the Washington, D.C., firm that lobbies for the Natural Products Association. The extensive entanglements of the lobbying industry in our nation's capital are more complexly interconnected than most citizens realize.

In any case, such laws serve to severely undercut the FDA's ability to properly fulfill its duty to provide, oversee, and enforce protective regulatory functions. It certainly doesn't help matters when executive refugees from the food, drug, and supplements industries are appointed, one after another after another, as chief agency regulators and, subsequently, have no real interest or desire in doing it either. More recently, the NPA has turned its aggressive and powerful lobbying juggernaut against the Dietary Supplement Labeling Act, which would require supplement labels to carry what in reality only amounts to the most basic information about potential side effects of these often-mysterious concoctions. The Act would also require the labels to provide warnings about ingredients that could be harmful to children and pregnant women, a requirement that would seem to be in everyone's interest—even the people at the NPA.

All of this becomes particularly frustrating to local and state health authorities desperately trying to address sometimes epidemic public health concerns but getting no help whatsoever from the federal government regulatory "authorities" in Washington. In April 2015, for example, 14 state attorney generals, led by New York's Eric Schneiderman, called on Congress to provide the FDA with greater power to more forcefully and more meaningfully regulate dietary supplements. With little likelihood of serious recourse from congressional leaders, Schneiderman's office has tried to fight the battle on the state level by accusing four major retailers of selling contaminated herbal products. That action gained, at least, the cooperation of one of the companies, GNC, which agreed to perform extensive new testing and heightened quality control procedures for its in-store brand of herbal products.

Of course, the problem of inaction on the part of government regulatory agencies like the FDA and all the others is not limited to dietary supplements. There are a growing number of cases in which local officials have become convinced that they have no other choice but to fight the battles that the FDA is too timid or too influentially constricted by outside forces (or simply refuses) to engage in for political reasons. In June 2017, exasperated with the continued combined failure of the both the FDA and the pharmaceuticals industry to do anything to stem the flood of prescription painkillers responsible for the local opioid epidemic, Nassau County in Long Island filed suit in New York State court against 19 pharmaceutical companies and five local doctors. Earlier that year, Suffolk County had filed a similar suit against 11 Big Pharma companies.

The Nassau County suit alleges the companies and the physicians knew about the addictiveness of prescription painkillers and didn't properly inform patients. The suit seeks millions of dollars to recoup costs for its drug rehab programs, Narcan trainings, and police overtime, yet further contends the companies should also pay for expenses related to the county's exploding heroin epidemic, alleging that many people who were addicted to prescription opioids have made the downward-spiral transition to heroin.

Returning once more to the scandalous BMPEA fiasco, perhaps the most ironic reaction to the whole affair may be seen in the response of Vitamin Shoppe, a New Jersey-based retailer of nutritional supplements with nearly 800 stores nationwide. Upon learning of Dr. Pieter Cohen's BMPEA study, Vitamin Shoppe released the following statement:

> *We are concerned by the findings outlined in the study [and have] decided to remove these products because the safety of these products is now in question and may not be in compliance with F.D.A. regulations. In addition, the Vitamin Shoppe*

continues to encourage the FDA to use its authority to remove any dietary supplements from the market which it deems unsafe.[131] (emphasis mine)

Here, against a backdrop of a "henhouse guarded by foxes," we have an apparently conscientious product retailer trying its best to do the right thing and, at the same time, imploring the FDA/ODSP to do *its* job of protecting them (Vitamin Shoppe, the retailer) from selling dangerous and potentially addictive products to their customers!

In sum, the BMPEA saga in microcosm has all of the earmarks of a perfect storm of regulatory failure. That is, first we have an FDA subagency in the guise of ODSP that is administered from the very top by former industry executives whose conflicts of interest are plainly illustrated by the revolving door through which most of these individuals eventually return—often, as we have seen, after a tenure of only two to three years—to the same industry. Historically, these individuals are ineffectual, industry-leaning regulators disinclined (for all practical purposes) to bite the hand that feeds. That "hand," of course, consists of both companies and the powerful trade organizations that represent them by relentlessly lobbying Congress and many others on the industry's behalf.

In addition, we have an FDA subagency in ODSP that is far too small to oversee the vast, expanding universe of dietary supplements on the market today. Nor is ODSP alone in this regard, as understaffing is a serious problem across many government regulatory agencies. This presents a difficult problem, as one is reluctant to suggest that simply adding more staff, with the concomitant additional bureaucracy that seems to inevitably entail, is the proper solution. My recommendation is that greater openness and better cooperation between industry and regulators within the context of the Proactive Safety Triad may be the best solution to the

---

[131] Ibid.

staffing dilemma that exists at most regulatory agencies. For the mutually beneficial cause of protecting consumer safety through informed consent, wouldn't it be more effective for industry and regulators to operate as partners rather than adversaries?

Finally, and perhaps most ominously, we have the substantial power of influence through political pressure exerted by the legislative branch through adopted laws prohibiting certain powers of restriction by the FDA. There is also formidable political pressure not necessarily grounded in specific legislation, but just as palpable and influential as law itself. At the top of the influence-peddling funnel sits all of the money that the lobbying groups give to the campaign funds of senators and representatives on both sides of the aisle. When Robert Califf was confirmed as commissioner of the FDA, despite being about as transparently tainted by literally a dozen or more separate conflicts of interest, the vote in favor was 99 to zero. The only senator who did not vote in favor of the candidate was Bernie Sanders. However, even the typically courageous senator from Vermont could only muster enough will to abstain. Even Sanders could not bring himself to vote no. That's because the powerful lobbying interests are equal opportunity campaign donors. They give equally to both Republicans and Democrats. What better way to cover your bets?

In this section we have seen how the legislative leaders of our government often exert undue influence over regulators largely at the behest of industry lobbyists and trade groups. In the final section of this chapter, we will look at undue influence exerted even more directly—and arbitrarily—by the executive branch. It represents a kind of double-whammy even for those regulators trying to do their jobs. In point of fact, there is no more alarming example of executive obstruction of regulatory authority and agency autonomy than the earliest appointments and actions of the Trump administration and in particular, as we will see, the disturbing directives in the form of executive orders issued by the president himself.

A POLITICAL FOOTBALL

Government regulation of business and industry is a perennial hot-button, highly politicizing concept that far too often gets caught up in the hopelessly polarizing debate over big government versus capitalist free enterprise. It's an argument often carried on the tongues of constituencies who understand neither. I do not wish to wade into a debate that is both too ideologically simplistic and too broadly vague to be meaningful and constructive, other than to assert that prudent government regulation of industry really has nothing to do with big government and everything to do with public safety. And to the critics of federal and state regulatory authority, who so often cite the rubric that government should not be allowed to meddle in the affairs or the conduct of business and industry, I would say that, conceptually at least, I could agree with that proviso. But only if it was truly the case that business and industry could be trusted—of its own volition—to do the right thing by fully engaging in principled disclosure of the hidden hazards that exist in their products that would be aimed at providing consumers with informed consent. But they cannot.

Time and time again, we have explored case after case in which companies failed to warn consumers about the hazards hidden in their products (like aluminum electrical wiring in our homes) or environments (like the alligators swimming in Disney World's lagoons). We have seen companies deliberately conceal from the consumer-public hidden hazards that they unquestionably knew existed—like GM's faulty ignition switch or the sugar industry's efforts to disguise unhealthy added sugar in processed foods through the invention of no less than 30 different confusing and largely meaningless terms.

If anything, industry's temerity in snubbing its nose at public safety and the appalling extent to which it is apparently willing to put people at risk has, in recent years, only gotten worse. So great was the eye-blinking magnitude of Takata's and VW's recent reckless arrogance and appalling disregard for human life that federal courts in the U.S. have gone to the extreme of handing down criminal indictments against top-echelon executives in both companies, a move that is almost unprecedented. We also looked at how both low-tech and high-tech industries put profits over worker safety in the coal industry and in the manufacture of high-strength beryllium for the Department of Defense.

Incredibly, this is all happening within the context of, and despite, an exponentially morphing information age, in which the instantaneous communicating ability of virtually anyone with a cell phone in their hand anywhere on Earth is making it increasingly difficult, even impossible, to keep this kind of incendiary information away from consumers and the general public for very long. And you want to trust industry to do the right thing?

When you consider the full significance of these glaring examples, it is really not an exaggeration to say that, were it not for government regulation of industry, we might conceivably still have child labor and sweatshops with people helplessly locked inside. The bottom line is that the regulation of business and industry to protect its citizens and to promote their health and welfare will always be an important and necessary function of government in a democratic society.

With that said, the fact remains that the regulatory leg has done no better. From its early days of existence when it put a monetary value on human life in the Ford Pinto scandal, NHTSA has been historically slow to order automakers to warn consumers against dangerous conditions in their vehicles or to force them to initiate mandatory recalls when such defects make their cars too dangerous to drive. The Federal Railroad Administration (FRA) has for decades consistently failed to require the installation of positive train control on all commuter and freight rail lines in the country, bowing to cost concerns lamented by the railroad industry. Political pressure brought to bear on congressional representatives by the barons of industry has effectively induced OSHA to relax or completely overlook strict enforcement of critical worker safety rules—often in extremely dangerous industries like coal mining, where low-paid workers have nowhere else to turn for protection. The FDA has allowed food companies to use deceptive practices like listing health-endangering ingredients in grams rather than the traditional apothecaries' system that most Americans are familiar with. Worse, the agency has kowtowed to Big Pharma's aggressive and unrelenting direct-to-consumer broadcast advertising blitz. It is pushing a perilous regression to self-medication by consumers that many experts believe is one factor in America's burgeoning opioid addiction crisis. The list goes on and on, and it makes quite clear that carefully crafted and targeted government regulation of industry is needed just as critically today as it was 100 years ago.

THE REGULATORY LEG OF THE PROACTIVE SAFETY TRIAD IS WALKING BACKWARD

Despite the real and demonstrable benefits of prudent government regulation by the agencies I have discussed in this book, we seem today—after a decade of some positive progress and rather suddenly—to be headed in the wrong direction, toward wholesale deregulation. Not simply deregulation of business and industry, but also of environmental rules as well as legal protections and rules and requirements for patient health care coverage designed to protect all Americans. And while the responsibility for this policy reversal may be laid at the feet of the administration in Washington ushered in by the election of President Trump, it illuminates quite vividly the ways that regulatory agencies remain under the powerful thumb of political power embodied in the executive branch no matter who sits in the White House. That said, the plain fact of the matter is that, right from the start of his administration, President Trump has alarmingly become a virtual wrecking ball to the regulatory function of government in ways that will have a demonstrably detrimental impact on consumer and public safety. This will ultimately cost the country billions of dollars in both lost wages and productivity, burdensome health care costs due to workplace injuries, and legal and settlement fees resulting from product liability and failure to warn lawsuits brought against industry. In the next section, we look at just a few examples from a long and growing list of worrisome and downright dangerous executive actions already taken by the president. These representative examples are presented in no particular order.

TRUMP THE DESTROYER

Let's begin with our food. As we saw in Chapter 3, after almost a decade of delays and squabbling, in 2016, the FDA finalized plans to change our food supply's nutritional and ingredients labels to make them more readable for consumers, with the intent that ultimately the readily available information would positively affect consumers' health. For example, in one part of the label that I advised the FDA, they agreed to eliminate all of the confusing terms that actually defined a certain amount of sugar in each product. Names such as "high-fructose corn syrup" or "evaporated cane juice"—to cite but two of the 30 confusing and deceptive names for sugar now in use—would all be much more accurately combined into one basket labeled "added sugar." The ultimate hoped-for impact on the millions of obese and diabetic consumers in the U.S. would be that, with a clear understanding of the actual amount of added sugar in a product, consumers would alter their diets and include more foods without high amounts of added sugar. This, in turn, would hopefully lead to fewer cases of diabetes, cardiovascular problems, obesity, and even tooth decay.

However, the current administration is working to water down, delay, or even eliminate altogether the implementation of the language clarifying the amount of sugar in a food product. They claim it would place undue pressure on the food industry and might cause damaging job layoffs. Without any evidence at all, Trump's actions, should they be passed by Congress, would most certainly place at serious risk the lives of millions of Americans, particularly diabetics, who MUST have an accurate understanding of the amount of sugar per day they consume. Their lives depend on this information.

On the work front, after 68 years of operating with a falsely determined and unacceptably inadequate air quality standard for airborne contamination of beryllium dust resulting from processing (2.0 micrograms/cubic meter of air), OSHA and the Department of Defense, along with the sole player in the beryllium processing industry, Materion Corporation (formerly known as Brush Wellman) and the union representing their workers, finally agreed on reducing the beryllium standard to a more medically scientific 0.2 micrograms per cubic meter of air. The new rule was expected to go into effect on May 20, 2017, with OSHA projecting that the measure would save as many as 90 lives each year, as well as preventing many others from suffering from beryllium-related diseases like chronic beryllium disease (CBD and lung cancer). Also, the new standard would have prevented 46 new cases of CBD from occurring each year.

Beryllium exposure is not limited to union workers at Materion. Other people at risk include workers and technicians employed by private companies and U.S. military workers who shape and sand the high-strength metal in the manufacture of jet aircraft, missiles, and other weaponry. Exposure is also an issue for some 11,500 construction and shipyard workers, because trace amounts of beryllium show up in the sand-based mixture used to sandblast the hulls and interiors of ships being built or refurbished. OSHA estimates that as many as 62,000 workers in the U.S. alone are exposed to some form of beryllium in their workplaces.

Nevertheless, the administration in Washington has once again intervened and delayed implementation of this hard-fought-for standard twice and seems intent on blocking it indefinitely. Experts estimate that, for every four days that the standard is delayed, at least one beryllium worker will die. In similar fashion, and again on executive orders from the administration, OSHA has also put off enforcement of another recently adopted standard designed to safeguard workers against yet another serious respiratory hazard—silica, a mineral linked to a disabling lung disease as well as cancer.

The Trump administration's rollback of rules governing the coal mining industry includes repeal of the Stream Protection Rule, which was designed to prohibit the dumping of hazardous waste known as slag into rivers and streams. Further easing of rules governing coal mines will put miners at increased risk of health issues like black lung and emphysema. Ironically, this about-face comes at a time when the administration is also seeking to repeal the Affordable Care Act and its protections for pre-existing conditions. That and other coverage restrictions will mean ending health care coverage for those very same mineworkers exposed to greater risk of serious illness and death.

In the logging industry, certainly another very dangerous occupation, the administration struck down a newly enacted OSHA regulation that extended the statute of limitations "allowing OSHA to cite employers for up to five years for failing to make and maintain injury and illness records."[132] The resolution reinstated a much more lenient recordkeeping requirement issued by the U.S. Department of Labor, stating that the new OSHA rule would have imposed excessive "costs on employers resulting from continuing recordkeeping obligations."

Moving on to other areas of concern, the administration has also rolled back regulations that had restricted disabled persons from buying and possessing firearms. On the surface, the notion of restricting "disabled persons" from owning firearms does indeed sound like it might be potentially discriminatory; that is, until you dig down to understand what the legislation really says. As Representative Mike Thompson, D-Calif., explains, this regulation didn't cover "people just having a bad day. These are not people simply suffering from depression or anxiety or agoraphobia." Rather, Thompson said, "These are people with a severe mental illness who can't hold any kind of job or make any decisions about their affairs. So the law says very clearly they shouldn't have a firearm."[133]

I could go on and on citing the suspension or elimination of one consumer or worker protection regulation after another. However, what is really the most alarming about this administration's deregulatory mania is that it is arguably dangerously irrational. That is to say, in many instances, the administration seems intent on pursuing deregulation simply for the sake of deregulation itself, and without any regard to an objective assessment of the potential benefits versus costs. For example, in January 2017 just days after his inauguration, the president issued a blanket order that requires all regulatory agencies to kill two existing rules for each new one

---

[132] Seyfarth Shaw LLP, "OSHA."
[133] Lopez, "Congress."

they wish to adopt. The order also arbitrarily caps the permitted costs of new regulations—even ones unanimously backed by industries, lawmakers, and the public.

This is dangerous and utterly irresponsible. At numerous agencies, this reckless, inflexible policy has brought a near halt to the regulatory process itself. The order has forced delays, or the rethinking of innovative rules brokered through years-long efforts at compromise—ideas that achieved at least some, if tacit, support from typically reluctant industry leaders, and which were expected by all parties to create significant benefits.

Not only that, but some of these regulatory rollbacks will actually hurtfully impact people while not only *not* saving federal government funds, but quite to the contrary, potentially costing it much more money going forward. As part of its continuing and widening assault on regulations focused on even some of the most localized issues, in August 2017, the Trump administration repealed stringent building standards aimed at protecting government-financed projects in flood-prone areas primarily among eastern seaboard states. The new building standards for public and private infrastructure projects were put in place to account for sea-level rise associated with climate change, which, of course, is a widely accepted scientific fact that the present administration nevertheless holds in singular dispute.

But here is the perplexing thing. By overturning the two-year-old regulation, this executive order rolls back protections for infrastructure projects funded *with federal aid*. In other words, viewed as one of the most significant steps taken in decades to reduce exposure to more frequent flooding due to sea-level rise and climate change, the rule would have ensured taxpayers' dollars would not be wasted on infrastructure projects subject to repeated flooding. We are talking here about substantial amounts—billions of dollars—of federal money paid out by FEMA and the National Flood Insurance Program to homeowners and shorefront businesses every time they are damaged or destroyed by storm-related flooding.

Meanwhile, the president's actions ignore the human cost of these events. "This anti-regulatory agenda is really going to put lives, first responders, and property at risk," said Tim Dillingham, executive director of the American Littoral Society. "Economically, it is going to increase costs for disaster bailout and storm recovery efforts."[134]

Earlier, in June 2017, Interior Secretary Ryan Zinke announced that his department would cut over 4,000 full-time staff within the next year, while at about the same time the *Washington Post* reported that the EPA would also cut some 1,200 jobs, or about eight percent of the agency's 15,000 employees, by September 2017.[135] Independent national polls invariably indicate that a vast majority of Americans are strongly in favor of protecting our environment and national resources, yet among the first people to be shown the door at the EPA were the entire Board of Scientific Counselors. This critical body consists of dozens of independent scientists charged with the responsibility of providing actionable advice and recommendation to the agency's Office of Research and Development and helps steer the EPA's research programs.

Of course, the reason for this wholesale housecleaning is anything but scientifically motivated. Critics among the scientific community and elsewhere, including several past members of the Board, have expressed deep shock and concern that the move will allow the Trump administration to appoint scientists or others—even nonscientists—more friendly to industry, especially companies that are regulated by the agency. Ultimately, the firing of the existing members of the Board diabolically cuts the unbiased, purely scientifically grounded legs right out from under the EPA. In effect, the hiring of industry-sympathetic replacements merely greases the wheels of the revolving door.

The list continues. According to a *U.S. News and World Report* article in July 2017, the Trump administration had withdrawn or delayed 860 proposed regulations in just its first five months in office.[136] Here again, what is most troublesome about this abrupt and wholesale suspension or

---

[134] Johnson, "Trump."
[135] Dennis, "EPA."
[136] Reuters, "Trump."

outright rejection of long sought-after consumer, worker, health, and environmental protections is that little or no consideration is being given to their potential merit, and no effort is being made to undertake a cost/benefit re-evaluation on an itemized basis. Sadly, it seems that in the minds of the Trump administration, all regulation is inherently bad. One thing seems abundantly clear: Through no fault of its own, the regulatory leg of the Proactive Safety Triad is currently running—not walking—in the wrong direction. As such, the regulatory leg will be the hardest one to fix, if that is even possible, at least as long as Trump remains in the presidency.

CHAPTER 11

CONSUMERS: FOOL ME TWICE

Late in August in the summer of 1949, in the workingman's town of Jersey City, New Jersey, 68-year-old Emilio Caruso was crossing a huge parking lot the size of two football fields and lined with over a hundred shipping docks owned by the McLean Trucking Company. Suddenly, and without warning, he was struck and knocked to the pavement by a tractor trailer moving at a slow speed through the lot.

The son of Italian immigrants, Caruso had retired only three years earlier from American Can Company. For more than 35 years, he toiled in its massive, city-block-long manufacturing facility on Dey Street, never missing a single day of work. His working days happily over, Caruso had settled into a leisurely and distinctly predictable daily walking routine that started with making his rounds visiting extended family members in the mornings and early afternoons, one house at a time in his close-knit neighborhood. Later in the day, he would head off to his favorite local tavern to meet up with a cordial group of also recently retired coworkers, spending the better part of the afternoon in camaraderie and conversation over a couple of beers or perhaps a large glass of Chianti. His routine had quickly become as clockwork precise as the mass production lines in the factory that had enabled Caruso to earn a comfortable and easy retirement.

That is, until the August day when the temperature soared above 100 degrees, the searing heat undulating in mirage-like waves off the hot concrete sidewalks and macadam streets of the factory town. Caruso decided to take a shortcut to the tavern and walked across the McLean Trucking Company parking lot.

Caruso's encounter, first with the gleaming front grill of the huge semi and subsequently with the rock-hard pavement, left him with numerous cuts and bruises, but fortunately nothing worse than that. An ambulance was immediately summoned, and Caruso was treated for his injuries by a pair of young paramedics, but he refused transport to the hospital and eventually made his way home on his own.

About a week later, Caruso found himself sitting in the executive offices of McLean Trucking, having been invited there by company officials to discuss the unfortunate incident that had occurred in the parking lot of their shipping depot. McLean's president and CEO was there along with the company's vice president, the trucking firm's attorney, and the most somber-looking person in the room, the Managing Supervisor of the Jersey City facility—the guy in charge of the lot where Caruso had been hit.

The CEO began by apologizing profusely for the accident and the injuries that Caruso had suffered. When he asked Caruso, with apparently sincere concern, how he was feeling, Caruso smiled and said simply, "I'm fine." However, the next person to speak was the attorney.

The attorney put some legal papers in front of Caruso. As he did this, he also expressed to Caruso that everyone in the company felt very bad about his accident. And then, much to Caruso's shock, on behalf of the company, the attorney offered the retiree an immediate, on-the-spot payment of $1,000 in return for Caruso's agreement not to sue the company over the incident. Standing halfway out of his chair to reach across the table and holding out a pen, he told Caruso all he had to do was sign the papers in front of him and take the already executed check that was alongside them.

Incredulous, Caruso looked hard at the attorney, then at the CEO. There was a discernable expression of utter bafflement in his face.

"I'm not signing those papers," Caruso said, a firm resoluteness in his voice as he pushed them away.

The attorney slowly sat back down. The CEO turned uncomfortably in his leather chair, deeply exhaling a sigh. There was a long, silent pause.

"Then you're planning on suing?" the attorney finally asked.

"No," Caruso said, and then added emphatically, "I was trespassing on *your* property!" Whereupon he stood up and walked quietly out of the room.

OF PERSONAL RESPONSIBILITY AND RECKLESSNESS

The first thought that might come to mind for many people today upon reading this true story is probably something like, "Boy, times have really changed!" It is certainly true, like it or not, that the U.S. has become the most litigious society on the face of the Earth. Yet, there remains an object lesson to be learned from the preceding tale that is as applicable today as it was nearly 70 years ago. As consumers using manufactured products or simply as members of the general public navigating through a dangerous world, each of us must take responsibility for our own actions and for trying to use good judgment. In part, this means enlightening yourself about the hazards that exist all around you.

The dual paradox of modern civilization is that, on the one hand, our environment is in some respects no less perilous than it was for humankind 10,000 years ago during the hunter-gatherer age, and on the other hand, the dangers are far more sophisticated and far less obvious. Primitive man had to worry about the lion or tiger lurking in the jungle or learn to differentiate between the color ring markings of the venomous coral snake and those of the harmless scarlet king snake ("Red touches yellow, kills a fellow; red touches black, venom lack."). As a modern consumer, you have a great many more hazards to learn about and protect yourself from. Not only that, but they can exist much more subtly in things that are supposed to be good for your health, like your prescription medicine or your food, or things that are supposed to make your life easier, like your household water heater or the autonomous features built into your computerized car.

Practically speaking, industry will continue to manufacture products that turn out to have hidden hazards, employers will continue to create work environments where danger lurks, and our recreational pursuits will continue to expose us to risk because that's what things like thrill rides and giant water slides at the nation's theme parks are supposed to simulate. Also, as we have seen, new technology that eliminates some hazards will inevitably bring more hazards that no one might have imagined or anticipated. People will continue to be injured or killed by product or environmental hazards regardless of whether manufacturers and employers are legitimately unaware of the existence of hazards, whether they are aware of them and failed to warn the general public, or whether they are aware of them and did take proactive steps—principled disclosure—to warn the general public.

And those are only the best-case scenarios. Because as we have seen throughout this book, there are and will likely always be bad actors in the world of business and industry. On the one hand, there will always be companies that are willing to deliberately ignore the hidden hazards in their products and cling to the Reactive Economic Model of product development described in Chapter 9, which puts profits ahead of public safety. On the other hand, even among those companies that attempt to embrace the concept of principled disclosure, there will be those that do so too timidly for anyone's good. I'm talking about companies and organizations that will continue to play hide-and-seek with the content, size, and strategic placement of warning labels based on the unfounded fear that such labels will adversely affect sales and, consequently, decrease profits. In other words, there will always be a segment of the industry leg of the Proactive Safety Triad that isn't going to hold up its end of the bargain.

Unfortunately, the same appears to be true of the regulatory leg. As long as the revolving door continues to spin, seamlessly transporting former industry executives to top leadership positions with regulatory agencies—and back to their beloved industries again—it is unlikely that there will ever be much will on the part of government regulators to take swifter and stronger action against companies that fail to warn consumers about hidden hazards in their products. Moreover, there will always be employers who fail to promote and protect the health and safety of their workers. To this corrupt culture of ignoring patently obvious conflicts of interest, when you add in the often anti-regulatory pressure that even well-intended regulators receive from congressional representatives—who annually receive millions of dollars in campaign fund contributions from lobbyists and trade group organizations—you may only conclude that regulatory reform in the U.S. is not going to happen any time soon.

Finally, as we saw in the previous chapter, less than a year into office, Trump the Destroyer and his administration are responsible—I would refer to it as "irresponsible"—for undertaking the most far-reaching rollback in federal regulation since the entire two-term tenure of Ronald Reagan. This administration's destructive policies have catastrophic consequences for consumer and worker health and safety in the short term. Additionally, the president's devastating budget and personnel cuts to regulatory agencies like the EPA and FDA, as well as to whole departments like Transportation and Labor, will make it difficult for his successor, whether Democratic or Republican, to revive and reaccelerate the safety rule-making apparatus, potentially for years to come.

In light of all of these facts, as an American consumer, it is fair to say that for the foreseeable future, you are not going to get a lot of help from government regulatory agencies, either in terms of requiring industries or employers to provide warnings about hidden hazards, or in terms of the regulatory agencies issuing their own warnings direct to the general public. In other words, when it comes to looking out for your safety and that of your family, you're going to be more on your own than perhaps ever before.

At the same time, however, today's consumers have more tools at their disposal to find the critical information needed to learn about the hidden hazards in the manufactured products we buy and use, the questionable ingredients in the foods we eat, the potentially dangerous side effects of the prescriptions we take, and even the provocative or subversive hidden messages in the relentless barrage of discrete communications we receive on our computers and smart devices. As well, today there are more information channels for learning about the hazards that may exist in our homes, our places of work, the recreational places we go to play or enjoy leisure time, and the travel environments we all must navigate to get to all of those locations.

The great equalizer, of course, is the internet and the infinite opportunities it affords for information-sharing among people everywhere. Admittedly, not all the information pulsing through the World Wide Web is always truthful or completely accurate. However, there is a good deal of reliable information that is posted through independent sources—whether by consumer organizations or just concerned citizens—and it is possible, with a little digging, to ferret out useful, factual information. The point is that being in a better position than ever to research and learn about hidden hazards in products or environments means that consumers are more able to exercise informed consent through their own persistent efforts. The other side of the coin, however, is that knowing about hidden hazards is no excuse for careless or reckless behavior by consumers. I will detail examples of both in the following section.

THE 12 STEPS TO BECOMING AN ACTIVE INFORMATION SEEKER

In the remainder of this chapter, I outline 12 steps that consumers and workers may adopt to take control of their own safety in our dangerous world. Think of this as a 12-step, how-to-do-it manual for informing yourself of the hidden hazards all around you so that you will be able to act accordingly to avoid becoming a victim. This is the very essence of the concept of informed consent. Once you know the hazards, you should be able to operate deliberately in a safe manner to avoid being injured. Alternatively, you will have the option of avoiding the dangerous product or environment altogether.

I wish to point out that it is not my goal to turn every U.S. citizen into a rabid, consumer activist willing to hold up a picket sign and march in a protest line in front of the collective headquarters of the American industrial complex, though that wouldn't necessarily be a bad thing. Rather, my goal is to turn every American into what we might call an "Active Information Seeker." By now, the mere handful of stories presented in this book ought to be enough to convince you to *not assume* that the products you buy or the environments you enter are inherently safe. Rather, you need to proactively question whether they are safe and to not cease asking that question until you find or receive a definitive answer to that question. Only then, when you know all the facts, will you be in a position to operate with true informed consent.

Indeed, my research has shown that Active Information Seekers are more likely to use dangerous products safely and are less likely to become accidental injury victims due to hidden and even undisclosed hazards. The reasons are quite simple. First of all, Active Information Seekers are more likely to read and abide by warning labels and signs. They are also more likely to actually read those boring and interminable product instruction manuals to learn the proper way to use the product—and to endeavor to follow those instructions responsibly. Not surprisingly then, that is the first of the 12 steps to becoming an Active Information Seeker:

1.   Read all product labels very carefully, both on the front and back. Even if deceptive language and terminology will continue to be used on product labels—for example, to describe ingredients as well as nutritional values in processed foods—consumers are in a position to learn the real meanings behind those terms. For instance, if you have been paying attention, you already know that there are in excess of 30 terms used by the food industry to describe added sugar. Don't let those deceptive terms deceive you any longer! Learn what they really mean in label-speak so that you are better informed when you are in the supermarket aisles evaluating what products to buy for yourself and your family. You might even post a note on your refrigerator door to remind every person who opens it that 4 grams of sugar equals 1 teaspoon, and that the average 20-ounce soft drink contains over 16 teaspoons of added sugar.

Similarly, when using power tools or appliances and a host of other household products, you should make a point of looking for any warning labels that are either affixed to the units themselves or posted on the packaging. Remember that manufacturers that are very nervous about scaring off potential purchasers are apt to hide warning labels, so you may want to seek them out for your own safety. And by the way, YouTube has thousands of short handyman videos that demonstrate how to do all sorts of do-it-yourself projects. I will have more to say about the internet later in this section.

2. **If you don't understand the language, call the company's consumer hotline and ask questions, or seek the advice of trusted professionals (doctors, lawyers, teachers, etc.).**

Along with informing yourself about the peculiar language and terminology that industries so often use deceptively to hide certain facts, I recommend that you actively question any terms that you do not fully understand or any claim that might seem implausible. Where this proviso might be most crucial for your health and welfare as well as that of your family is in connection with prescription and over-the-counter medications. There are a lot of medical and quasi-medical terms on those labels that nobody short of a trained doctor or nurse is likely to fully understand. These might be the names of chemical ingredients or of clinically defined and potentially detrimental side effects.

It is also important for consumers to resist the regressive trend toward self-medication that direct-to-consumer prescription drug advertising covertly promotes—even if Big Pharma denies that inducing patients to insist on receiving advertised drugs from their doctors is part of their marketing strategy. Which it unequivocally is. Perhaps the best way of avoiding falling into Big Pharma's trap in this example is to know and keep in mind the learned intermediary rule when it comes to areas in which you are not the expert. If you must choose a prescription medication for some ailment, consult your physician and fully involve him or her in the final decision. If you are an employer looking to bring new and powerful machinery into your plant operation, insist that the manufacturer provide formal operational safety training on the equipment for your employees or consult with your attorney about liability issues—you probably ought to do both.

3. Use the internet to research product safety information.

While the internet may certainly be many things to many people, I believe that one extremely positive thing that may be said is that the internet has the potential to be the greatest tool for consumer advocacy and for the dissemination of consumer product-related information ever invented. The basic fact of the matter is that you can look up information about anything. It remains to be seen whether industry will fully embrace the internet and the raw potential it has—not just for promoting the variety and the particular advantages of the products they make—but also as a means of responsibly keeping consumers informed of any hazards or other issues that might be discovered, in order to help their customers avoid injury. Many smart entrepreneurs have already learned that keeping their customers informed of product improvements and upgrades, either through postings on company websites or through subscription-based email blogs and newsletters, serves to increase customer loyalty, even if those notifications occasionally alert consumers to a problem or defect with a particular product.

Fortunately, many companies do post safety warnings information as well as provide instructions for the proper use of their products to avoid injuries. Consumers still need to be wary, however. For example, one pitfall is for companies to post *too much* information regarding product safety procedures, thereby potentially obfuscating the dangers or making it difficult for consumers to precisely zero in on exactly what the specific hazard is, what to look for, and what steps or precautions to take to avoid injury or worse.

4. Use social media both to research and share with others important product safety information.

Should industry fail to take a proactive approach to informing consumers of hidden hazards via the internet, there are millions of consumers out there who have no compunction about posting scads of information—and much more likely—detailed complaints and warnings, about bad or dangerous products.

Recently, a friend of mine had a problem with his 2006 Buick Lacrosse in which the headlights suddenly died while he was driving in the middle of the night. A very scary thing, although fortunately, he was able to flip on the high beams which did work, so no crash occurred and no one was injured. The next day, however, before taking his car to the mechanic, he googled the problem on his computer. He wasn't the least bit surprised when he immediately found a site containing a stream of more than two dozen complaints about the exact same headlight failure in the exact same GM model and year. The sheer number of similar complaints posted by different individual owners on this one site alone clearly suggested a much wider problem with a faulty or defective part affecting who knows how many vehicles? GM certainly wasn't telling. When my friend contacted the dealership to ask them about the problem, he was told that they were unaware of any systemic defect concerning the operation of the headlights and that there was no recall in effect to fix or replace any parts at the time.

But the story doesn't end there, because the website also provided a link to another site that showed the fix, which involved the easy replacement of a computer control module (a $40 part) in the vehicle's circuit box, a repair that didn't require a single tool. So, my friend bought the part at an auto parts store and replaced it himself. Some months later, he received a recall notice from General Motors instructing him to go to the dealership, where they would replace the defective computer control module. (Interestingly, GM later issued a limited-time offer to reimburse consumers who had completed the repair themselves for the cost of the module—and then promptly retracted the offer with no further explanation.)

The moral of the story, of course, is that when it comes to looking for verifiable or validated consumer product complaints on the internet: Seek, and ye shall find!

5. Blog about product safety information.

If blogging is not your thing, I nevertheless recommend that you make your voice be heard (or seen in electronic print, as the case may be) by posting your own two cents on "grassroots" internet complaint boards or websites. I hope, for example, that my friend added some choice words concerning his frightening, late-night headlight failure experience to the growing list posted by other consumers who had the same thing happen to them. While there is no direct evidence in this particular case to suggest that the growing numbers of consumer complaints posted on the internet ultimately induced or in any way pressured GM to issue its eventual recall, one can easily see the potential for "average" consumer action to have a significant impact on an individual company or even a whole industry. Imagine hundreds or thousands—imagine hundreds of thousands!—of consumers across the country all posting complaints about the same problem with the same car make and model, or any consumer product for that matter, on the same website or internet forum. Deniability of the problem for industry would go right out the window, and consumer advocacy attorneys would have a very handy list of class action plaintiffs right at their fingertips, all theoretically without the need of regulatory oversight by some government agency.

6. Write to government agencies responsible for regulating a product to ask questions and report product-related injuries (by law, the agency must open a file upon receipt of a complaint).

I acknowledge I have described these 12 steps as ways to become an Active Information Seeker rather than a rabid, protest-sign-carrying, rabble-rousing, troublemaking consumer advocate walking the picket line hurling epithets against corporate America. But the truth is, while true consumer activism has always been as simple and easy as writing a letter to the proper regulatory agency, once again, the internet has made doing so much easier. You can file complaints electronically right on the official websites of virtually all U.S. regulatory agencies. Just pick one or two:

CPSC, FDA, EPA, NHTSA, OSHA, CDC, NIOSH, FRA, ATF, FAA, FTC, FCC, FMHSRC. You won't even need a stamp or an envelope!

I do not mean to trivialize electronic letter-writing by joking about it. Given the current and disturbing anti-regulatory fever gripping our nation's capital, it ought to be clear to every concerned citizen that today it is even *more* critical than ever before in our history for consumers to speak up and be heard. Consumer activism may be the only way to force Congress and government regulators to keep their eyes on the ball when it comes to proactively requiring industries and employers to engage in principled disclosure of hidden hazards in products and workplaces. Indeed, in the current climate, if not consumers themselves, then who?

7. **Attend government hearings about product safety (most agencies widely advertise their planned hearings and the process for giving comments).**

This is not as difficult or complicated as it may seem. When the FDA announced it had decided to reexamine the ingredient and nutrition labels on processed foods sold in the U.S., the agency also indicated that it would convene open hearings to receive input from interested parties among the general public. That could be nutritionists or physicians or simply concerned citizens.

When I read about the hearings, I thought they should hear from me, not just as an expert in product hidden hazards and the deceptive advertising practices employed to keep them hidden, but as one of those concerned citizens frustrated with the metric system smoke screen and alarmed at the obesity epidemic in our country, to which excess added sugar in our food is a major contributor. My feeling today is the same as it was then: if ordinary people don't speak up and make their dissatisfaction known, nothing will change.

I went to the FDA website and filled out the proper forms online. You may file written comments or a "brief" for the committee or you may petition to appear before the committee in person to make your presentation orally. I chose the latter.

On the appointed day of the hearing, my son and I traveled to Washington, D.C., on Amtrak and gave my presentation before the committee along with perhaps a dozen other people. I have to say that the committee members were all very gracious and appeared to be sincerely interested in what each speaker had to say on the matter. It is worth noting that every single one of the speakers ardently and compellingly called for greater transparency in food labeling. Moreover, a majority of them singled out the deceptive use of grams in ingredients listings and called for a separate line in the "Nutrition Facts" label for total *Added Sugar* rather than the current practice of lumping together natural and added sugars.

Being the hidden hazards consumer agitator I am, and having no love for the lies of the sugar industry, I decided not to leave things just with my public testimony before the committee. I figured, "What the hell, I'm here now." So, I approached each of the committee members and, somewhat to my surprise, I got a chance to chat further with each of them, one on one. Here again, each member appeared to take my input seriously to heart, and it was truly a marvelous experience.

Did my testimony and the comments of the other concerned citizens who spoke at this or any other hearings have any impact on the committee's decision-making process? That's hard to say. Although, as I noted in Chapter 3, when the FDA promulgated its new labeling rules in May 2016, the agency did indeed institute a new rule requiring "Added Sugars" to be listed as a separate line item in the Nutrition Facts label, while refusing to abolish the practice of using grams instead of teaspoons or ounces. Yet, as I indicated earlier, if you win one battle at a time, at least you are making progress in the right direction.

Moreover, it is a valuable exercise in participatory government, such that I recommend you might even bring your children to such hearings when they are old enough to understand what is going on. This is more feasible than you may think, because regulatory agencies very often hold multiple hearings in various convenient locations across the country to make it easier for citizens to attend and make their voices heard.

Too often it seems we rely on our elected officials and government to do the right thing, only to be sorely disappointed, and sometimes outraged, by how ineffectual and out of touch they become. Perhaps by exposing our children in this way to the democratic operations of government, younger generations will do a better job of holding politicians and legislators accountable to the will of the people they are supposed to serve.

8. **Organize boycotts of unsafe products and work with local media and local elected officials, including your congress people, to promote your actions.**

Well, of course, if you *do* want to become a rabid, protest-sign-carrying, rabble-rousing, trouble-making consumer advocate walking the picket line hurling epithets against corporate America, then do so by all means. There are numerous time-honored ways of becoming a gadfly to industries that fail to put consumer safety ahead of profits, or to foot-dragging elected congressional representatives when broad-based consumer-protective legislation is warranted. You certainly have the constitutional right to do it. What the heck? It worked for Ralph Nader!

9. **Pay attention to and participate in National Safety Awareness Campaigns (e.g., NOAA's national lightning awareness campaign).**

Despite my fairly extensive criticism of the federal regulatory agencies and my deep dissatisfaction with many of the same-industry executives who are often chosen to lead them, I do have to acknowledge that many regulators post a surprising amount of useful information for consumers on their official websites. For example, the CPSC posts a daily list of recent product recalls, as well as numerous statistical product safety reports, and information about current legal actions and pending legislation related to consumer safety. The FDA similarly provides a daily rundown of product recalls, market withdrawals, and safety alerts, as well as product approvals and clearances. The NHTSA website provides an interactive vehicle safety ratings module that consumers may use by plugging in different car models when searching for their next automobile purchase. All of these sites feature the full text of news articles, press releases, and official actions and documents that contain a wealth of safety and other valuable information for consumers and businesses alike.

Here again, it is up to consumers to hold up their leg of the Proactive Safety Triad by educating themselves about the hazards, hidden or otherwise, inherent in some products and environments. My suggestion, if you'll forgive a little sarcasm, is that the next time you think you'll share a cat video on Facebook or post a picture of your lunch on Pinterest, why not use that time to peruse a government regulatory website for a few minutes. You may find that you learn something astounding you didn't previously know about an everyday appliance in your home that you use all the time. The next time you fire up that appliance, you'll actually be doing so with informed consent!

10. **At work, be sure you read all labels and Material Safety Data Sheets (MSDS) of hazardous products you may encounter, and that you are offered adequate safety training about these hazards.**

Whether you read the business and financial section of your favorite newspaper or any of the dozens of business magazines from *Forbes* to *Inc.*, you should know that one significant sector of our economy that is quite happy with the deregulatory frenzy that swept into Washington with the new administration—and which has, in many cases, done little to hide their glee—are many of the nation's largest employers. Let's call it like it is: If you are an employee and not a business owner, you must bear in mind the fact that your employer's number one concern is making a profit, plain and simple. Your safety on the job, while a legitimate concern for your employer, is categorically not the principal one. In fact, your employer's concern for your safety on the job is much more likely to be a matter of how much it will cost them—in health coverage and disability premiums and workplace mandates to meet compliance with OSHA, EPA, and other regulators or, if you're injured on the job, the potential costs resulting from lost productivity, legal fees, and settlement monies should you sue for negligence or for failure to warn—than a matter of their humanistic concern for your health and well-being.

So, it is really your responsibility, if only by default. You must make sure you read and understand whatever safety information is provided by your employer. You must also ensure that you and your coworkers receive adequate instruction and training in the operation of any machinery used in your place of work or on the job site. Moreover, if you suspect that either the safety information or on-the-job training is inadequate, you may need to petition your employer to do a better job of warning employees about hidden hazards in the workplace.

Here's a converse reason: Suppose your employer does properly post safety warnings, but you simply choose to ignore them and you become seriously injured as a result. In such a case, your failure to inform yourself and heed the warnings makes you the negligent party. Consequently, if your employer can demonstrate principled disclosure of the hazard in a court of law, your chances of winning a lawsuit may be nil. Your chances of winning a sizeable settlement may also be severely hampered. So, it is in your best interests to be proactive on your own behalf.

11. **For all recreational activities, make sure you are informed about dangers you may face (e.g., ask the pool owner if diving is safe, ask the gym trainer or manager about all risks at the gym).**

In Chapter 5, we looked at some of the more typical circumstances that have led to serious injury and some deaths at America's most popular recreation and theme parks. The majority of these incidents involve the failure of ride operators to enforce the rules of the ride, like the strict use of seat belts and other safety restraints (a factor in which park visitors are sometimes complicit) or the failure of park owner-operators to adequately warn parkgoers of hidden hazards, like alligators swimming in a lagoon just yards from the beach.

It bears repeating that, on the whole, fixed-ride amusement parks represent a rather unique example of a federally unregulated industry that does a very good job of self-regulation and self-policing through routine safety inspections of thrill rides and other attractions. As we noted in Chapter 5, the chance of being seriously injured in a fixed-site amusement park ride is one in 16 million.

However, as for some of the sanity-challenging decisions made by some amusement park guests, self-regulation or self-policing, if I may call it that, has not been quite so good.

A sober and rigorously objective examination of what are often the goriest and most grotesquely violent accidents that occur at amusement parks reveals that they are most often the result of parkgoers who blatantly ignore well-designed and prominently placed warning signage, and worse, who physically surmount barriers designed specifically to keep people out of highly dangerous areas in and around fast-moving rides. For example, in June 2008 at Six Flags Over Georgia, 17-year-old Asia Ferguson was decapitated by the Batman: The Ride rollercoaster when he tried to retrieve the hat he had lost earlier on the very same ride. Ferguson had scaled not one, but two six-foot chain-link fences and passed right by big red signs that said the restricted area was both off-limits and dangerous to visitors. In August 2015 at the Cedar Point Amusement Park in Sandusky, Ohio, 45-year-old special education teacher James Young was also decapitated, this time by the Raptor rollercoaster ride. Young had done the exact same thing as Ferguson by climbing over two six-foot fences and passing warning signage, all to try to retrieve his cell phone.

While I consider myself a consumer advocate and I try hard to come down on the side of consumers wherever possible, it is undeniable that the actions of these two park attendees was blatantly irresponsible behavior of the highest order. It stands to reason that not only must you, as a consumer, ask questions to inform yourself about potential hazards, you also need to be responsible for heeding prominent warnings to stay out of danger. A cynic might say that Ferguson and Young exercised informed consent to having their heads cut off.

12. Finally, when you have adequate information about the risks and hazards you may confront, you will be able to make your own informed choices.

Sometime during the latter half of the 20th century, an extremely ingenious and business-savvy off-price clothing retailer by the name of Sy Syms grew his chain of stores to 11 thriving outlets in the tri-state metropolitan area of New York, New Jersey, and Connecticut. Something of a shameless impresario, Syms also acquitted himself very ably as the star of his own television advertising commercials for his establishments. That was, until one day, when he got himself into some very hot water with formal grammarians everywhere, especially the local elementary and high school teachers, when, to their horror of horrors, Sy looked straight into the camera with sincerity and conviction and concluded his 30-second pitch by saying, "You, the educated consumer, *is* our best customer."

Notwithstanding Sy Sym's egregious syntactical faux pas (and its pretty hilarious reception), your responsibility as a consumer is indeed to educate yourself as much as you possibly can about the hazards, hidden or otherwise, in the products you use and the environments you occupy or travel through. As an informed consumer, your responsibility as a member of the third leg of the Proactive Safety Triad is to follow the rules. You must act with due caution in abiding by posted or promulgated safety instructions to avoid being injured or harmed, or to avoid causing damage as a result of falling victim to those hazards. Alternatively, you may decide not to use the hazardous product or enter the dangerous environment altogether. Either way, you will be acting completely within the realm of informed consent.

THE BEAT GOES ON

One of the biggest challenges I faced in writing this book has been deciding which among the legions of liability cases to include and which there was simply no room for. I could fill ten books equal in size to this one, and probably a lot more than that, with story after story of companies that failed to warn consumers about hidden hazards in their products, workplaces, or recreational environments. I could write volumes more about the failure of regulatory agencies. How they do not fulfill their mandates to require industries to exercise principled disclosure in the form of hazard warnings and safety information that would enable consumers and workers to operate with the informed consent that is their right.

For the past eleven years, and every single month since March 2009, I have published an issue of *The Goldhaber Warnings Report*, and never once have I been without a wealth of safety warnings issues or some heretofore unrevealed hidden hazard to choose from and to inform my readers about. Instead, the opposite is true: I never have enough room to cover all of the issues that consumers, workers, commuters, parents, and homeowners should know about. There are literally thousands upon thousands of new cases every year, though most of them aren't in the national news like Takata's exploding airbags or Disney World's alligators. Some do, of course.

Just over the course of writing this book, for example, a jury in St. Louis awarded a woman $110 million after linking her ovarian cancer to years of using talcum powder products, like Shower-to-Shower and baby powder, manufactured by Johnson & Johnson. The award added to over $197 million in judgments that J&J was hit with in three previous cases. One Alabama law firm has reported that it alone has 867 cases pending against the health products giant.

Meanwhile, in New York State, the parents of two children seriously injured while playing in an inflatable bounce house filed a lawsuit against the owner of the bounce house, the toy store that sold it, and the manufacturer. Despite being set up properly according to manufacturer's instructions and secured to the ground through a system of straps and steel spikes, the structure was blown into the air by a strong gust of wind, causing injury to the children when they subsequently fell out of it. What sounds like a fluke occurrence is actually more common than most people might imagine: There are, on average, about 30 bounce house injuries daily in the U.S.

In the New York case, as well as in many of the others, the questions will be: Did the manufacturer and the toy store adequately warn consumers of the wind-related hazard? Did the owner of the bounce house use adequate caution on what conceivably may have been too windy a day to allow the neighborhood children to play in the bounce house? Remember that, as with the private swimming pool, this appears to be a paradigm case in which the homeowner shares some significant responsibility for providing an authoritative regulatory control (second leg of the triad) over the use of the product. Now, it appears the courts will have to decide these issues to determine if there was negligence on the part of the manufacturer or the retailer for failure to warn or, if proper warning was given, whether the owner of the bounce house is at fault for negligently failing to heed the warnings by allowing the kids to play in the bounce house under hazardous conditions.

The decades-long national campaign to inform consumers of the serious health risks associated with smoking cigarettes has met with significant success in reducing cigarette use among some demographic populations of Americans. However, it has also led to the rise of alternative forms of smoking. Enter the e-cigarette and the hookah parlor. Make that the *exploding* e-cigarette. It's just amazing how many different weird things are capable of exploding these days!

Very recently, a jury awarded $1.9 million to a woman who was seriously injured when the battery-powered e-cigarette she was smoking exploded in her face. When these things blow up, it's not just smoke and flames, because battery acid is often spewed outward, causing even worse second- and third-degree chemical burns. Not surprisingly, given this recent rise in popularity, the past year has also seen a spike in lawsuits stemming from injuries caused by exploding e-cigarettes. Do manufacturers adequately warn about this danger? Are there prominent warning labels printed on the outside of the packages to inform consumers of this particularly harmful and nasty hidden hazard?

As for the growing popularity of hookah lounges, the Centers for Disease Control and Prevention (CDC) warns that hookah smoking delivers the addictive drug nicotine and is just as toxic as cigarette smoking. But it can actually be a lot worse. In linking hookah smoke to cancer risk, the CDC warns that the charcoal used to heat tobacco in the hookah increases the health risks by producing smoke that contains high levels of carbon monoxide, metals, and cancer-causing chemicals. The agency also points out that a typical one-hour-long hookah smoking session involves 200 puffs, while an average cigarette is 20 puffs. If you do the math, that's like smoking ten cigarettes—half a pack—within one hour. The volume of smoke inhaled during a typical hookah session is about 90,000 milliliters, compared with 500 to 600 milliliters inhaled when smoking a cigarette.

Here's my question: Is anybody—the manufacturers of hookah products and paraphernalia, the smoke shops that sell these products to the general public for private use; the hookah parlor proprietors, or the regulators like CPSC or the FDA—doing anything to warn consumers of the serious risk to their health that comes from hookah smoking? I seriously doubt it.

But the scariest statistic of all is the profile of the typical hookah enthusiast. Consider the following statistics published in a recent report on the CDC website and citing the findings of the Monitoring the Future survey conducted annually by the Institute for Social Research at the University of Michigan:

> *In 2014, about 23% of 12ᵗʰ grade students in the United States had used hookahs in the past year, up from 17% in 2010. In 2014, this rate was slightly higher among boys (25%) than girls (21%). CDC's National Youth Tobacco Survey found that from 2013 to 2014, hookah smoking roughly doubled for middle and high school students in the United States. Current hookah use among high school students rose from 5.2% (770,000) to 9.4% (1.3 million) and for middle school students from 1.1% (120,000) to 2.5% (280,000) over this period.*[137]

To make matters worse, as with the Young Turks diving every-which-way into an unfamiliar pool to impress the ladies, here again we are dealing with a population that is inherently disinclined to read warning labels at all and is equally likely to ignore them even when they do bother to read them. Manufacturers' and regulators' warnings aside, are parents and school administrators doing enough to inform and protect this vulnerable population segment? Not only do I tend to doubt that as well, I'll wager that the vast majority of consumers, let alone parents and administrators, have no idea whatsoever about the serious health risks posed by hookah smoking. The fact is, hookah smoking by minors should be prohibited by law, just as smoking cigarettes is, yet the statistics above suggest that more effective enforcement is urgently needed.

The amazing thing is that, while I have been researching and reporting on hidden hazards in products and environments for nearly 42 years, I am still astounded when I routinely discover hazards that—even as an expert dedicated to actively looking for them—I previously had no idea even existed. Such was the case recently when dangerously toxic chemicals

---

[137] CDC, "Hookah."

began a chain reaction of fiery explosions at the Arkema chemical plant located 30 miles northeast of Houston, Texas. The explosions occurred when the massive flooding caused by Hurricane Harvey knocked out the electrical power. Eventually, the backup power generators on site, which were specifically designed to maintain the volatile chemicals at a safe temperature, also failed.

The incident shed renewed light on long-standing concerns over risk disclosure, disturbingly large gaps in regulatory oversight and abysmal disaster preparedness and emergency planning at the nation's major chemical plants. First, it turns out that the EPA ignores a whole class of chemicals (like the ones stored at the Arkema plant) that experts have warned for years pose serious explosion hazards. Yet, when the Obama administration sought to strengthen the nation's chemical laws by requiring companies to make information about these dangerous chemicals more easily available to the public, as well as giving the EPA more regulatory power, the industry objected.

Their reasoning? Arkema's senior process safety engineer, Susan Lee-Martin, argued that audits of the company's safety plans by third parties would, first, be too costly. No surprise in that response, of course, although it should be noted that Arkema enjoyed worldwide sales of $8.9 billion in 2016 alone. But Lee-Martin also admonished that third-party audits would require "exposing proprietary information" that could be harmful to citizens. What exactly does that mean?

Well, it represents the chemical industry's fear, real or imagined—or simply trumped up—that if the wrong people got wind of the fact that chemical plants across the country house or process *the* most dangerous, *the* most explosive, and *the* most deadly chemicals on Earth, those plants would instantly become vulnerable targets for both foreign and domestic terrorists. In other words, the chemical industry wants you to believe that it is actually *protecting the public* by *not disclosing* the dangerous chemicals housed in plants right in our own back yards.

If you analyze their logic, this reasoning is not based simply on the remote chance that a terrorist might try to blow up a chemical plant.

As we all know, that chance exists today regardless of what particular chemicals are actually in the plant. Rather, what the chemical industry is purportedly saying is that the discriminating terrorist will be more likely to try to blow up a chemical plant if he or she knows that it contains really, really deadly chemicals. (Never mind that they could just beef up essential security at all chemical plants to begin with.)

And for this we should allow thousands of residents surrounding hundreds of chemical plants across the country to remain blithely uninformed and ignorant of the nature and toxicity of the chemicals within the plant. We should further be okay, apparently, with allowing those residents to be at serious risk of exposure to these unknown dangerous chemicals should another natural disaster cause leaks or explosions like the one we saw in Texas during Hurricane Harvey. But it's nice to know that the chemical industry is taking such a proactive role in protecting us from acts of terrorism.

But industry leaders and lobbyists went even further by managing to get a number of states to side with the chemical manufacturers in opposing the proposed Obama-era rules that would have forced them to disclose the kinds of chemicals stored in the plants. Ostensibly buying into this nonsensical proprietary information/terrorism argument, in July 2016, the Republican attorneys general of 11 states, led by none other than Scott Pruitt of Oklahoma, sent a letter to then EPA administrator Gina McCarthy, in which they argued the newly proposed rules would harm citizens. The letter read in part:

> *The safety of these manufacturing, processing and storage facilities should be a priority for us all, but safety encompasses more than preventing accidental releases of chemicals, it also encompasses preventing intentional releases caused by bad actors seeking to harm our citizens.*[138]

---

[138] Krauss et al., "Crisis."

In June 2017, barely three months before the explosion and fire at the Arkema plant in the wake of Hurricane Harvey, the same Scott Pruitt, who—from February 2017 to July 2018—was the chief EPA administrator appointed by President Trump, officially delayed the proposed rule changes by 20 months, until February 2019. Eleven states led by former New York Attorney General Eric Schneiderman had sued over the decision. However, such litigation is likely to take years to sort out.

The Arkema plant's emergency contingency plans, which the company is required to file every four years with the EPA, failed to include specific logistical measures to raise critical equipment like backup generators above flood levels. The plans provided no workable strategies for isolating or protecting hazardous materials from high wind or water—or practical methods for trucking them quickly away from the plant and the flooding altogether if that became necessary. Incredibly, Gilles Galinier, Arkema's vice president of communications, insisted that the conflagration was "not an industrial accident," but was caused by the unprecedented nature of the "hurricane and torrential rains" that he further claimed no one could have prepared for.[139]

However, there are a number of obvious reasons why that argument doesn't hold water (no pun intended). Consider the following established geographical and meteorological facts:

- Crosby, Texas, lies on a flat plain that is only 46 feet above sea level and prone to flooding. In fact, the entire Houston metropolitan region contains several dams and levees designed specifically to try to control historic, prevalent flood risks;
- Crosby is only about 50 miles inland, as the crow flies, from the Gulf of Mexico, a virtual witches' cauldron for brewing tropical storms and hurricanes, and less than two hours' drive from the port of Galveston;

---

[139] Ibid.

- Galveston and the surrounding region have, throughout history, been hit repeatedly by some of the severest hurricanes Americans have ever experienced;
- The Great Galveston Hurricane of 1900, a ferocious Category 4 storm packing winds of 145 mph, took between 6,000 and 12,000 lives.

All of these facts ought to lead any reasonable person to see the need for definitive emergency plans to deal with not just the chance, but the likelihood of similar natural hurricane disasters in the future. Yet, it took another disaster in 2008, when Hurricane Ike made landfall over Galveston killing 103 people and causing more than $50 billion in damage, for Arkema to even go so far as to identify, for the first time in its emergency plans, that floods and hurricanes potentially leading to power failures and loss of cooling capacity were threats to the Crosby site.

According to Tom Neltner, chemical policy director at the Environmental Defense Fund, Arkema identified the "new hazards but [didn't] change anything in their plans." What should have happened in their revision, Neltner added, was that the company should have provided definitive, specific, disaster-preventative actions the plant operators proactively would undertake immediately once it was determined that "they have to evacuate because of flooding."[140]

Does all this sound to you like strictly an entirely unpredictable, entirely natural disaster that no one could have prepared for? Or does it sound a lot more like an industrial accident just waiting to happen?

Finally, the Arkema explosion and fire also served to expose a gap in federal environmental law through which chemical companies are not even required to address (in the emergency plans that are submitted to federal regulators) the inherent risks that are posed by the properties of this class of highly unstable chemicals—and not just for the sake of the general public. Even more urgently, this is information of vital, life-threatening

---

[140] Ibid.

concern to first responders reacting to save lives and property in just about any natural disaster in this country.

What this meant during Hurricane Harvey was that first responders to the Arkema plant fire had no idea what they were up against. Many of the very first police, fire, and emergency medical technicians to arrive on the scene were overcome by toxic fumes from the burning chemicals that burned their eyes and faces and caused severe nausea and vomiting. Even more alarmingly, these first responders were sickened even though they were manning a "safe" evacuation perimeter a mile and a half away from the burning plant!

Just try to picture that:

Courageous first responders—emergency fire, police, national guard, medical personnel, potentially including many volunteers (possibly your neighbors)—risking their own lives trying to save other people (perhaps you or your family) and to reduce or prevent property damage in the face of a colossal disaster, only to be unwittingly poisoned, burned, or even killed by whatever happens to be contained within the very manufacturing facilities they are trying to save.

I can think of no better example that should convince every American consumer to see the positive advantages and the absolute necessity of demanding that all industries provide full and forthright principled disclosure either to the general public, or in the case of sensitive information, to government regulators and those authorities charged with public safety. Further, it should also convince every American that measured, responsible, and effective regulatory oversight by appropriately empowered government agencies is also a necessity to ensure continued public safety in an ever-dangerous world.

RESOURCES

INTRODUCTION

Grimshaw v. Ford Motor Company. Civ. No. 20095. Court of Appeals of California, Fourth Appellate District, Division Two. May 29, 1981.

Dowie, Mark. "Pinto Madness." *Mother Jones*, September 1977, http://www.motherjones.com/politics/1977/09/pinto-madness.

Leggett, Christopher. "The Ford Pinto Case: The valuation of life as it applies to the negligence-efficiency argument." Spring 1999, https://users.wfu.edu/palmitar/Law&Valuation/Papers/1999/Leggett-pinto.html.

Eilperin, Juliet. "Trump undertakes most ambitious regulatory rollback since Reagan." *Washington Post*, February 12, 2017, https://www.washingtonpost.com/politics/trump-undertakes-most-ambitious-regulatory-rollback-since-reagan/2017/02/12/0337b1f0-efb4-11e6-9662-6eedf1627882_story.html?utm_term=.345f6dc97f8c&wpisrc=nl_headlines&wpmm=1.

CHAPTER 1

Isadore, Chris. "Death toll for GM ignition switch: 124." *CNN Business*, December 10, 2015, https://money.cnn.com/2015/12/10/news/companies/gm-recall-ignition-switch-death-toll/index.html.

Muller, Joann. "GM Profit Plunges on Recall Costs: $400 Million Set Aside for Victims." *Forbes*, July 24, 2014, https://www.forbes.com/sites/joannmuller/2014/07/24/gm-profit-plunges-on-recall-costs-400-million-set-aside-for-victims/#35c2fdd330b7.

Ewing, Jack and Hiroko Tabuchi. "Volkswagen Set to Plead Guilty and to Pay U.S. 4.3 Billion in Deal." *New York Times*, January 10, 2017, https://www.nytimes.com/2017/01/10/business/volkswagen-diesel-settlement.html.

Spector, Mike. "Takata Executives Criminally Charged in U.S. Probe of Faulty Airbags." *Wall Street Journal*, January 13, 2017, https://www.wsj.com/articles/takata-executives-criminally-charged-in-u-s-probe-of-faulty-air-bags-1484325097.

Tajitsu, Naomi. "Japanese airbag maker Takata files for bankruptcy, gets Chinese backing." *Reuters*, June 25, 2017, https://www.reuters.com/article/us-takata-bankruptcy-japan/japanese-airbag-maker-takata-files-for-bankruptcy-gets-chinese-backing-idUSKBN19G0ZG.

Weiman, Darryl S. "The McDonald's Coffee Case." *Huffington Post*, January 7, 2018, https://www.huffpost.com/entry/the-mcdonalds-coffee-case_b_14002362.

Wikipedia. "Liebeck v. McDonald's Restaurants." https://en.wikipedia.org/wiki/Liebeck_v._McDonald%27s_Restaurants.

Chemical Industry Archives. "H.G. Piper Memo." http://www.chemicalindustryarchives.org/dirtysecrets/beryllium/1.asp.

Mangan, Douglas. "Majority of youth sports injuries can be prevented, here's how to keep kids safe." *USA Today*, September 5, 2018, https://www.usatoday.com/story/life/allthemoms/2018/09/05/majority-youth-sports-injuries-can-prevented-heres-how/1139104002/.

National Collegiate Athletic Association Student-Athlete Concussion Injury Litigation, Case No. 1:13-cv-09116 (N.D. Ill.).

Wikipedia. "Marshall McLuhan." https://en.wikipedia.org/wiki/Marshall_McLuhan.

CHAPTER 2

United States Consumer Product Safety Commission. https://www.cpsc.gov/About-CPSC

CPSC. "2015 Annual Report to the President and Congress." https://www.cpsc.gov/s3fs-public/FY15AnnualReport.pdf

Hogan, Bill. "Government Recalls Bed Rails After Reported Deaths." American Association of Retired Persons (AARP), May 20, 2014, https://blog.aarp.org/bulletin-today/government-recalls-bed-rails-after-reported-deaths.

Gromicko, Nick and Kenton Shepard. "Inspecting Aluminum Wiring." International Association of Certified Home Inspectors. https://www.nachi.org/aluminum-wiring.htm.

U.S. Consumer Product Safety Commission (CPSC). "Repairing Aluminum Wiring." U.S. CPSC Publication 516, June 2011, https://www.cpsc.gov/s3fs-public/516.pdf.

Bob Schiffmann, personal communication, August 2019.

West Bend. "Ladder Safety." Culture of Safety. https://cultureofsafety.thesilverlining.com/safety-tips/ladder-safety.

The Goldhaber Warnings Report. Vol. IV, February 2012, https://irp-cdn.multiscreensite.com/760d2a66/files/uploaded/Goldhaber-Warnings-Report-February-20127.pdf.

CHAPTER 3

Bomey, Nathan. "Philadelphia soda tax caused 'substantial decline' in soda sales, study finds." *USA Today*, May 19, 2019, https://www.usatoday.com/story/money/2019/05/15/philadelphia-soda-tax-sales-study/3677713002/.

Moreira, Paula I. "High-sugar diets, type 2 diabetes and Alzheimer's disease." *Current Opinion in Clinical Nutrition and Metabolic Care*. http://journals.lww.com/co-clinicalnutrition/Abstract/2013/07000/High_sugar_diets,_type_2_diabetes_and_Alzheimer_s.12.aspx

Franco, Michael. "Excess sugar linked to Alzheimer's in new study." *New Atlas*, February 24, 2017, https://newatlas.com/sugar-linked-to-alzheimers/48098/.

National Institutes of Health (NIH). "NIH study identifies ideal body mass index." December 1, 2010, https://www.nih.gov/news-events/news-releases/nih-study-identifies-ideal-body-mass-index.

Feldscher, Karen. "Sickly sweet." *The Harvard Gazette*, March 18, 2019, https://news.harvard.edu/gazette/story/2019/03/higher-consumption-of-sugary-beverages-linked-with-increased-risk-of-mortality.

Schulte, Erica M., N.M. Avena, and A.N. Gearhardt. "Which foods may be addictive? The roles of processing, fat content, and glycemic load." Public Library of Science (PLOS), February 18, 2015, https://doi.org/10.1371/journal.pone.0117959.

Wilmut, Roger, ed. *The Complete Monty Python's Flying Circus: All the Words, Volume One.* New York: Pantheon Books, 1989.

Hungry for Change. "How to Spot Sugar on Food Labels." http://www.hungryforchange.tv/article/how-to-spot-sugar-on-food-labels.

U.S. Food and Drug Administration. "FDA Modernizes Nutrition Facts Label for Packaged Foods." May 19, 2016, https://www.fda.gov/NewsEvents/Newsroom/PressAnnouncements/ucm502182.htm.

Editorial Board. "Coke Tries to Sugarcoat the Truth on Calories." *New York Times*, August 14, 2015, https://www.nytimes.com/2015/08/14/opinion/coke-tries-to-sugarcoat-the-truth-on-calories.html.

O'Connor, Anahad. "Research Group Funded by Coca-Cola to Disband." *New York Times*, December 1, 2015, https://well.blogs.nytimes.com/2015/12/01/research-group-funded-by-coca-cola-to-disband/?mtrref=www.google.com&gwh=1F40D1CB9F20BBC730CB4D10AF4C166A&gwt=pay&assetType=REGIWALL.

Erickson, Jennifer, Behnam Sadeghirad, Lyubov Lytvyn, Joanne Slavin, and Bradley C. Johnston. "The Scientific Basis of Guideline Recommendations on Sugar Intake: A Systematic Review." *Annals of Internal Medicine.* 2017; 166(4): 257–267.

Kearns, Cristin and Dean Schillinger. "In response to 'Guidelines to Limit Added Sugar Intake.'" *Annals of Internal Medicine*, 2017; 176(3): 220. https://annals.org/aim/article-abstract/2646643/guidelines-limit-added-sugar-intake?searchresult=1.

O'Connor, Anahad. "Study Tied to Food Industry Tries to Discredit Sugar Guidelines." *New York Times*, December 19, 2016, https://www.nytimes.com/2016/12/19/well/eat/a-food-industry-study-tries-to-discredit-advice-about-sugar.html?ref=business&_r=2%22.

O'Connor, Anahad. "How the Sugar Industry Shifted Blame to Fat." *New York Times*, September 13, 2016, https://www.nytimes.com/2016/09/13/well/eat/how-the-sugar-industry-shifted-blame-to-fat.html.

UPI. "Man Awarded $1 Million Because of Exploding Pop." *United Press International*, November 16, 1984, http://www.upi.com/Archives/1984/11/16/Man-awarded-1-million-because-of-exploding-pop/1730469429200/.

Zerbe, Leah. "How Much Toxic Roundup Are You Eating?" *Rodale's Organic Life*, March 13, 2017, http://www.rodalesorganiclife.com/food/how-much-toxic-roundup-are-you-eating.

Zhang, Luoping, Iemaan Rana, Rachel M. Shaffer, Emanuela Taioli, and Lianne Sheppard. "Exposure to glyphosate-based herbicides and risk for non-Hodgkin lymphoma: A meta-analysis and supporting evidence." *Mutation Research/Reviews in Mutation Research*, (781) July-September 2019, pp.186–206, https://doi.org/10.1016/j.mrrev.2019.02.001.

Levin, Sam. "USA: Monsanto found liable in lawsuit alleging its weed killer causes cancer; co. ordered to pay $289m in damages." Business and Human Rights Resource Centre, October 23, 2018, https://www.business-humanrights.org/en/usa-monsanto-faces-lawsuit-alleging-its-weed-killer-causes-cancer-co-claims-product-is-safe.

Rosenblatt, Joel, Lydia Mulvany, and Peter Waldman. "EPA Official Accused of Helping Monsanto 'Kill' Cancer Study." *Bloomberg*, March 14, 2017, https://www.bloomberg.com/news/articles/2017-03-14/monsanto-accused-of-ghost-writing-papers-on-roundup-cancer-risk.

Benbrook, Charles. "Impacts of genetically engineered crops on pesticide use in the U.S.-the first sixteen years." *Environmental Sciences Europe*, 2012; (24) 1–24, https://enveurope.springeropen.com/articles/10.1186/2190-4715-24-24.

CHAPTER 4

Segal, David. "The People v. The Coal Baron." *New York Times*, June 21, 2015, https://www.nytimes.com/2015/06/21/business/energy-environment/the-people-v-the-coal-baron.html.

Mine Safety and Health Administration. "MSHA Executive Summary Big Branch Mine disaster." U.S. Department of Labor. https://arlweb.msha.gov/Fatals/2010/UBB/ExecutiveSummary.pdf

Jervey, Ben. "Don Blankenship, Fresh Out of Prison, Begs Trump to Have Mercy on Coal Execs." *DESMOG*, May 19, 2017, https://www.desmogblog.com/2017/05/19/don-blankenship-fresh-out-prison-begs-trump-have-mercy-coal-execs.

National Safety Council. "Former mine CEO Blankenship asks Trump to reject calls for harsher punishments for safety violators." *Safety & Health Magazine*, May 8, 2017, https://www.safetyandhealthmagazine.com/articles/print/15648-bobby-scott-calls-for-stronger-criminal-penalties-after-former-mine-ceo-blankenship-leaves-prison.

The Cleveland Clinic. "Beryllium Disease." https://my.clevelandclinic.org/health/diseases/13807-beryllium-disease

Piper, H.G. "H.G. Piper Memo." Chemical industry Archives. http://www.chemicalindustryarchives.org/dirtysecrets/beryllium/1.asp.

Kreiss, Kathleen, Margaret M. Mroz, Boguang Zhen, Herbert Wiedemann, and Barbara Barna. "Risks of beryllium disease related to work processes at a metal, alloy, and oxide production plant." *Occupational and Environmental Medicine, 54*, 605–612.

Eisenbud, Merril. "Origins of the standards for control of beryllium disease (1947–1949)." *Environmental Research, 27*(1), 79–88.

Kolenz, Marc. Beryllium letter. http://www.chemicalindustryarchives.org/dirtysecrets/beryllium/pdfs/doc-o.pdf.

Occupational Safety and Health Administration (OSHA). "Final Rule to Protect Workers from Beryllium Exposure." U.S. Dept. of Labor, May 20, 2017, https://www.osha.gov/berylliumrule/.

CHAPTER 5

Madhani, Aamer. "Treadmill injuries send thousands to the ER every year." *USA Today*, May 4, 2015, https://www.usatoday.com/story/news/2015/05/04/treadmill-emergency-room-injuries-exercise-equipment/26898487/.

Association of Pool and Spa Professionals (Pool & Hot Tub Alliance). http://
apsp.org/about/what-we-do.

Crichton, Michael, dir. *Westworld*. Beverly Hills, CA: Metro-Goldwyn-Mayer,
1973.

CHAPTER 6

Wert, Ray. "Toyota Settles for $10 million in Deadly San Diego Crash." *Jalopnik*,
December 23, 2010, https://jalopnik.com/toyota-settles-for-10-million-
in-deadly-san-diego-cras-5717045.

U.S. Travel Association. "Domestic Travel Market Report 2015." https://www.
ustravel.org/research/domestic-travel-market-report-2015

U.S. Department of Transportation. Bureau of Transportation Statistics. https://
www.rita.dot.gov/bts/press_releases/bts018_16.

Hammer, Joshua. "The Real Story of Germanwings Flight 9525."
Gentlemen's Quarterly, February 22, 2016, https://www.gq.com/story/
germanwings-flight-9525-final-moments.

Association of American Railroads. "Freight Railroads & Positive Train
Control." https://www.aar.org/policy/positive-train-control

Zambito, Thomas C. and Jorge Fitz-Gibbon. "Derailment engineer $10M suit
blames Metro-North." *lohud*, December 1, 2016, https://www.lohud.com/
story/news/transit/2016/12/01/metro-north-derailment-engineer-
sues/94733180/.

Federal Bureau of Investigation. "Criminal Charge Against Toyota Motor
Corporation and Deferred Prosecution Agreement with $1.2 Billion
Financial Penalty." *New York Field Office*, March 19, 2014, https://archives.
fbi.gov/archives/newyork/press-releases/2014/criminal-charge-against-
toyota-motor-corporation-and-deferred-prosecution-agreement-with-
1.2-billion-financial-penalty.

SDNews. "Toyota Quietly Settles Lawsuit with San Diego's Saylor Family,
Following Deadly Crash." https://www.youtube.com/watch?v=ZYuSu3Rcbx0.

Wallace, Gregory, Poppy Harlow, and Amanda Hobor. "How Brooke Melton's death led to the GM recall." *CNN Money*, June 4, 2014, http://money.cnn.com/2014/06/04/autos/general-motors-melton-crash/index.html.

Associated Press. "Cost to fix faulty General Motors ignition switch behind 13 deaths was 57 cents: congress." *Daily News*, April 1, 2014, http://www.nydailynews.com/news/national/cost-fix-faulty-gm-ignition-switch-57-cents-congress-article-1.1742342.

Sorokanich, Bob. "Volkswagen USA CEO: 'We Totally Screwed Up.'" *Road and Track*, September 22, 2015, http://www.roadandtrack.com/new-cars/car-technology/news/a26774/volkswagen-ceo-we-screwed-up/.

Reynolds, Jerry. "Takata Pleads Guilty, Executives Charged Criminally." *CarProUSA*, January 18, 2018, https://www.carprousa.com/Takata-Pleads-Guilty-Executives-Charged-Criminally/a/337.

Kiley, David. "The Takata Airbag Recall Is Now a Full-Blown Crisis." *Fortune*, June 10, 2016, https://fortune.com/2016/06/10/the-takata-airbag-recall-is-now-a-full-blown-crisis/.

Tabuchi, Hiroko. "Takata Saw and Hid Risk in Airbags in 2004, Former Workers Say." *New York Times*, November 6, 2014, https://www.nytimes.com/2014/11/07/business/airbag-maker-takata-is-said-to-have-conducted-secret-tests.html?referrer=&_r=0.

Palmer, Shelly. "Can Self-Driving Cars Ever Really Be Safe?" April 16, 2017, https://www.shellypalmer.com/2017/04/can-self-driving-cars-ever-really-safe/.

AAA Newsroom. "Americans Feel Unsafe Sharing the Road with Fully Self-Driving Cars." March 2017, http://newsroom.aaa.com/2017/03/americans-feel-unsafe-sharing-road-fully-self-driving-cars.

Boudette, Neal E. "Tesla Self-Driving System Cleared in Deadly Crash." *New York Times*, January 19, 2017, https://www.nytimes.com/2017/01/19/business/tesla-model-s-autopilot-fatal-crash.html.

CHAPTER 7

Brooks, Mel, dir. *Spaceballs*. Beverly Hills, CA: Metro-Goldwyn-Mayer, 1987.

Robbins, Rebecca. "Drug makers now spend $5 billion a year on advertising. Here's what that buys." *Stat*, March 9, 2016, https://www.statnews.com/2016/03/09/drug-industry-advertising/.

Reyes v. Wyeth Labs., 498 F.2d 1264, 1276 (5th Cir. 1974).

Donohue, Julie. "A History of Drug Advertising: The evolving roles of consumers and consumer protection." *The Millbank Quarterly*, Dec; 84(4): 659–699, https://www.ncbi.nlm.nih.gov/pmc/articles/PMC2690298/.

Public Law 82-215, 65 Stat. 648. https://www.govinfo.gov/app/details/STATUTE-65/STATUTE-65-Pg648/summary.

AARP Bulletin. "Why Our Drugs Cost So Much." *AARP*, May 1, 2017, http://www.aarp.org/health/drugs-supplements/info-2017/rx-prescription-drug-pricing.html.

Picchi, Aimee. "Drug ads: $5.2 billion annually—and rising." *CBS News*, March 11, 2016, http://www.cbsnews.com/news/drug-ads-5-2-billion-annually-and-rising/.

Wilson, Christy. "New technologies are accelerating drug development, bringing hope to patients." Elsevier, June 3, 2016, https://www.elsevier.com/connect/new-technologies-are-accelerating-drug-development-bringing-hope-to-patients.

OpenSecrets.org. "Pharmaceuticals/Health Products—Industry Profile: Summary, 2019." Center for Responsive Politics. https://www.opensecrets.org/lobby/indusclient.php?id=h04.

Kaufman, Joanne. "Think You're Seeing More Drug Ads on TV? You Are, and Here's Why." *New York Times*, December 24, 2017, https://www.nytimes.com/2017/12/24/business/media/prescription-drugs-advertising-tv.html.

Lo, Chris. "Big Pharma and the Ethics of TV Advertising." *Pharmaceutical Technology*, November 27, 2013, https://www.pharmaceutical-technology.com/features/feature-big-pharma-ethics-of-tv-advertising/.

Ehrlich, Bob. "DTC in Perspective: Media Misreporting Advertising Off-label Use." *DTC Perspectives*, February 17, 2017, http://www.dtcperspectives.com/dtc-perspective-media-misreporting-advertising-off-label-use/.

Rosenberg, Martha. "Disgraced former FDA official Now Marketing Lilly Drug." CommonDreams.org, December 27, 2017, https://www.commondreams.org/views/2007/12/27/disgraced-former-fda-official-now-marketing-lilly-drug.

Rosenberg, Martha. "The FDA now officially belongs to Big Pharma." *Salon*, February 27, 2016, https://www.salon.com/2016/02/27/the_fda_now_officially_belongs_to_big_pharma_partner/.

Tavernise, Sabrina. "F.D.A. Nominee Califf's Ties to Drug Makers Worry Some." *New York Times*, September 19, 2015, https://www.nytimes.com/2015/09/20/health/fda-nominee-califfs-ties-to-drug-industry-raise-questions.html.

CHAPTER 8

Wikipedia. "Casualties of the Syrian Civil War." https://en.wikipedia.org/wiki/Casualties_of_the_Syrian_Civil_War.

Wikipedia. "Marshall McLuhan." https://en.wikipedia.org/wiki/Marshall_McLuhan.

IGN. "Obsessed EverQuest Fan found Guilty of Manslaughter." January 3, 2001, https://www.ign.com/articles/2001/01/04/obsessed-everquest-fan-found-guilty-of-manslaughter.

Miller, Stanley A. "Sucked Deep into Cyberworld fantasy of EverQuest, man commits suicide." *Milwaukee Journal Sentinel*, April 8, 2002, https://billingsgazette.com/business/technology/sucked-deep-into-cyberworld-fantasy-of-everquest-man-commits-suicide/article_718a9277-68f5-5ae7-a5a1-f10be9c3a5ab.html.

LevelSkip. "Virtual Addiction: The Hidden Dangers of Online Gaming." Updated on March 29, 2017, https://levelskip.com/misc/Virtual-Addiction-Dangers-of-Online-Gaming.

Wikipedia. "Suicide of Tyler Clementi." https://en.wikipedia.org/wiki/
Suicide_of_Tyler_Clementi.

Phillips, Kristine. "An 11-year-old boy killed himself after his girlfriend faked
her death. She's now facing charges." *Washington Post*, April 11, 2017,
https://www.washingtonpost.com/news/education/wp/2017/04/09/an-11-
year-old-boy-killed-himself-after-his-girlfriend-faked-her-death-shes-
now-facing-charges/?utm_term=.eba5e9269151.

Shapiro, Emily and Doug Lantz. "Michelle Carter sentenced to 2.5 years for
texting suicide case." *ABC News*, August 3, 2017, https://abcnews.go.com/
US/michelle-carter-set-sentenced-texting-suicide-case/story?id=48947807.

IMDb. *War Games* (Movie). https://www.imdb.com/title/tt0086567/.

CHAPTER 9

Krisher, Tom. "16.7 Million Recalled Takata Airbags Still Unrepaired and
on U.S. Roads." *Insurance Journal*, December 27, 2018, https://www.
insurancejournal.com/news/national/2018/12/27/512907.htm#.

NHTSA. "Takata Recall Spotlight." https://www.nhtsa.gov/equipment/
takata-recall-spotlight.

CHAPTER 10

Baram, Marcus and Andrea Stone. "Triangle Shirtwaist Factory Fire's Legacy
Under Threat." *Huffington Post*, December 6, 2017, https://www.huffpost.
com/entry/triangle-shirtwaist-co-factory-fire-legacy_n_840835?guccoun
ter=1&guce_referrer=aHR0cHM6Ly93d3cuZ29vZ2xlLmNvbS8&guce_
referrer_sig=AQAAAKZtSuUF6M_cYc9jqwWvNm9LdypmUkzFnd-
349i9EVX-R4AEiXuqUbCrnKSrgL1iTSLAhbwNvHsRxoHXmG9DZ0j
geAMuhG9nEg-txMJ1EKwFeMI3AwQNEL5KiBWAAtRgBl5ONMK8v
5S6yl1l_1xaYlHNIC5SrcGgmR2Iu4uOSJem.

Cullen, David. "Feds Withdraw Sleep Apnea Pre-Rule." *HDT Truckinginfo*,
August 4, 2017, https://www.truckinginfo.com/141584/feds-withdraw-
sleep-apnea-pre-rule.

Rosenblatt, Joel, Lydia Mulvany, and Peter Waldman. "EPA Official Accused of Helping Monsanto 'Kill' Cancer Study." *Bloomberg*, March 14, 2017, https://www.bloomberg.com/news/articles/2017-03-14/monsanto-accused-of-ghost-writing-papers-on-roundup-cancer-risk.

Zion Market Research. "Dietary Supplements Market To Register Humungous Growth, Revenue To Surge To US\$ 220.3 Bn By 2022." September 6, 2018, https://www.zionmarketresearch.com/news/dietary-supplements-market.

O'Connor, Anahad. "Study warns of Diet Supplement Dangers Kept Quiet by F.D.A." *New York Times*, April 7, 2015, https://well.blogs.nytimes.com/2015/04/07/study-warns-of-diet-supplement-dangers-kept-quiet-by-f-d-a/.

Advisory Board. "Study: Popular diet supplements contain amphetamine-like chemical." April 10, 2015, https://www.advisory.com/daily-briefing/2015/04/10/bmpea-in-supplements.

Cohen, Pieter A., Clayton Bloszies, Caleb Yee, and Roy Gerona. "An amphetamine isomer whose efficacy and safety in humans has never been studied, β-methylphenylethylamine (BMPEA), is found in multiple dietary supplements." *Drug Testing and Analysis*; 8, 328–333.

Seyfarth Shaw LLP. "OSHA 'Removes' Late Term Rule Which Allowed OSHA to Cite Injury Recordkeeping Violations Going Back Five-Years." Seyfarth's Workplace Safety and Environmental Law Alert blog, May 9, 2017, https://www.environmentalsafetyupdate.com/investigationsinspections/osha-removes-late-term-rule-which-allowed-osha-to-cite-injury-recordkeeping-violations-going-back-five-years/.

Lopez, German. "Yes, Congress did repeal a rule that made it harder for people with mental illness to buy a gun." *Vox*, October 3, 2017, https://www.vox.com/policy-and-politics/2017/2/3/14496774/congress-guns-mental-illness.

Johnson, Tom. "Trump Weakens Protections for Buildings in Flood-Prone Areas." *Essex County Politics*, August 16, 2017, http://www.essexcountypolitics.com/trump_weakens_protections_for_buildings_in_flood_prone_areas.

Dennis, Brady. "EPA plans to buy out more than 1,200 employees this summer." *Washington Post*, June 20, 2017, https://www.washingtonpost.com/news/energy-environment/wp/2017/06/20/epa-plans-to-buy-out-more-than-1200-employees-by-the-end-of-summer/?utm_term=.a9a499de0f59.

Reuters. "Donald Trump Stops Hundreds of Planned Regulations." *U.S. News and World Report,* July 20, 2017, https://www.news18.com/news/world/donald-trump-stops-hundreds-of-planned-regulations-1466787.html.

AFTERWORD

Centers for Disease Control and Prevention. "Hookah smoking." *CDC Features.* https://www.cdc.gov/features/hookahsmoking/index.html.

Krauss, Clifford, Hiroko Tabuchi, and Henry Fountain. "Crisis Is Over at Texas Plant, but Chemical Safety Flaws Remain." *New York Times,* September 5, 2017, https://www.nytimes.com/2017/09/05/us/harvey-arkema-crosby-chemicals.html.